1/03

The

Reference

Shelf

Representative American Speeches 2001–2002

Editors

Calvin M. Logue, Ph.D.

and

Lynn M. Messina, Ph.D.

The Reference Shelf
Volume 74 • Number 6

The H.W. Wilson Company
2002

The Reference Shelf

The books in this series contain reprints of articles, excerpts from books, addresses on current issues, and studies of social trends in the United States and other countries. There are six separately bound numbers in each volume, all of which are usually published in the same calendar year. Numbers one through five are each devoted to a single subject, providing background information and discussion from various points of view and concluding with a subject index and comprehensive bibliography that lists books, pamphlets, and abstracts of additional articles on the subject. The final number of each volume is a collection of recent speeches, and it contains a cumulative speaker index. Books in the series may be purchased individually or on subscription.

Library of Congress has cataloged this serial title as follows:

Representative American speeches. 1937 / 38–
    New York, H. W. Wilson Co.
        v. 21 cm.—The Reference Shelf
Annual
Indexes:
    Author index: 1937/38–1959/60, with 1959/60;
    1960/61–1969/70, with 1969/70; 1970/71–1979/80,
    with 1979/80; 1980/81–1989/90, 1990.
Editors: 1937/38–1958/59, A. C. Baird.—1959/60–1969/70, L. Thonssen.—1970/71–1979/80, W. W. Braden.—1980/81–1994/95, O. Peterson.—1995/96–1998/99 , C. M. Logue and J. DeHart.—1999/2000– , C. M. Logue and L. M. Messina.
    ISSN 0197-6923 Representative American speeches.
        1. Speeches, addresses, etc., American. 2. Speeches, addresses, etc.
        I. Baird, Albert Craig, 1883–1979 ed. II. Thonssen, Lester, 1904–
        III. Braden, Waldo Warder, 1911–1991 ed.
        IV. Peterson, Owen, 1924– ed. V. Logue, Calvin McLeod, 1935– , Messina, Lynn M., and DeHart, Jean, eds. VI. Series.
PS668.B3   815.5082   38-27962
                                                                            MARC-S
Library of Congress [8503r85] rev4

Cover: New York City Mayor Rudolph Giuliani addresses the United Nations General Assembly, Monday, October 1, 2001. (AP Photo/Richard Drew)

Visit H. W. Wilson's Web site: www.hwwilson.com

Printed in the United States of America

Contents

Preface vii

I. Responses to September 11th 1

1) George E. Pataki. Joint Session of the New York State Legislature 3
2) Galen J. Guengerich. The Shaking of the Foundations 6
3) George W. Bush. Address to a Joint Session of Congress and the
   American People 11
4) Rudolph W. Giuliani. United Nations General Assembly Special
   Session on Terrorism 19
5) Laura Welch Bush. Taliban Oppression of Women and Children 26
6) Jonathan F. Fanton. Chicago Council on Foreign Relations 28
7) Shaykh Muhammad Hisham Kabbani. Muslims Within the
   Democratic Framework 33

II. Character and Heroism 41

1) Christopher J. "Gus" Loria. In Defense of Liberty 43
2) Mary O. Donohue. Maria College Commencement 50
3) Zayed Muhammed Yasin. Of Faith and Citizenship: My American Jihad 57
4) Colin L. Powell. Acceptance of the 14th Annual Philadelphia Liberty Medal 59
5) Mark Schweiker. Flight 93 Patriots: Our Heroes, Our Family 66
6) Donald H. Rumsfeld. Arlington National Cemetery Funeral Service
   for the Unidentified Victims of the Attack on the Pentagon 68

III. Immigration 71

1) Dan Stein. U.S. Asylum Policy: Reforms Needed in Current System 73
2) Linda Chavez-Thompson. Immigration Reform 86
3) Mark Krikorian. Immigration and Civil Rights in the Wake of September 11 90
4) Wade Henderson. Statement at SEIU Immigration Press Conference 97
5) John Ashcroft. Remarks on the National Security Entry-Exit Registration
   System 99

IV. Labor and the Economy 103

1) Elaine L. Chao. State of the Workforce 105
2) Thomas Daschle. America's Economy: Rising to Our New Challenges 110
3) Harvey L. Pitt. Remarks Before the Economic Club of New York 123
4) John J. Sweeney. Remarks on the Wall Street Rally 128

V. Food Safety 133

1) Janet Abrams and Laurie Girand. S.T.O.P.'s Position on FDA's
   Prevention Efforts Toward BSE to Date 135
2) Gregory Conko. Behind the Headlines: What Laymen Should Know
   About Everyday Issues in Science and Health 139
3) John D. Dingell. Food Safety and Bioterrorism Legislation 149
4) Elsa Murano. Taking Food Safety to the Next Level 155

VI. Stem Cell Research and Cloning 161

1) Carl B. Feldbaum. Keeping the Faith 163
2) James R. Langevin. Testimony at the Hearing on Stem Cell Research 171
3) Stuart A. Newman. Testimony at the Hearing on Human Cloning 174
4) Nigel M. de S. Cameron. Biotechnology and the Struggle for
   Human Dignity: Whatever Happened to the Human Race? 178

Cumulative Speaker Index: 2000–2002 189

Preface

For most people living in the United States today, there will always be two Americas—the one before September 11, 2001, and the one after. People will contrast a time of peace with a time of war, a time of security with a time of fear, a time of complacency with a time of action, and a time of carefree existence with a time of mourning. From the moment the first of four hijacked airliners hit the north tower of the World Trade Center at 8:46 A.M., roughly 30,000 innocent civilians working there became soldiers in a war they were not trained to fight and for which they were thoroughly unprepared. They were unexpectedly indoctrinated into unimaginable horror and asked to muster the kind of courage they had never known they possessed.

Within hours, the country was transformed. New York City and Washington, DC, where another plane had struck the Pentagon, suddenly didn't seem so far from Los Angeles or Chicago. After all, Americans lived there. Besides, if it could happen there, it could happen anywhere. Vendors quickly sold out of American flags, which became ubiquitous across the land on houses, cars, T-shirts, and lapels. Taking a cue from the United States Congress, whose members stood hand-in-hand on the steps of the Capitol Building that September night and sang "God Bless America," sporting venues made the singing of the song part of their games, alongside the national anthem and "Take Me Out to the Ballgame." When 343 New York firefighters, 73 police officers, and other emergency personnel died trying to rescue others from the Twin Towers, people gained a new appreciation and respect for the jobs they do across the nation, and they became the new American heroes.

At the turn of the last century, W. E. B. DuBois wrote of the "double-consciousness" of African Americans, who seemed to live with one foot in two worlds. Since September 11, at the dawn of the 21st century, Americans of all races and walks of life have learned to live with their own double-consciousness, as they have tried to go about their normal lives while remaining vigilant of enemies living among them. Americans have always assumed—perhaps naively—that immigrants see the United States as a refuge, that those who come here from abroad cannot help but love this country and value the freedom and opportunity promised in Emma Lazarus's poem inscribed on the Statue of Liberty. On the morning of September 11, Americans were rudely awakened to the startling reality that some whom they had welcomed from abroad had used their open society to destroy them. That reality is inescapable for New Yorkers, who daily pass makeshift memorials to the dead and see, when they look downtown, what Bruce Springsteen calls an "empty sky" where a familiar landmark used to stand, their beloved skyline forever altered. The sense of loss is palpable across the nation, where so many people kissed their loved ones good-bye that morning, never to see them again. Americans' sense of security and invulnerability was severely shaken that day, as the nation and 80 other countries lost more than 3,000 of their citizens, whose only crime was showing up for work.

The speeches contained in this book, most of them given between September 11 of 2001 and 2002, address the concerns of pre-9/11 America and reflect upon the terrible events of that day and its aftermath. Although other issues—particularly the economy, stem cell research, and human cloning—were also significant topics of conversation and debate during this period, September 11 is mentioned in some context in nearly every speech delivered after that day, illustrating the extent to which this tragic event has affected American thinking about numerous issues.

The book's first section is devoted to speeches that directly address the terrorist attacks on the United States. New York Governor George Pataki, the Reverend Galen Guengerich, President George W. Bush, New York Mayor Rudolph Giuliani, First Lady Laura Bush, historian Jonathan Fanton, and Shaykh Muhammad Hisham Kabbani touch on several common themes as they encourage citizens of New York and the nation, console the grieving, analyze the aftermath of the attacks, and inform the public and the world about the state of the nation and its policies in the new war on terrorism. Praise echoes throughout several speeches for ordinary citizens who displayed extraordinary courage and selflessness on September 11, including New York City rescue and relief workers, those who provided aid in the days, weeks, and months following the attacks, and the passengers on Flight 93, who valiantly tried to overcome their hijackers, causing their plane—possibly bound for the White House or the Capitol—to crash in a field in Shanksville, PA. More than any speaker here, Mayor Giuliani—*Time* magazine's Person of the Year for 2001—embodies the resiliency and determination of his city and the nation during this crisis in his address to the United Nations. As he reminds the foreign dignitaries how many of their countrymen call New York home, he portrays the city as a shining example of America's strength through diversity, the very pluralism so despised by the terrorists. Many speakers point out that America's greatness must be measured in the power of its ideals of liberty and justice, not in its wealth or the height of its buildings, and Shaykh Kabbani discusses how those principles are in many respects congruous with true Islamic ideals. In addition, Mrs. Bush alerts the nation to the oppression of Afghanistan's women and children by the Taliban, with whom the nation had gone to war on October 7 in response to the September 11 attacks.

All of the speeches in the second section on character and heroism were delivered in 2002 and express views that are either colored by the events of September 11 or commemorate them. Astronaut "Gus" Loria lauds members of what Tom Brokaw has called the "Greatest Generation" at a gathering commemorating the raising of the American flag at Iwo Jima. Loria compares the marines of nearly 60 years earlier with firefighters at Ground Zero, who hoisted a flag on this latest battle site as a sign of hope and eventual victory. New York Lieutenant Governor Mary O. Donohue urges schools to teach character and virtue, pointing to the spontaneous acts of kindness performed by

Americans across the country in response to the 9/11 attacks as examples of virtuous behavior. Newly minted Harvard graduate Zayed Muhammed Yasin caused great controversy when he announced his speech's title would be "My American Jihad," but Yasin surprised many when his definition of *jihad* turned out to be fairly consistent with American values. In a speech given on the 4th of July, U.S. Secretary of State Colin Powell asserts that the principles of liberty and equality upon which the nation was founded continue to shape the American character, and no act of terrorism can destroy them. The final two speeches, by Pennsylvania Governor Mark Schweiker and Secretary of Defense Donald Rumsfeld memorializing the passengers of Flight 93 and the victims of the Pentagon respectively, were given on the first anniversary of the attacks and praise the patriotism of those who were among the first casualties of the new war on terrorism.

Immigration, the subject of the third section, became an extremely important topic after September 11, although reform of American immigration policies had been of great concern in the months before the attacks as well. Dan Stein, who represents an organization advocating reduced immigration into the United States, describes ways of curbing illegal immigration and easing the transition of those already here legally into American society. The issue of the immigrants' civil rights is addressed from several angles, first by labor leader Linda Chavez-Thompson, who champions the cause of undocumented workers, then by immigration scholar Mark Krikorian, who insists that the right to immigrate is not a civil right and that the U.S. should devise criteria by which to exclude certain individuals from immigrating. Wade Henderson next asks that Americans respect the civil rights of immigrants already here, despite the actions of the nineteen September 11 hijackers, while John Ashcroft considers immigration restrictions from the standpoint of national security.

The economy, which had started to slow during the spring of 2001 and was seriously crippled by two man-made disasters—the September 11 attacks and the corporate scandals involving Enron and WorldCom which followed—is the subject of the fourth chapter. Labor Secretary Elaine Chao, speaking barely two weeks before the attack on the World Trade Center, refers in passing to "tremors on the economic landscape," which seems in hindsight to be an eerie foreshadowing of the full-scale corporate earthquakes that would rattle the nation before the end of the year. By the time Senator Tom Daschle spoke before the Center for National Policy in January of 2002, the combination of the terrorist attacks and the Enron bankruptcy scandal had cost thousands their jobs and had shaken investors' confidence in American industry. While Daschle addresses the unavoidably negative effects of September 11 on the economy, he blames the Bush administration for the policies that precipitated the Enron collapse and the fraudulent actions of Enron's accounting firm, Arthur Andersen. The spring of 2002 brought yet another corporate scandal, this one involving WorldCom, which would put the administration further on the defensive and prompt officials like former SEC chairman Harvey Pitt to launch investigations into corporate misconduct. In his speech in late June,

Pitt sounds as exasperated as the American public and describes strategies to clean up corporate America. A month later, in an impassioned speech, AFL-CIO president John Sweeney calls for greater accountability and more severe penalties for CEOs whose criminal actions result in their companies' demise, the unemployment of thousands of workers, and the near disappearance of their employees' retirement funds.

The issue of food safety, to which we turn our attention in the fifth chapter, had been hotly debated since the 1990s, largely due to outbreaks of *E. coli* and *Salmonella* in the United States and mad cow disease in the United Kingdom, and interest in this subject continued in 2001. In an April speech, Janet Abrams and Laurie Girand call for stricter enforcement of food safety measures by the FDA and USDA. One year later, Gregory Conko accuses many of overstating the dangers of chemically treated and genetically engineered foods. However, when the September 2001 terrorist attacks were followed in October by the appearance of anthrax in mail sent to various media outlets and government offices, many more people began worrying about America's ability to prevent an attack of bioterrorism through our food supply. Congressman John Dingell, for instance, fears that our nation's food inspection service is insufficient to stop a bioterrorist attack, and although Elsa Murano of the Food Safety and Inspection Service does not directly mention September 11, she discusses, among other things, the concern for "biosecurity"—safeguarding against contamination by naturally occurring and artificially introduced pathogens.

The final section in the book looks at two revolutionary scientific breakthroughs that have the potential to greatly benefit humankind but which pose serious ethical and moral dilemmas: stem cell research and human cloning. President Bush's decision in the summer of 2001 to allow limited research into the use of adult stem cells—as opposed to embryonic stem cells—for curing diseases was met with favor by many but with concern and even outrage by others. Carl Feldbaum and Congressman James Langevin find no moral conflict in the use of stem cells and believe the medical benefits from that research far outweigh the risks. Others, such as scientist Stuart Newman, while not opposed to stem cell research or human cloning in principle, do fear the irresponsible use of cloning technology to harvest organs or embryonic stem cells (the most easily molded cells in the human body). Right-to-life advocate Nigel M. de S. Cameron, however, opposes all attempts at human cloning which, he believes, is an act of the utmost hubris that violates human dignity.

We would like to thank those who generously gave us permission to reprint their speeches here. We would also like to thank Sandra Watson, Rich Stein, Eugene F. Miller, and Gray Young for their assistance in producing this book.

December 2002

I. Responses to September 11th

Joint Session of the New York State Legislature[1]

George E. Pataki

Governor of New York State, 1995– ; born Peekskill, NY, June 24, 1945, on his family farm; B.A., Yale University, 1967; J.D., Columbia Law School, 1970; mayor of Peekskill, NY, 1981–1984; New York state assemblyman, 1985–1992; New York state senator, 1992–1995; founder and chair, 21st Century Freedom PAC, 1999– . He is New York State's first Republican-Conservative chief executive.

Editors' introduction: During the 48 hours after terrorists flew two hijacked airplanes into the World Trade Center in New York City, destroying the Twin Towers and those remaining inside, Governor George E. Pataki was an almost constant presence at the disaster site and in other locations around the city. In the ensuing weeks, he acted swiftly to provide assistance to the victims' families and to expedite New York's recovery. He also coordinated efforts between the Federal Emergency Management Agency (FEMA) and state and local search and rescue teams. Governor Pataki established the World Trade Center Relief Fund to benefit all victims and established a World Trade Center Memorial Scholarship guaranteeing a free college education for the children and spouses of those who perished in the attacks. In the speech below, just two days after the tragic event, the governor, who had had little rest since the attack, praised New Yorkers' courageous response to the crisis and promised to lead them to their "greatest day."

George E. Pataki's speech: Today, we join together as a state, and as a nation, to pray for the victims who were lost on one of the darkest days in American history.

We pray for the children who will go to bed this evening without their mothers and fathers.

We pray for the mothers and fathers who've lost the children they loved.

We pray for the husbands and wives who will return to empty homes.

We pray for the firefighters, police officers, and rescue workers who died while committing extraordinary acts of heroism.

---

1. Delivered on September 13, 2001, in the Assembly Chamber of the New York State Capitol building at Albany, NY.

We pray, also, for this great nation of ours, a nation that is free, a nation that is strong, a nation that is united in grief.

For we know that the freedom we so cherish for which countless thousands have sacrificed their lives exposes us to the wicked, the murderous, the cowardly forces of hate.

December 7th will always be known as a "Day of Infamy." So, too, September 11th forever will be known as the day a dark cloud descended across America.

But clouds always pass. The sun always breaks through. And we know as Americans that God's light will again shine across this great land, and that our free and strong people will prevail.

The forces of evil that committed this atrocity have caused pain that will last for generations, pain that has claimed the lives of innocent men, women, and children.

But evil never prevails. Freedom, despite its vulnerabilities, will always prevail.

And I am confident that President Bush and a united American Congress will strike back—swiftly and strongly—against the forces of terror, and the nations that harbor them.

We will stand with the president in those actions.

> *Ultimately, the courageous and resilient spirit of our people will prevail over this cowardly act of hatred.*

New Yorkers have always stood strong, firm and together in times of crisis and human hardship.

Already, we've seen the extraordinary heroism of our firefighters, police officers, emergency service workers, and everyday citizens.

We've seen the indomitable spirit of New Yorkers, pulling together to overcome the most horrendous, destructive and murderous act of terrorism in history.

We owe a deep debt of gratitude for the heroism of the thousands who have been risking, and continue to risk, their lives to help with the relief effort.

We thank President Bush for the extraordinary aid he has provided.

And we owe profound thanks to Mayor Giuliani, and to his team, for the tremendous leadership they have shown.

This crisis has tested and will continue to test the resolve and the resilience of New Yorkers like never before.

But ultimately, the courageous and resilient spirit of our people will prevail over this cowardly act of hatred.

Yesterday I was at Bellevue Hospital visiting injured firefighters. I stood at the bedside of a lieutenant, thanked him for his courage, and told him he was a hero.

He smiled and said, in a thick New York accent: "What'd you expect? I'm a New Yorker."

But then the smile left his face as he spoke about his partner, who was missing. With tears in his eyes, he told me his partner was the father of ten children.

I told him that those children will not be alone. We will stand with them. We will stand with all of these heroes, and we will stand with the children and family members they left behind.

They are now a part of us. They will be a part of New York, and America, forever.

The people of this state are united as never before.

I've seen New Yorkers lined up for blocks, waiting to donate blood at Cabrini Hospital.

I asked one woman why she was there and she said, "I have to be here."

I've seen injured firefighters at St. Vincent's, begging to leave their hospital beds, so they could go back and rejoin their comrades in the rescue effort.

All across our State, people are volunteering to help however and wherever they can.

In this time of crisis, we can draw strength from that spirit of unity, and from the compassion of our people.

There is nothing we cannot accomplish when we are united behind a common purpose. It is that common purpose that brings us here today. For today, the issues that occasionally divide seem small.

Today, we are united in our commitment to rebuild the greatest City in the world. And we are united in our commitment to rekindle the spirit of our people.

And because we are unified, I know we will be unanimous in the action we take today to begin putting this crisis behind us.

Make no mistake: We will not just survive this disaster. Nor will we simply overcome it.

We, the people of New York, will join together, united in strength, and lift New York to its greatest day.

We face a long and difficult road. But we face it together.

These unspeakable acts have shattered our City and shocked our nation.

But they have not weakened the bonds that unite us as New Yorkers, as Americans, as those who love freedom, and, ultimately, as those who love one another.

Our strength will defeat this evil. Our spirit will overcome this atrocity. And, together, this land of the people, and by the people, will soar higher than even our beloved Twin Towers.

Thank you. God bless the great people of New York. And God bless America.

The Shaking of the Foundations[2]

Galen J. Guengerich

Co-Minister, All Souls Unitarian Church; born Milford, DE, September 3, 1957; B.A., Phi Beta Kappa, Franklin and Marshall College, 1982; M.Div., Princeton Theological Seminary, 1985; candidate for Ph.D., University of Chicago Divinity School; Acting Senior Minister, First Unitarian Church, Monmouth County, NJ; appeared on National Public Radio's All Things Considered *and* In Depth *and* On Religion *on the Fox News Channel; appears on* Morning Meditations, *semimonthly half-hour radio program, WQXR, New York; visiting scholar, Union Theological Seminary, New York City, 1996–97; Advisory Board,* Musica Viva of New York; *Board of Directors, Unitarian Universalist Service Committee; authored two volumes of* The Twentieth Century, *1982; contributing writer,* World Explorers and Discoverers, *1992; coeditor,* A History of Virginia, *1991; has published articles in* UUWorld, *the magazine of the Unitarian Universalist Association.*

Editors' introduction: During the week of September 11, with New York City still reeling from the terrorist attacks on the World Trade Center, Reverend Galen Guengerich delivered this sermon to 400 worshippers attending the 10:00 A.M. service, and 1,100 at the 11:15 A.M. service at the Unitarian congregation at All Souls Church. Established in 1819, the church serves the community as a nondogmatic religious environment that, among other things, sponsors 25 social outreach programs. "What we need," Reverend Guengerich advised, "is something that remains firm when all else is crumbling. . . . We also need love—for our country, for each other, and even for our enemies." Margot Adler of National Public Radio recorded the service, and replayed a brief excerpt of the sermon on NPR at a later date.

Galen J. Guengerich's speech: We have seen so much sorrow this week. The first fruits of hate have been bitter indeed. Some of you lived through the attack in person; the rest of us witnessed it on television. All of us smelled the smoke. Together, we've listened to the silence of subways shut down, the scream of fighter jets overhead, the lament of the sixteen-year-old still searching for both of his parents, and the woman desperately looking for her son and her daughter. Then there are the images: the fireball, people jumping, firefighters sobbing, hordes of people walking north along the ave-

---

2. Delivered on September 16, 2001, at New York at the 10:00 A.M. and 11:15 A.M. services. Reprinted with permission of Galen J. Guengerich.

nues, Times Square deserted, and ashes falling like snow. The financial district looks more like Baghdad or Beirut than the Capital of the World. Then there are the numbers: hundreds known dead, many thousands still missing, thousands more injured. Everything is more serious now.

We have also witnessed acts of unbelievable bravery. As one commentator said yesterday, "New Yorkers may be the most cynical of people, but their heroism this week has been one for the history books." Even with their comrades dead by the battalion, our police and firefighters have risen to their mottos: New York's Finest, and New York's Bravest. Our mayor has been tireless, compassionate, effective and ever present. There were heroes in the towers, heroes on the ground, and even heroes on the planes—especially United Flight 93, the one headed for Washington that crashed in Pennsylvania. Thomas Burnett and Jeremy Glick, the two men who apparently led the mutiny against the hijackers, have been cited for possible posthumous Medals of Freedom. What incredible heroes.

Our city and our nation have been shaken to their very foundations. The images and sounds of the week recall to mind a passage from the Hebrew prophet Jeremiah:

> I looked on the earth, and lo, it was waste and void,
> And to the heavens, and they had no light.
> I looked on the mountains, and lo, they were quaking,
> And all the hills moved to and fro.
> I looked, and lo, there was no one,
> And all the birds of the air had fled.
> I looked, and lo, the fruitful land was a desert,
> And all its cities were laid in ruin.
>
> *Jeremiah 4:23–26*

During the late 1940s, the theologian Paul Tillich invoked this biblical text in a sermon about the terrors of the Second World War. It is also an apt description of the onset of what many are now calling World War III. The term is not an overstatement. As the historian Richard Reeves said, when asked by CNN Senior Analyst Jeff Greenfield to put the attack in historical context, "Your generation has been misled. This has been building since the Crusades. It was inevitable that East would eventually meet West."

Benjamin Barber's 1995 book *Jihad vs. McWorld* explores the radical difference between these two worlds, yet demonstrates their paradoxical interdependence. Anyone who reads the daily papers carefully, Barber says, knows that the world is caught between two eternities, Jihad and McWorld. Jihad reflects the tribal past, and McWorld anticipates the cosmopolitan future. They operate with equal strength in opposite directions, one driven by parochial hatreds, the other by universalizing markets. Jihad forges communities of blood rooted in exclusion and hatred, while McWorld forges global markets rooted in consumption and profit.

In this sense, fundamentalism is not a religion. It is a worldview that requires the annihilation of all contrary convictions. Six years ago, Osama bin Laden declared war on the evil empire of the West, and thus on the United States as its leading exemplar. His mission is clear and his disciples are unwavering. Our enemy is not a coward, nor is the violence inflicted on our nation senseless, at least not on their terms. Osama bin Laden's form of fundamentalism will be fiendishly difficult to stamp out. It will certainly take years—a long commitment in the same direction. The battle will shake our nation and our world to its very foundations. Indeed, it already has.

> *What we need is something that remains firm when all else is crumbling.*

What we need is something that remains firm when all else is crumbling. In the wake of the horrors of the Holocaust, Paul Tillich described his experience of discovering strength in life that emerged despite the fire of trials and tribulations. "There is something immovable and unshakable which becomes manifest in the crumbling of our world. On the boundaries of the finite, the infinite becomes visible. This is why the prophets were able to face the shaking of the foundations. It is the only way to look at the shaking without recoiling from it." In other words, when everything comes tumbling down, it is a good time to look around and see what does not.

This strength that rises from the source of life has many names. The Hebrew prophets understandably called it God; any power that can withstand the shaking of the foundations is surely divine. But the New Testament is more specific about the nature of the strength that endures. In a familiar passage from the first letter to the Corinthians, the Apostle explains that almost everything will eventually pass away, except three things: faith, and hope, and love. These will always hold us steady when trouble comes. Faith lifts us up, hope keeps us going, and love holds us together.

If we are to persevere in the days ahead, we need faith: faith in our leaders, faith in ourselves. After a slow start, President Bush has done a laudable job in the past few days of balancing his dual roles of Mourner in Chief and Commander in Chief. We need to rally around him and trust that he will be president for all of us. His stern censure of Jerry Falwell's hate-filled words—did you hear that Falwell blames homosexuals, feminists, and abortionists, among others, for Tuesday's attack on America?—is surely a sign of his commitment to lead in a way that unites rather than divides.

We also need faith in ourselves. Doubts about our national character have been raised repeatedly in recent days. Many people wonder whether the children of prosperity have the stomach and the attention span to make the sacrifices necessary to uphold our ideals. But not everyone wonders. On Friday afternoon, a New York City police officer appeared unannounced at the door of my office. He had attended the candle-lighting service here on Wednesday night and wanted to say thank you. He also told me that as a child he had lived across the street from the church, and had attended church school here. But mostly he talked about the events of the previous three days, and his time down at the scene: the horrific carnage, the dogged determination of the searchers, and the anguish of the victims' friends and relatives. He talked about how

> *We need faith that we too can be heroes by acting in ways that make a difference.*

upsetting the smell was, but even more the swirling shreds of paper in the streets: torn photos, charred calendar pages, partial memos, unreadable degrees, incomplete lists.

But he also said that he has never felt better about being a cop. "The people have been wonderful to us and to each other," he said. "Everyone offers to help and applauds what we do. If I could go to work every day and feel like I do now, I wouldn't worry how the contract negotiations were going. The city could keep the extra money. Today, everyone is concerned about the right things and angry about the right things and happy about the right things. I just want it to last after the crisis is past."

We need faith that we too can be heroes by acting in ways that make a difference. We need to keep the foundations strong. We also need hope, which is grounded in a sense of that to which we as a nation have been called. One of the most powerful photos I have seen in the past few days shows the smoldering ruins of the World Trade Center, with the Statue of Liberty in the foreground. The statue represents the best of who we are. She is . . .

> A mighty woman with a torch, whose flame
> Is the imprisoned lightning, and her name Mother of Exiles.
> From her beacon-hand
> Glows worldwide welcome. . . .
> Give me your tired, your poor,
> Your huddled masses yearning to breathe free,
> The wretched refuse of your teeming shore.
> Send these, the homeless, tempest-tost to me,
> I lift my lamp beside the golden door!
>
> *Emma Lazarus*

Our mission as a nation is not to amass wealth or exert power or exact revenge. It is to be Mother of Exiles, a golden door for all who yearn to breathe free. When we go to war, we fight in freedom's name for all whom fundamentalism and tyranny have enslaved. We need to keep the foundations strong.

We also need love—for our country, for each other, and even for our enemies. We have done something extraordinary over the past five days. We have paid attention to each other in ways we usually never do. We have listened and cried and phoned and given and hugged as though it really mattered. And it did matter. I want that same spirit to continue. As your minister, I give you permission to grieve what we have lost. Stress, fear, anger, uncertainty, and grief are entirely normal reactions to what we have endured. Working through these feelings will take time. Don't try to go it alone. Reach out. Call me, or Forrest, or Jan, or anyone close to you who can help.*

Also, I give you permission to care about ordinary things. Even though the World Trade Center has been destroyed and thousands of people have died, you need to care about ordinary things that aren't ultimately important but that help keep your foundation strong. Life persists, and most of what bears it along is perfectly ordinary and mundane. Care about ordinary things again. Have a picnic in the park. Buy a new book. Buy some stock—tomorrow morning. We need to keep the foundation strong.

We have seen much sorrow this week, and many acts of courage and bravery. We must mourn our dead and celebrate the heroes among us. And have faith, keep hope, and give love. That is what will keep the foundation strong.

---

* Forrest Church is senior minister at All Souls Church; Jan Carlsson-Bull is assistant minister.

Address to a Joint Session of Congress and the American People[3]

George W. Bush

President of the United States, 2001– ; born New Haven, CT, July 6, 1946, and raised in Midland and Houston, TX; attended Phillips Academy, Andover, MA; B.A., Yale University; M.B.A., Harvard Business School, 1975; F-102 pilot, Texas Air National Guard, 1968–73; oil and gas business, Midland, TX, 1975–86; senior advisor in father's presidential campaign, 1987–88; one of the partners that purchased the Texas Rangers baseball franchise, 1989, and managing general partner of the team, 1989–1994; Governor of Texas, 1995–2000.

Editors' introduction: As President George W. Bush entered the House chamber on the night of September 20, 2001, to make the most important speech of his young presidency, the nation was still reeling from the events of September 11. Those citizens who experienced the dramatic tragedies firsthand and others who witnessed them replayed hourly on television looked to the commander in chief for an appropriate response. None of the president's initial responses, in the judgment of D. T. Max (*New York Times*, Oct. 7, 2001), "soothed the public." However, all that changed with this formal, televised address to Congress and the nation. In a speech that could define his presidency, President Bush praised the heroic responses of citizens in New York, at the Pentagon, and in the air over Pennsylvania, explained the nature and scope of the enemy, and assured Congress and other Americans that "we will direct every resource at our command . . . to the destruction and to the defeat of the global terror network."

George W. Bush's speech: Mr. Speaker, Mr. President Pro Tempore, members of Congress, and fellow Americans:

In the normal course of events, Presidents come to this chamber to report on the state of the Union. Tonight, no such report is needed. It has already been delivered by the American people.

We have seen it in the courage of passengers, who rushed terrorists to save others on the ground—passengers like an exceptional man named Todd Beamer. And would you please help me to welcome his wife, Lisa Beamer, here tonight. (Applause.)

---

3. Delivered on September 20, 2001, in the House of Representatives chamber of the U.S. Capitol building, at Washington, D.C.

We have seen the state of our Union in the endurance of rescuers, working past exhaustion. We have seen the unfurling of flags, the lighting of candles, the giving of blood, the saying of prayers—in English, Hebrew, and Arabic. We have seen the decency of a loving and giving people who have made the grief of strangers their own.

My fellow citizens, for the last nine days, the entire world has seen for itself the state of our Union—and it is strong. (Applause.)

Tonight we are a country awakened to danger and called to defend freedom. Our grief has turned to anger, and anger to resolution. Whether we bring our enemies to justice, or bring justice to our enemies, justice will be done. (Applause.)

I thank the Congress for its leadership at such an important time. All of America was touched on the evening of the tragedy to see Republicans and Democrats joined together on the steps of this Capitol, singing "God Bless America." And you did more than sing; you acted, by delivering $40 billion to rebuild our communities and meet the needs of our military.

> *Whether we bring our enemies to justice, or bring justice to our enemies, justice will be done.*

Speaker Hastert, Minority Leader Gephardt, Majority Leader Daschle, and Senator Lott, I thank you for your friendship, for your leadership and for your service to our country. (Applause.)

And on behalf of the American people, I thank the world for its outpouring of support. America will never forget the sounds of our National Anthem playing at Buckingham Palace, on the streets of Paris, and at Berlin's Brandenburg Gate.

We will not forget South Korean children gathering to pray outside our embassy in Seoul, or the prayers of sympathy offered at a mosque in Cairo. We will not forget moments of silence and days of mourning in Australia and Africa and Latin America.

Nor will we forget the citizens of 80 other nations who died with our own: dozens of Pakistanis; more than 130 Israelis; more than 250 citizens of India; men and women from El Salvador, Iran, Mexico, and Japan; and hundreds of British citizens. America has no truer friend than Great Britain. (Applause.) Once again, we are joined together in a great cause—so honored the British prime minister has crossed an ocean to show his unity of purpose with America. Thank you for coming, friend. (Applause.)

On September the 11, enemies of freedom committed an act of war against our country. Americans have known wars—but for the past 136 years, they have been wars on foreign soil, except for one Sunday in 1941. Americans have known the casualties of war—but not at the center of a great city on a peaceful morning. Americans have known surprise attacks—but never before on thousands of civilians. All of this was brought upon us in a single day—and night fell on a different world, a world where freedom itself is under attack.

Americans have many questions tonight. Americans are asking: Who attacked our country? The evidence we have gathered all points to a collection of loosely affiliated terrorist organizations known as al Qaeda. They are the same murderers indicted for bombing American embassies in Tanzania and Kenya, and responsible for bombing the USS *Cole*.

Al Qaeda is to terror what the mafia is to crime. But its goal is not making money; its goal is remaking the world—and imposing its radical beliefs on people everywhere.

The terrorists practice a fringe form of Islamic extremism that has been rejected by Muslim scholars and the vast majority of Muslim clerics—a fringe movement that perverts the peaceful teachings of Islam. The terrorists' directive commands them to kill Christians and Jews, to kill all Americans, and make no distinction among military and civilians, including women and children.

This group and its leader—a person named Osama bin Laden—are linked to many other organizations in different countries, including the Egyptian Islamic Jihad and the Islamic Movement of Uzbekistan. There are thousands of these terrorists in more than 60 countries. They are recruited from their own nations and neighborhoods and brought to camps in places like Afghanistan, where they are trained in the tactics of terror. They are sent back to their homes or sent to hide in countries around the world to plot evil and destruction.

The leadership of al Qaeda has great influence in Afghanistan and supports the Taliban regime in controlling most of that country. In Afghanistan, we see al Qaeda's vision for the world.

Afghanistan's people have been brutalized—many are starving and many have fled. Women are not allowed to attend school. You can be jailed for owning a television. Religion can be practiced only as their leaders dictate. A man can be jailed in Afghanistan if his beard is not long enough.

The United States respects the people of Afghanistan—after all, we are currently its largest source of humanitarian aid—but we condemn the Taliban regime. (Applause.) It is not only repressing its own people, it is threatening people everywhere by sponsoring and sheltering and supplying terrorists. By aiding and abetting murder, the Taliban regime is committing murder.

And tonight, the United States of America makes the following demands on the Taliban: Deliver to United States authorities all the leaders of al Qaeda who hide in your land. (Applause.) Release all foreign nationals, including American citizens, you have unjustly imprisoned. Protect foreign journalists, diplomats and aid workers in your country. Close immediately and permanently every terrorist training camp in Afghanistan, and hand over every terrorist, and every person in their support structure, to appropriate authorities. (Applause.) Give the United States full access to terrorist training camps, so we can make sure they are no longer operating.

These demands are not open to negotiation or discussion. (Applause.) The Taliban must act, and act immediately. They will hand over the terrorists, or they will share in their fate.

I also want to speak tonight directly to Muslims throughout the world. We respect your faith. It's practiced freely by many millions of Americans, and by millions more in countries that America counts as friends. Its teachings are good and peaceful, and those who commit evil in the name of Allah blaspheme the name of Allah. (Applause.) The terrorists are traitors to their own faith, trying, in effect, to hijack Islam itself. The enemy of America is not our many Muslim friends; it is not our many Arab friends. Our enemy is a radical network of terrorists, and every government that supports them. (Applause.)

Our war on terror begins with al Qaeda, but it does not end there. It will not end until every terrorist group of global reach has been found, stopped and defeated. (Applause.)

Americans are asking, why do they hate us? They hate what we see right here in this chamber—a democratically elected government. Their leaders are self-appointed. They hate our freedoms—our freedom of religion, our freedom of speech, our freedom to vote

---

The terrorists are traitors to their own faith, trying, in effect, to hijack Islam itself.

---

and assemble and disagree with each other.

They want to overthrow existing governments in many Muslim countries, such as Egypt, Saudi Arabia, and Jordan. They want to drive Israel out of the Middle East. They want to drive Christians and Jews out of vast regions of Asia and Africa.

These terrorists kill not merely to end lives, but to disrupt and end a way of life. With every atrocity, they hope that America grows fearful, retreating from the world and forsaking our friends. They stand against us, because we stand in their way.

We are not deceived by their pretenses to piety. We have seen their kind before. They are the heirs of all the murderous ideologies of the 20th century. By sacrificing human life to serve their radical visions—by abandoning every value except the will to power—they follow in the path of fascism, and Nazism, and totalitarianism. And they will follow that path all the way, to where it ends: in history's unmarked grave of discarded lies. (Applause.)

Americans are asking: How will we fight and win this war? We will direct every resource at our command—every means of diplomacy, every tool of intelligence, every instrument of law enforcement, every financial influence, and every necessary weapon of war—to the disruption and to the defeat of the global terror network.

This war will not be like the war against Iraq a decade ago, with a decisive liberation of territory and a swift conclusion. It will not look like the air war above Kosovo two years ago, where no ground troops were used and not a single American was lost in combat.

Our response involves far more than instant retaliation and isolated strikes. Americans should not expect one battle, but a lengthy campaign, unlike any other we have ever seen. It may include dramatic strikes, visible on TV, and covert operations, secret even in success. We will starve terrorists of funding, turn them one against another, drive them from place to place, until there is no refuge or no rest. And we will pursue nations that provide aid or safe haven to terrorism. Every nation, in every region, now has a decision to make. Either you are with us, or you are with the terrorists. (Applause.) From this day forward, any nation that continues to harbor or support terrorism will be regarded by the United States as a hostile regime.

Our nation has been put on notice: We are not immune from attack. We will take defensive measures against terrorism to pro-

---

From this day forward, any nation that continues to harbor or support terrorism will be regarded by the United States as a hostile regime.

---

tect Americans. Today, dozens of federal departments and agencies, as well as state and local governments, have responsibilities affecting homeland security. These efforts must be coordinated at the highest level. So tonight I announce the creation of a cabinet-level position reporting directly to me—the Office of Homeland Security.

And tonight I also announce a distinguished American to lead this effort, to strengthen American security: a military veteran, an effective governor, a true patriot, a trusted friend—Pennsylvania's Tom Ridge. (Applause.) He will lead, oversee and coordinate a comprehensive national strategy to safeguard our country against terrorism, and respond to any attacks that may come.

These measures are essential. But the only way to defeat terrorism as a threat to our way of life is to stop it, eliminate it, and destroy it where it grows. (Applause.)

Many will be involved in this effort, from FBI agents to intelligence operatives to the reservists we have called to active duty. All deserve our thanks, and all have our prayers. And tonight, a few miles from the damaged Pentagon, I have a message for our military: Be ready. I've called the armed forces to alert, and there is a reason. The hour is coming when America will act, and you will make us proud. (Applause.)

This is not, however, just America's fight. And what is at stake is not just America's freedom. This is the world's fight. This is civilization's fight. This is the fight of all who believe in progress and pluralism, tolerance and freedom.

> *We are in a fight for our principles, and our first responsibility is to live by them.*

We ask every nation to join us. We will ask, and we will need, the help of police forces, intelligence services, and banking systems around the world. The United States is grateful that many nations and many international organizations have already responded—with sympathy and with support. Nations from Latin America, to Asia, to Africa, to Europe, to the Islamic world. Perhaps the NATO Charter reflects best the attitude of the world: An attack on one is an attack on all.

The civilized world is rallying to America's side. They understand that if this terror goes unpunished, their own cities, their own citizens may be next. Terror, unanswered, can not only bring down buildings, it can threaten the stability of legitimate governments. And you know what—we're not going to allow it. (Applause.)

Americans are asking: What is expected of us? I ask you to live your lives, and hug your children. I know many citizens have fears tonight, and I ask you to be calm and resolute, even in the face of a continuing threat.

I ask you to uphold the values of America, and remember why so many have come here. We are in a fight for our principles, and our first responsibility is to live by them. No one should be singled out for unfair treatment or unkind words because of their ethnic background or religious faith. (Applause.)

I ask you to continue to support the victims of this tragedy with your contributions. Those who want to give can go to a central source of information, *libertyunites.org*, to find the names of groups providing direct help in New York, Pennsylvania, and Virginia.

The thousands of FBI agents who are now at work in this investigation may need your cooperation, and I ask you to give it.

I ask for your patience, with the delays and inconveniences that may accompany tighter security; and for your patience in what will be a long struggle.

I ask your continued participation and confidence in the American economy. Terrorists attacked a symbol of American prosperity. They did not touch its source. America is successful because of the hard work, and creativity, and enterprise of our people. These were the true strengths of our economy before September 11, and they are our strengths today. (Applause.)

And, finally, please continue praying for the victims of terror and their families, for those in uniform, and for our great country. Prayer has comforted us in sorrow, and will help strengthen us for the journey ahead.

Tonight I thank my fellow Americans for what you have already done and for what you will do. And ladies and gentlemen of the Congress, I thank you, their representatives, for what you have already done and for what we will do together.

Tonight, we face new and sudden national challenges. We will come together to improve air safety, to dramatically expand the number of air marshals on domestic flights, and take new measures to prevent hijacking. We will come together to promote stability and keep our airlines flying, with direct assistance during this emergency. (Applause.)

> *We will not tire, we will not falter, and we will not fail.*

We will come together to give law enforcement the additional tools it needs to track down terror here at home. (Applause.) We will come together to strengthen our intelligence capabilities to know the plans of terrorists before they act, and find them before they strike. (Applause.)

We will come together to take active steps that strengthen America's economy, and put our people back to work.

Tonight we welcome two leaders who embody the extraordinary spirit of all New Yorkers: Governor George Pataki and Mayor Rudolph Giuliani. (Applause.) As a symbol of America's resolve, my administration will work with Congress, and these two leaders, to show the world that we will rebuild New York City. (Applause.)

After all that has just passed—all the lives taken, and all the possibilities and hopes that died with them—it is natural to wonder if America's future is one of fear. Some speak of an age of terror. I know there are struggles ahead, and dangers to face. But this country will define our times, not be defined by them. As long as the United States of America is determined and strong, this will not be an age of terror; this will be an age of liberty, here and across the world. (Applause.)

Great harm has been done to us. We have suffered great loss. And in our grief and anger we have found our mission and our moment. Freedom and fear are at war. The advance of human freedom—the great achievement of our time, and the great hope of every time—now depends on us. Our nation—this generation—will lift a dark threat of violence from our people and our future. We will rally the world to this cause by our efforts, by our courage. We will not tire, we will not falter, and we will not fail. (Applause.)

It is my hope that in the months and years ahead, life will return almost to normal. We'll go back to our lives and routines, and that is good. Even grief recedes with time and grace. But our resolve must not pass. Each of us will remember what happened that day, and to whom it happened. We'll remember the moment the news came—where we were and what we were doing. Some will remember an image of a fire, or a story of rescue. Some will carry memories of a face and a voice gone forever.

And I will carry this: It is the police shield of a man named George Howard, who died at the World Trade Center trying to save others. It was given to me by his mom, Arlene, as a proud memorial to her son. This is my reminder of lives that ended, and a task that does not end. (Applause.)

I will not forget this wound to our country or those who inflicted it. I will not yield; I will not rest; I will not relent in waging this struggle for freedom and security for the American people.

The course of this conflict is not known, yet its outcome is certain. Freedom and fear, justice and cruelty, have always been at war, and we know that God is not neutral between them. (Applause.)

Fellow citizens, we'll meet violence with patient justice—assured of the rightness of our cause, and confident of the victories to come. In all that lies before us, may God grant us wisdom, and may He watch over the United States of America.

Thank you. (Applause.)

United Nations General Assembly Special Session on Terrorism[4]

Rudolph W. Giuliani

Mayor of New York City, 1994–2001; born Brooklyn, NY, 1944; graduated Bishop Loughlin Memorial High School, Brooklyn, 1961; graduated Manhattan College, the Bronx, 1965; graduated magna cum laude, New York University Law School, 1968; upon graduation, clerked for Judge Lloyd MacMahon, U.S. District Judge for the Southern District of New York; office of the U.S. Attorney, 1970, and named chief of the Narcotics Unit and Executive U.S. Attorney; Associate Deputy Attorney General and chief of staff to Deputy Attorney General, Washington, DC, 1975–76; with Patterson, Belknap, Webb and Tyler law firm, 1977–81; Associate Attorney General, Department of Justice, 1981; U.S. Attorney for Southern District of New York, 1983–1992.

Editors' introduction: Mayor Rudolph W. Giuliani confronted the tragic events of September 11 and its dire consequences with heroic determination. He seemed to be everywhere at once, as he comforted grieving families of the victims, supported the search and recovery effort, and briefed the City and the nation with frequent press conferences, announcing within hours of the attack that New York City would emerge stronger than ever from this horrific disaster. In addressing delegates to the United Nations, Mayor Giuliani admonished, "Let those who say that we must understand the reasons for terrorism come with me to the thousands of funerals we are having in New York City. . . . Moral relativism does not have a place in this discussion and debate."

Rudolph W. Giuliani's speech: Thank you, President of the General Assembly Dr. Han Seung-Soo. Thank you, Secretary-General Kofi Annan.

Thank you very much for the opportunity to speak, and for the consideration you've shown the City in putting off your General Session. As I explained to the Secretary-General and the President of the General Assembly, our city is now open, and any time we can arrange it, we look forward to having your heads of state and your foreign ministers here for that session.

---

4. Delivered on October 1, 2001, in the United Nations building, at New York City.

On September 11, 2001, New York City—the most diverse city in the world—was viciously attacked in an unprovoked act of war. More than 5,000 innocent men, women, and children of every race, religion, and ethnicity are lost. Among these were people from 80 different nations. To their representatives here today, I offer my condolences to you as well on behalf of all New Yorkers who share this loss with you. This was the deadliest terrorist attack in history. It claimed more lives than Pearl Harbor or D-Day.

This was not just an attack on the City of New York or on the United States of America. It was an attack on the very idea of a free, inclusive, and civil society.

It was a direct assault on the founding principles of the United Nations itself. The Preamble to the UN Charter states that this organization exists "to reaffirm faith in fundamental human rights, in the dignity and worth of the human person . . . to practice tolerance and live together in peace as good neighbors . . . [and] to unite our strength to maintain international peace and security."

This was not just an attack on the City of New York or on the United States of America. It was an attack on the very idea of a free, inclusive, and civil society.

Indeed, this vicious attack places in jeopardy the whole purpose of the United Nations.

Terrorism is based on the persistent and deliberate violation of fundamental human rights. With bullets and bombs—and now with hijacked airplanes—terrorists deny the dignity of human life. Terrorism preys particularly on cultures and communities that practice openness and tolerance. Their targeting of innocent civilians mocks the efforts of those who seek to live together in peace as neighbors. It defies the very notion of being a neighbor.

This massive attack was intended to break our spirit. It has not done that. It has made us stronger, more determined and more resolved.

The bravery of our firefighters, our police officers, our emergency workers, and civilians we may never learn of, in saving over 25,000 lives that day—carrying out the most effective rescue operation in our history—inspires all of us. I am very honored to have with me, as their representative, the Fire Commissioner of New York City, Tom Von Essen, and the Police Commissioner of New York City, Bernard Kerik. [Applause]

The determination, resolve, and leadership of President George W. Bush has unified America and all decent men and women around the world.

The response of many of your nations—your leaders and people—spontaneously demonstrating in the days after the attack your support for New York and America, and your understanding of what needs to be done to remove the threat of terrorism, gives us great, great hope that we will prevail.

The strength of America's response, please understand, flows from the principles upon which we stand.

Americans are not a single ethnic group.

Americans are not of one race or one religion.

Americans emerge from all your nations.

We are defined as Americans by our beliefs—not by our ethnic origins, our race or our religion. Our beliefs in religious freedom, political freedom, and economic freedom—that's what makes an American. Our belief in democracy, the rule of law, and respect for human life—that's how you become an American. It is these very principles—and the opportunities these principles give to so many to create a better life for themselves and their families—that make

---

The best long-term deterrent to terrorism . . . is the spread of our principles of freedom, democracy, the rule of law, and respect for human life.

America, and New York, a "shining city on a hill."

There is no nation, and no city, in the history of the world that has seen more immigrants, in less time, than America. People continue to come here in large numbers to seek freedom, opportunity, decency, and civility.

Each of your nations—I am certain—has contributed citizens to the United States and to New York. I believe I can take every one of you someplace in New York City, where you can find someone from your country, someone from your village or town, that speaks your language and practices your religion. In each of your lands there are many who are Americans in spirit, by virtue of their commitment to our shared principles.

It is tragic and perverse that it is because of these very principles—particularly our religious, political and economic freedoms—that we find ourselves under attack by terrorists.

Our freedom threatens them, because they know that if our ideas of freedom gain a foothold among their people it will destroy their power. So they strike out against us to keep those ideas from reaching their people.

The best long-term deterrent to terrorism—obviously—is the spread of our principles of freedom, democracy, the rule of law, and respect for human life. The more that spreads around the globe, the safer we will all be. These are very powerful ideas and once they gain a foothold, they cannot be stopped.

In fact, the rise that we have seen in terrorism and terrorist groups, I believe, is in no small measure a response to the spread of these ideas of freedom and democracy to many nations, particularly over the past 15 years.

The terrorists have no ideas or ideals with which to combat freedom and democracy. So their only defense is to strike out against innocent civilians, destroying human life in massive numbers and hoping to deter all of us from our pursuit and expansion of freedom.

But the long-term deterrent of spreading our ideals throughout the world is just not enough, and may never be realized, if we do not act—and act together—to remove the clear and present danger posed by terrorism and terrorists.

The United Nations must hold accountable any country that supports or condones terrorism, otherwise you will fail in your primary mission as peacekeeper.

It must ostracize any nation that supports terrorism.

It must isolate any nation that remains neutral in the fight against terrorism.

> *There is no room for neutrality on the issue of terrorism. You're either with civilization or with terrorists.*

Now is the time, in the words of the UN Charter, "to unite our strength to maintain international peace and security." This is not a time for further study or vague directives. The evidence of terrorism's brutality and inhumanity—of its contempt for life and the concept of peace—is lying beneath the rubble of the World Trade Center less than two miles from where we meet today.

Look at that destruction, that massive, senseless, cruel loss of human life . . . and then I ask you to look in your hearts and recognize that there is no room for neutrality on the issue of terrorism. You're either with civilization or with terrorists.

On one side is democracy, the rule of law, and respect for human life; on the other is tyranny, arbitrary executions, and mass murder.

We're right and they're wrong. It's as simple as that.

And by that I mean that America and its allies are right about democracy, about religious, political, and economic freedom.

The terrorists are wrong, and in fact evil, in their mass destruction of human life in the name of addressing alleged injustices.

Let those who say that we must understand the reasons for terrorism come with me to the thousands of funerals we are having in New York City and explain those insane, maniacal reasons to the children who will grow up without fathers and mothers, to the parents who have had their children ripped from them for no reason at all.

Instead, I ask each of you to allow me to say at those funerals that your nation stands with America in making a solemn promise and pledge that we will achieve unconditional victory over terrorism and terrorists.

There is no excuse for mass murder, just as there is no excuse for genocide. Those who practice terrorism—murdering or victimizing innocent civilians—lose any right to have their cause understood by decent people and lawful nations.

On this issue—terrorism—the United Nations must draw a line. The era of moral relativism between those who practice or condone terrorism, and those nations who stand up against it, must end. Moral relativism does not have a place in this discussion and debate.

There is no moral way to sympathize with grossly immoral actions. And by trying to do that, unfortunately, a fertile field has been created in which terrorism has grown.

The best and most practical way to promote peace is to stand up to terror and intimidation. The Security Council's unanimous passage of Resolution 1373, adopting wide ranging antiterrorism measures in the international community is a very good first step. It's necessary to establish accountability for the subsidizing of terrorism.

As a former United States Attorney, I am particularly encouraged that the UN has answered President Bush's call to cut terrorists off from their money and their funding. It's enormously important. We've done that successfully with organized crime groups in America. By taking away their ability to mass large amounts of money, you take away their ability to have others carry on their functioning for them, even if they are removed, arrested, prosecuted, or eliminated through war or through law enforcement. It cuts off the lifeblood of the organization. So I believe this is a very good first step.

But now it's up to the member states to enforce this and other aspects of the resolution, and for the United Nations to enforce these new mechanisms to take the financial base away from the terrorists. Take away their money, take away their access to money, and you reduce their ability to carry out complex missions.

Each of you is sitting in this room because of your country's commitment to being part of the family of nations. We need to unite as a family as never before—across all our differences, in recognition of the fact that the United Nations stands for the proposition that we human beings have more in common than divides us.

If you need to be reminded of this, you don't need to look very far. Just go outside for a walk in the streets and parks of New York City. You can't walk a block in New York City without seeing somebody that looks different than you, acts different than you, talks different than you, believes different than you. If you grow up in New York City, you learn that. And if you're an intelligent or decent person, you learn that all those differences are nothing in comparison to the things that unite us.

We are a city of immigrants—unlike any other City—within a nation of immigrants. Like the victims of the World Trade Center attack, we are of every race, religion, and ethnicity. Our diversity has always been our greatest source of strength. It's the thing that renews us and revives us in every generation—our openness to new people from all over the world.

So from the first day of this attack, an attack on New York and America, and I believe an attack on the basic principles that underlie this organization, I have told the people of New York that we should not allow this to divide us, because then we would really lose what this city is all about. We have very strong and vibrant Arab and Muslim communities in New York City. They are an equally important part of the life of our city. We respect their religious beliefs. We respect everybody's religious beliefs—that's what America's about, that's what New York City is about. I have urged New Yorkers not to engage in any form of group blame or group hatred. This is exactly the evil that we are confronting with these terrorists. And if we are going to prevail over terror, our ideals, principles, and values must transcend all forms of prejudice. This is a very important part of the struggle against terrorism.

Our diversity has always been our greatest source of strength. It's the thing that renews us and revives us in every generation.

This is not a dispute between religions or ethnic groups. All religions, all decent people, are united in their desire to achieve peace, and understand that we have to eliminate terrorism. We're not divided about this.

There have been many days in New York when I was running for Mayor, and then since I've been Mayor, when I would have a weekend in which I would go to a mosque on Friday, and a synagogue on Saturday, and a church—sometimes two churches—on a Sunday. And by the time I finished, I would say to myself, "I know that we're through to God." We're talking to him in every language that He understands, we're using every liturgy that exists, and I know that we are getting through to the same God, even though we may be doing it in slightly different ways. God is known by many different names and many different traditions, but identified by one consistent feeling, love. Love for humanity, particularly love for our children. Love does eventually conquer hate, but it needs our help. Good intentions alone are not enough to conquer evil.

Remember British Prime Minister Neville Chamberlain, who—armed only with good intentions—negotiated with the Nazis and emerged hopeful that he had achieved peace in his time. Hitler's wave of terror was only encouraged by these attempts at appeasement. At the cost of millions of lives, we learned that words—though important—are not enough to guarantee peace. It is action alone that counts.

For the UN, and individual nations, decisive action is needed to stop terrorism from ever orphaning another child.

That's for nations. For individuals, the most effective course of action they can take to aid our recovery is to be determined to go ahead with their lives. We can't let terrorists change the way we live—otherwise they will have succeeded.

In some ways, the resilience of life in New York City is the ultimate sign of defiance to terrorism. We call ourselves the Capital of the World in large part because we are the most diverse city in the world, home to the United Nations. The spirit of unity amid all our diversity has never been stronger.

On Saturday night I walked through Times Square, it was crowded, it was bright, it was lively. Thousands of people were visiting from all parts of the United States and all parts of the world. And many of them came up to me and shook my hand and patted me on the back and said, "We're here because we want to show our support for the City of New York." And that's why there has never been a better time to come to New York City.

I say to people across the country and around the world: if you were planning to come to New York sometime in the future, come here now. Come to enjoy our thousands of restaurants, museums, theaters, sporting events, and shopping . . . but also come to take a stand against terrorism.

We need to heed the words of a hymn that I, and the police commissioner, and the fire commissioner, have heard at the many funerals and memorial services that we've gone to in the last two weeks. The hymn begins, "Be Not Afraid."

Freedom from fear is a basic human right. We need to reassert our right to live free from fear with greater confidence and determination than ever before . . . here in New York City . . . across America . . . and around the world. With one clear voice, unanimously, we need to say that we will not give in to terrorism.

Surrounded by our friends of every faith, we know that this is not a clash of civilizations; it is a conflict between murderers and humanity.

This is not a question of retaliation or revenge. It is a matter of justice leading to peace. The only acceptable result is the complete and total eradication of terrorism.

New Yorkers are strong and resilient. We are unified. And we will not yield to terror. We do not let fear make our decisions for us.

We choose to live in freedom.

Thank you, and God bless you.

Taliban Oppression of Women and Children[5]

Laura Welch Bush

First Lady of the United States, 2001– ; born Midland, TX, November 4, 1946; B.S. in education, Southern Methodist University, 1968; Master of Library Science, University of Texas at Austin, 1973; teacher, Longfellow Elementary School, Dallas, 1968–69; teacher, John F. Kennedy Elementary School, Houston, 1970–72; librarian, Houston Public Library, 1973–74; librarian, Dawson Elementary School, Austin, 1974–77.

Editors' introduction: After the terrorist attacks of September 11, First Lady Laura Welch Bush sought to help children and their parents adjust to the losses suffered by the nation. In public appearances, Mrs. Bush had maintained that every human being should be treated with dignity, and that no child should be left behind in school or in life. She therefore joined a worldwide effort to end the Taliban's oppression of women and children in Afghanistan, where the United States was currently conducting a military campaign against the Taliban and the al Qaeda terrorist network. In what was the first weekly presidential radio address given by a First Lady of the United Sates, Mrs. Bush insisted that "fighting brutality against women and children is not the expression of a specific culture; it's the acceptance of our common humanity."

Laura Welch Bush's speech: Good morning. I'm Laura Bush. And I am delivering this week's radio address to kick off a worldwide effort to focus on the brutality against women and children by the al Qaeda terrorist network and the regime it supports in Afghanistan, the Taliban.

That regime is now in retreat across much of the country, and the people of Afghanistan, especially women, are rejoicing. Afghan women know through hard experience what the rest of the world is discovering: The brutal oppression of women is a central goal of the terrorists.

Long before the current war began, the Taliban and its terrorist allies were making the lives of children and women in Afghanistan miserable. Seventy percent of the Afghan people are malnourished.

---

5. Delivered on Saturday, November 17, 2001, as the weekly radio address regularly delivered by President George W. Bush.

One in every four children won't live past the age of five because health care is not available. Women have been denied access to doctors when they're sick.

Life under the Taliban is so hard and repressive, even small displays of joy are outlawed. Children aren't allowed to fly kites. Their mothers face beatings for laughing out loud. Women cannot work outside the home or even leave their homes by themselves.

The severe repression and brutality against women in Afghanistan is not a matter of legitimate religious practice. Muslims around the world have condemned the brutal degradation of women and children by the Taliban regime. The poverty, poor health, and illiteracy that the terrorists and the Taliban have imposed on women in Afghanistan do not conform with the treatment of women in most of the Islamic world, where women make important contributions in their societies.

Only the terrorists and the Taliban forbid education to women. Only the terrorists and the Taliban threaten to pull out women's fingernails for wearing nail polish.

The plight of the women and children in Afghanistan is a matter of deliberate human cruelty carried out by those who seek to intimidate and control.

Civilized people throughout the world are speaking out in horror, not only because our hearts break for the women and children in Afghanistan but also because, in Afghanistan, we see the world the terrorists would like to impose on the rest of us.

The severe repression and brutality against women in Afghanistan is not a matter of legitimate religious practice.

All of us have an obligation to speak out. We may come from different backgrounds and faiths, but parents the world over love their children. We respect our mothers, our sisters and daughters.

Fighting brutality against women and children is not the expression of a specific culture; it's the acceptance of our common humanity, a commitment shared by people of good will on every continent.

Because of our recent military gains, in much of Afghanistan women are no longer imprisoned in their homes. They can listen to music and teach their daughters without fear of punishment.

Yet, the terrorists who helped rule that country now plot and plan in many countries, and they must be stopped. The fight against terrorism is also a fight for the rights and dignity of women.

In America, next week brings Thanksgiving. After the events of the last few months, we will be holding our families even closer. And we will be especially thankful for all of the blessings of American life.

I hope Americans will join our family in working to ensure that dignity and opportunity will be secured for all the women and children of Afghanistan.

Have a wonderful holiday, and thank you for listening.

Chicago Council on Foreign Relations[6]

Jonathan F. Fanton

President, John D. and Catherine T. MacArthur Foundation, 1999– ; born Alabama, April 29, 1943, and raised in Connecticut; B.A., 1965, M.A. in philosophy, 1977, and Ph.D. in American history, 1978, Yale University; assistant to Yale president Kingman Brewster, 1970–73; associate provost, Yale University, 1976–78; vice president for planning and professor of American history, University of Chicago, 1978–82; president, New School University, New York City, 1982–99; chair, Human Rights Watch; advisory trustee, Rockefeller Brothers Fund; former cochair, 14th Street/Union Square Local Development Corporation, New York City.

Editors' introduction: Although terrorism had been of worldwide concern for decades, the hijacking of airliners in the United States on September 11 increased the threat felt by Americans in their own homeland and raised the call for greater security. While many were preoccupied with the installation of metal detectors and airport luggage scanners, some, such as the historian Dr. Jonathan F. Fanton, sought a better understanding of the causes of terrorism. In his speech to the Chicago Council on Foreign Relations, Fanton maintained that "fighting terrorism and respecting human rights are not mutually incompatible goals." The Chicago Council provides its 7,000 members, specialized groups, and the general public a forum for addressing all sides of significant international issues and their bearing on American foreign policy. President Fanton participated in a panel entitled "The Anatomy of Terrorism: Terrorism and Civil Society." The speech was Mr. Fanton's opening remarks. Attending the panel were Chicago Council members, businesspeople, university students, and leaders of of nongovernmental organizations in the area.

Jonathan F. Fanton's speech: When we speak of civil society we are also talking about democratic aspirations and building a culture that respects human rights. Where the three elements come together—democracy, civil society, and a respect for human rights—terrorism has a hard time finding sympathizers—let alone recruits.

---

6. Delivered on February 28, 2002, at Chicago, IL. Reprinted with the permission of Jonathan F. Fanton.

The reverse is also true: authoritarian regimes, sometimes wrongly praised for infusing stability—and supported for that purpose—are more likely to create the conditions that give rise to terrorism.

What I know outside the U.S. comes largely from 20 years of work with Human Rights Watch where my focus was East and Central Europe and the former Soviet Union, including Central Asia. And, as President of MacArthur, I have learned firsthand the critical role of civil society in three countries undergoing democratic transition: Mexico, Russia, and Nigeria. MacArthur has an office in each and supports civil society groups working on the environment, population, education and human rights.

In a recent *New York Times* op-ed piece, Michael Ignatieff asked a provocative and disturbing question: is the human rights era ending or at least in sharp recession, a victim of the U.S.-led war on terrorism? He wrote:

> The new element in determining American foreign policy is what assets—bases, intelligence and diplomatic leverage—it can bring to bear against Al Qaeda.
>
> Some veterans of the human rights campaigns of the cold war refuse to admit that the climate is any worse now than it was then. But in the Reagan years, the movement merely risked being unpopular. In the Bush era it risks irrelevance.

Despite Washington's tendency to subordinate human rights in fighting terrorism, human rights concerns are hardly irrelevant in the Bush era. I cite as one example the lengths to which this administration went to avoid civilian casualties in Afghanistan. But Ignatieff does identify an ongoing tension that challenges the human rights movement to sharpen its arguments.

I believe that fighting terrorism and respecting human rights are not mutually incompatible goals. Indeed, just the reverse is true. It is the body of international and humanitarian law—the philosophical foundation of the human rights movement—that establishes the principle that civilians are never a legitimate target of war for any cause.

Kenneth Roth, Executive Director of Human Rights Watch, put it this way, and I quote:

> The fight against terrorism should be seen only in part as a matter of security. It is also a matter of values. Police, intelligence units, even armies all have a role to play in meeting particular terrorist threats. But terrorism emanates as well from the realm of public morality. It is essential to understand the mores that would countenance such mass murder as a legitimate political tool. Building a stronger human rights culture—a culture in which any disregard for civilian life is condemned rather than condoned—is essential in the long run for defeating terrorism.

The U.S. and its allies must strengthen the culture for human rights, democracy and civil society through opposition to authoritarian regimes and by example.

This position is not inconsistent with strengthening our security and rooting out terrorist networks, which are both vital tasks. I would advocate, for example, aggressive physical and electronic surveillance of suspects, heightened intelligence sharing, vigorous prosecution of offenders under the myriad existing laws, and shutting down the bases that terrorists use to launch attacks on civilians. But I do not think security measures alone will get the job done. So I see it as a very pragmatic response to say that we need both better security and affirmative steps to build democracy and a human rights culture.

I would ask whether the United States has done enough in the Middle East and North Africa to support the growth of civil society, democracy and human rights. Take Saudi Arabia, home of Osama

---

I would ask whether the United States has done enough . . . to support the growth of civil society, democracy and human rights.

---

bin Laden and fifteen of the nineteen September 11 hijackers, a society that suppresses dissent and condones discrimination against women. Or Egypt, home of the accused ringleader and other al Qaeda leaders, which is also inhospitable to political opposition.

Citing the need for Egypt's partnership in pursuing a Middle East peace or in recognition of our dependence on Saudi oil, the U.S. has far too long given a free pass to those two countries to pursue oppressive policies.

Here is what we said in the Human Rights Watch annual report:

> In societies where basic freedoms flourish, citizens could have pressed their government to respond to grievances, on threat of being publicly scorned and voted out of power. But in Egypt, Saudi Arabia, and many of the other countries where Osama bin Laden strikes a chord of resentment, governments restrict debate about how to address society's ills. They close off avenues for peaceful political change. They leave people with the desperate choice of tolerating the status quo, exile, or violence. Frequently, as political options are closed off, the voices of non-violent dissent are upstaged by a politics of radical opposition.

That observation is likely to strike with special force in Uzbekistan, one of our new allies in the war against terrorism. I have been to Uzbekistan seven times, first in 1990, most recently last April. It is a good case in point. Civil society groups have a hard time in

Uzbekistan, their leaders harassed and jailed. There are no free elections, no independent media, no political opposition, no independent human rights groups.

In 1998, I visited Tashkent as part of a Human Rights Watch delegation looking into the problem of students expelled from the universities for practicing the Islamic faith, wearing head dresses, growing beards. I recall vividly a meeting with 20 students expelled from Tashkent State University and the Institute of Eastern Studies.

I asked the students if they were part of a campus organization or had engaged in any political activities. "We have the right to express our ideas," one student responded. "Sometimes we gather and talk about politics and religion just as students do everywhere. But we are not an organization." Another commented: "The government says we are Wahhabists—that we are all armed to the teeth, ready to kill—but we are not—Wahhabism is only something I hear about on radio and television."

"We have a dictatorship today," one student charged. "There are other countries where people can express their opinions freely but not in Uzbekistan." "If we speak our minds the government calls us fundamentalists," said another. Finally, one bearded man, destined to become a leader, said, "Karimov wants to keep power, playing on fear of fundamentalism in his strategy. But he will make Islam an oppositional political force, a force for protecting our rights."

Since that time the al Qaeda–linked rebel group, the Islamic Movement of Uzbekistan, has gained force—just as the students had predicted. It would not surprise me if one or two of them had been driven to the IMU.

Against this backdrop of religious repression—and there is much more than just these students—the United States government has never cited Uzbekistan as a country of concern for suppression of religious freedom on the annual list compiled under the International Religious Freedom Act.

I have no doubt that Uzbekistan, together with other repressive regimes like Turkmenistan, will produce tomorrow's terrorists shielded by ordinary people whose human rights have been denied.

Can strengthening civil society make a difference in fighting terrorism? Does it help to nurture local groups concerned about despoiling the environment, to fund partnerships for Uzbek universities with Western counterparts, to give technical advice to independent but nonpolitical newspapers? Yes it does. Is it useful for international NGOs to have offices in Tashkent, Human Rights Watch, the Eurasia Foundation, Open Society Institute, the Red Cross, and the Institute for War and Peace Reporting? No doubt.

But let us face the cold reality that allowing symbolic space for weak civil society does not inexorably lead to a more open and democratic society. We have been pursuing the civil society route for over a decade in Uzbekistan and conditions are more repressive today than they were five years ago.

A few civil society groups fortified by the presence of international NGOs is no substitute for a free press, an independent electronic media or a robust opposition party.

By now we should know that dictators like Karimov respond to power, not well-intended exhortation. What the World Bank and the IMF do matters. U.S. and Western economic pressure is critical. Even the largely symbolic act of being on the U.S. religious freedom watch list can help.

Private groups like the Council on Foreign Relations also have a role to play. I recall an unfortunate event at the New York Council several years ago at which President Karimov spoke unchallenged to a group of Council members eager to do business in Central Asia. That warm reception undercut the Human Rights Watch message that international business is wary of stability that comes at the price of human rights repression. Being informed about internal conditions in Uzbekistan and asking challenging questions would have been helpful that night.

I have spoken about an imbalance in the West's response to terrorism—too much weight on security and military means and an underinvestment in persuading authoritarian societies to pursue a more open and democratic path.

Now is the time to correct the imbalance—for sure by nurturing civil society groups in countries which are fertile ground for terrorists and their supporters. But also by mobilizing economic and political pressure on those same societies to open to the free market and democracy.

Now is not the time to issue free passes in exchange for air bases or energy. Now is not the time to set bad examples by compromising civil liberties and respect for international standards at home.

I am by nature an optimist—I feel good about the way our democratic system has worked in this difficult period—lots of vigorous discussion about antiterrorism regulations, the treatment of Taliban and al Qaeda prisoners, and the conduct of the war in Afghanistan. That discussion—here and around the world—has muted our government's one-dimensional first instincts—and demonstrated, I think, that human rights principles are by now deeply rooted and remarkably resilient.

The next step is to strengthen the implementation of these principles through a mix of building civil society and applying political and economic pressure to authoritarian regimes that are fertile ground for terrorists. That would constitute a more effective approach to fighting terrorism than the present course.

Muslims Within the Democratic Framework[7]

Shaykh Muhammad Hisham Kabbani

Founder and Chairman, Islamic Supreme Council of America; a naturalized citizen, 1996, born in the Middle East; B.S. in chemistry, American University of Beirut, Lebanon, 1968; medical studies in Louvain, Belgium, 1968–73; degree in Islamic Divine Law, Damascus, Syria; license to teach students in Islamic spirituality, from Hanafi scholar Shaykh Muhammad Nazim Adil, 1989; former co-developer and general manager, Jeddah Medical Center, Saudi Arabia, 1978–81; founded 23 Islamic spiritual study and meeting centers in the United States and Canada; advisor, Human Rights Council, U.S.A.; founder of several top-rated Islamic Web sites; author of articles and books about Islam, including Encyclopedia of Muhammad's Women Companions, Naqshbandi Way, Angels Unveiled, Pearls & Coral, *vols. I and II, and* Encyclopedia of Islamic Doctrine and Beliefs According to Ahl as-Sunna; *has appeared on National Public Radio and numerous TV and radio programs, including* Today *and* CNN Headline News.

Editors' introduction: The attack on the United States by a few Muslim extremists prompted some people to question the motives of most Muslims. President George W. Bush and many Muslim leaders, including Shaykh Muhammad Hisham Kabbani, assured Americans that most Muslims shared their own values. A prominent Islamic American scholar, Shaykh Kabbani has devoted his life to spreading the Islamic messages of peace, tolerance, respect and love throughout the world. He spoke to more than 100 persons at the Ethics and Public Policy Center's inaugural program on the future relationship between Islam and democracy, especially the desire of American Muslims "to live by truly democratic traditions." Attending were important U.S. policymakers, foreign representatives, NGOs, and media representatives. Some commentators noted that it was the first time they had heard many of the points raised by Shaykh Kabbani about the compatibility of Islam and Western-style democracy.

Shaykh Muhammad Hisham Kabbani's speech: The Muslim community in the United States continues to grow and, as it begins to occupy a greater role within the American political system, poli-

---

7. Delivered on July 11, 2002, at Washington, D.C., at a noon luncheon. Reprinted by permission of Shaykh Muhammad Hisham Kabbani.

cymakers, the media and the public are beginning to ask some of the fundamental questions about its political stance and composition. What motivates Muslims? Are their culture and beliefs in opposition to those of Western civilization, and, if so, are we moving inevitably towards a "clash of civilizations"?

Firstly, one must realize that Muslims are not monolithic. Interpretations of Islamic teachings are as diverse as the members of the global Muslim community, which spans 65 countries and, in the United States, is comprised of more than 40 cultures and languages. While core beliefs are essentially the same among all Muslims, the variations in interpretation are no fewer than those within the Jewish, Christian, Hindu, or Buddhist communities. This diversity is part of the great dynamism of the faith. The tendency of Islam is therefore to accommodate the developments and progress of society, despite the opinions put forth by underqualified or misinformed students and scholars of Islam. Over the centuries of Islamic history, Muslims moved towards a dynastic system of governance and away from the principles of justice, freedom and choice that marked the initial Islamic model prescribed by the Prophet Muhammad (S). These principles, similar in so many ways to the ancient Greek and contemporary Western models of democracy, are inherent in Islam.

> *Interpretations of Islamic teachings are as diverse as the members of the global Muslim community.*

Upon examining the democratic ideals present in early Islamic history, and thereby firmly establishing the existence of democracy within Islam, one can then ask why democratic principles are not present in modern Muslim states. Currently, many Islamic movements not only oppose the West and its influence on Muslim lands, but they reject the system of democracy outright. They contend that democracy and Islam are disparate and opposing systems, as in the Islamic model of governance the source of law is the will of God, while in democracy law is derived from the will of man. This assessment is inaccurate. A close examination of the Islamic tradition shows that God has revealed Islamic law, but the application of the law is based on human understanding and interpretation, and, moreover, demonstrates that the law is dynamic and adaptable to changing society. Clearly, the argument made in this paper does not coincide with some of the views of other Muslim speakers or organizations. But what is taking place today inside the Muslim community is as much a "clash of civilizations" as what many fear is impending between Islam and the West. One can hope that, out of this internal struggle, Muslims will familiarize themselves with their past political theories and practices and realize that there is no incompatibility between Islam and democracy.

Democracy in Light of Traditional Islamic Sources

A recent scholar of Islam, Imam Abu Zahra, discusses in his *History of the Islamic Schools of Thought* that there are more than 470 distinct schools of thought in Islam and all of them agree that the Muslim political leadership should be chosen by the Muslim community.[1] This assertion is supported by a well-known saying of the Prophet Muhammad (S), "If you are three, choose one from among you as the leader."[2] Whatever the size of the populace, Muslims should select a leader to rule and guide their community. Consequently, elections were carried out in the time of the first four caliphs of Islam, and independent, competitive political parties were present in the selection process.

The formation of parties with differing views as to who would be the best successor, along with the events that ensued in the selection process, provided a model for the transition of political leadership for future generations. When the Prophet Muhammad (S) passed away, he intentionally did not appoint a leader for the new Muslim state, leaving the Muslims to convene and elect a leader for themselves. The Muslim community discussed the situation and made their individual choices. Three parties emerged in the selection process, each with their own set of candidates. Ultimately, the three groups arrived at a consensus through a council of respected members of the community, and Abu Bakr as-Siddiq was selected as the designated successor. Once the majority decision had been reached, the selection was confirmed by the individual citizens who pledged their allegiance to the new ruler. Continuing and affirming this tradition, Umar ibn al-Khattab, the second caliph of the Muslim state, said, "whoever is chosen by the people after me will be the caliph, and you must listen to and obey him."[3] Thus, the Islamic precedent for peaceful transition between rulers was introduced.

Further examples of democracy in early Islam abound; the constitution of Medina and the Pact of Umar are among the clear examples of the practices of pluralism and the rule of law. The constitution of Medina was written by the Prophet Muhammad (S) while the Muslims ruled the city. A portion of the constitution reads, "The Jews of Banu 'Awf are one nation with the Muslims; the Jews have their religion and the Muslims have theirs, their freedmen and their persons shall be protected except those who behave unjustly."[4] This article of the constitution went on to include the same rights for the other Jewish tribes residing in Medina. It was a strong confirmation of the Prophet's ongoing position to provide Christian, Jewish and other religious communities with freedom of worship.

In the 7th century, the caliph Umar established a pact with the Christians of Syria whereby they would live under the protection of the Muslim state. This pact further illustrates the Islamic acceptance of a pluralistic society, wherein its citizens would enjoy the right to worship and receive security and social services provided by the Muslim state. The non-Muslim inhabitants were required to pay a tax, *jizya*, which was a similar amount to the Muslim tax, *zakat*, to cover the expenses of the army and social welfare for all the citizens. As the payment of *zakat* for the benefit of the Muslim commonwealth is a tenet of the Islamic faith, non-Muslims were not required to pay it as an act of religious worship, but rather paid a different tax based on their amount of wealth. The different requirements for the various religious communities under the caliph again demonstrate the presence and acceptance of religious freedom in Islam.

The status and codification of the body of Islamic law is a crucial and often misunderstood element in the discussion of Islamic political theory. A shaykh of Al-Azhar University in Cairo and prominent scholar of Islam, Dr. Abdul Halim Mahmoud has written on the adoption of societal, political and economic developments from other cultures into Islamic society, so long as they do not conflict with the tenets of Islamic belief.[5] The Qur'an did not abrogate the entirety of the rules by which pre-Islamic society lived, but rather corrected them and offered a perfected model of governance for which man could strive. Dr. Mahmoud continues that freedom, choice, and man's powers of deduction are clarified in the Qur'an and Hadith as gifts granted by God, and thus should be used in approaching Islamic law.[6] As the society in which Muslims live will inevitably change as they encounter new cultures and environments, the Prophetic traditions intentionally left the majority of Islamic law open to interpretation and adaptation within the limits of fundamental Islamic belief and obligatory worship.

Specifically, modifications to the law are presented to a *shura'*, or consultative body, a process similar to a referendum. The *shura'* gathers the opinions of the society and determines appropriate changes to the law based on the concensus of society. This council is established as a parliament or advisory committee with whom the Muslim ruler consults before implementing decisions or rules. Similar to the community's right to voice their opinion for choice of ruler, the Caliph must consult the *shura'* in decisions affecting the lives of the community. Accordingly, whenever the Prophet (S) had a significant decision to make, he gathered his followers and requested they consult amongst themselves and present him with their decision.

While these examples clearly illustrate the prominent role democratic principles—born out of Islamic belief—have played in the formation of the early Islamic polity, over time the Muslim world moved away from their historical political system. Today, one finds few remnants of the rule of the people crafted by the Prophet (S) and his succeeding generations.

Democracy in the Muslim World

As mentioned above, Islam mandated democratic choice through a council of leaders, a process through which members of a community convene, consult one another, and select a leader to represent them. This process was recently employed in Afghanistan where, despite the majority of the population adhering to conservative branches of Islam, the people convened and made arguments for their choice of leader. The recent *loya jirga*, which confirmed Hamid Karzai as president of Afghanistan, demonstrated that democratic principles could exist within a contemporary Muslim nation.

While the *loya jirga* was a positive sign for the reemergence of democracy in Muslim society, the majority of nations in which Muslims are a majority practice largely autocratic systems of governance. Centuries of Islamic political history were dominated by a dynastic model of rule, implemented by both the Muslim rulers and later adapted from British colonial rule following the collapse of the Ottoman Empire. The modern Turkish state born out of the

> *American Muslims, for the most part, view democracy as an acceptable means of political organization.*

Empire was built on exclusively Western and secular standards. This model, however, does not prove a useful one for other reform-minded Muslim nations, lest they completely remove religion from the political and legislative arena. Such separation of "church and state" in Muslim nations would be nearly impossible because, for the majority of the populace, the basis for the law throughout the centuries of their political history—from the inception of the religion to modernity—has been Islam.

Aside from the theoretical challenges, there are other, more practical obstacles facing democratic reform in the Muslim world. Movement towards free and fair elections and a legal system based on the rule of the people directly endangers the reigning monarchies of the Islamic world. Kingdoms, though they may employ the concept of divine right or entitlement on historical grounds, have no real basis for their authority in Islam. The establishment of truly free democratic states in the Muslim world will require an exhaustive campaign of educating Muslims on the benefits of the democratic system, not from the Western perspective but from that of their own Islamic heritage.

American Muslims and Democracy

American Muslims, for the most part, view democracy as an acceptable means of political organization. They have no misgivings towards it in either practical or theoretical terms. They participate in elections, meaningful debate, and on occasion communicate concerns to their elected officials. When organized efforts to affect policy occur, however, the situation becomes more complicated and problematic. At times, organized campaigns through mosques or national Islamic organizations clandestinely provide support for extremist groups actively opposed to the U.S. Moreover, the leadership of these organizations show a superficial willingness to work with policymakers, yet in their literature and internal discussions seem to fundamentally oppose the U.S. for its dominant role in the world arena and policies towards the Middle East, in particular vis-à-vis Palestine. These contradictions and duplicitous agendas present a serious obstacle to constructive engagement for the roughly 7 million Muslims living within the U.S., as well as a potential hazard in terms of their unwitting support for terrorism.

While the Qur'anic injunction to "Obey God, obey his Prophet (S) and obey those in authority among you" unquestionably applies to non-Muslim leaders, many groups operating within the U.S. nonetheless refuse to wholeheartedly participate within the framework of the American political system and seemingly oppose the government on as many issues as possible. These attitudes are reflected in the literature of many of the well-established Muslim organizations—even the so-called "mainstream" ones—and promote the idea among the Muslim community that hostility towards the government is the only approach to democracy.

The views of these organizations are not indigenous to this country, but rather are part of an extreme, imported ideology backed by significant overseas funding. Undoubtedly, Muslims feel pressure to support the vociferous nonmoderate platform or to disengage from American politics altogether. Indeed, American Muslims have few alternatives to political engagement aside from these radical-leaning organizations. Those who choose to participate, by means of active involvement or material support, are often moved by the causes they embrace but may not be fully aware of their agenda and activities. Muslims who organize themselves outside of the existing organizations and agendas to bring about changes in policy have little affect on the political system and are often ostracized, lacking the resources and strategic alliances of the established groups.

Since September 11, less moderate American Muslim groups have been more vocal, using issues like civil liberties, U.S. support for regimes and countries viewed as enemies to Islam, etc., as pretext for opposition to any accommodation within the community towards moderates. They bombard the political machinery with campaigns on controversial or volatile subjects within the Muslim community, relying on emotional incitement. The voice of nonmoderate Muslims has become increasingly shrill, as they attempt to paint every effort of the administration towards security as racial profiling, discrimination or anti-Muslim bias. The unfortunate result is that many moderate Muslims further disengage, avoiding the mosques and Islamic groups completely for fear of any association with terrorism or those who support it.

While the current political climate in the United States may have shied Muslims away from active involvement in democratic processes, the past actions of the Muslim community reflect their faith in and desire to live by truly democratic traditions. In the 1940–1950s, when the first significant numbers of Muslim immigrants began to arrive in America, communities from South Asia, Africa and the Middle East alike founded their mosques on democratic principles. They held elections for various positions within the mosque leadership and held discussions to resolve issues in the community. In time, however, new immigrants set out an aggressive takeover of these religious institutions. These groups or individuals came well prepared; often backed by oil wealth and religious training and clout, the initial leadership was removed and replaced by those with more active and extreme agendas. It was not that their electoral procedures failed them, but that no safeguards against intimidation or ensuring fairness existed.

Despite the fact that some Muslim leaders have used democratic concepts and procedures to effectively, but unfairly, gain power within organizations and mosques, by no means should American Muslims lose hope in the political process, as they can play a unique and important role in showing the larger Muslim community that they and Islam can in fact thrive within a democratic nation. For this to happen, however, Muslims must find new means of organizing themselves and effectively illustrating their true stances in the political arena.

Conclusion

By correcting the bias in the United States towards the established Islamic organizations and reducing their unfair influence over the political activities of the Muslim community, Muslims will be able to more freely participate in the policymaking process in this country. This constructive engagement, along with the ideas and historical examples provided in this paper, can encourage democratic reform in the global Muslim community.

Notes

1. Imam Abu Zahra, *Tareekh al-madahib al-Islamiyya fi al-siyasa wa al-`aqa'id wa tareekh al-madahib al-fiqhiyyah*, vol. 1, (Cairo: Dar al-Fikra al-`Arabi, 1989).
2. Hadith, from the collection of Sahih Imam Bukhari.
3. Hadith, Sahih Bukhari.
4. Chronicled by Ibn Ishaq, the first biographer of the Prophet Muhammad (S).

5. Abdul Halim, Mahmoud *al-tafkeer al-falsafi fil-Islam*, vol. 1 (Beirut: Dar al-Kitab al-Lubnani, 1985.)

6. *al-tafkeer al-falsafi fil-Islam*, p. 247. Vol 1.

II. Character and Heroism

In Defense of Liberty[1]

Christopher J. "Gus" Loria

NASA Astronaut and Lieutenant Colonel, USMC, 1996– ; born Belmont, MA, July 9, 1960; hometown, League City, TX; graduated Belmont High School, 1978, and U.S. Naval Academy Preparatory School, 1979; B.S. in general engineering, U.S. Naval Academy, 1983; completing thesis for M.S. in aeronautical engineering, Florida Institute of Technology; Naval Aviator, 1988; Strike Fighter Squadron 125, Naval Air Station, Lemoore, CA, 1988–89; Marine Fighter Attack Squadron 314, Marine Corps Air Station, El Toro, CA, 1989–92; Operations Desert Shield and Desert Storm, flying 42 combat missions, 1990–91; U.S. Air Force Test Pilot School, Edwards Air Force Base, 1992; Strike Aircraft Test Squadron, Naval Air Station, Patuxent River, MD, 1994–96; more than 2,500 hours of flight time in 35 different aircraft; Society of Experimental Test Pilots; Marine Corps Aviation Association; National Rifle Association; Who's Who in the World, 1995; Naval Test Wing Atlantic Test Pilot of the Year, 1995–96; Meritorious Service Medal; two Navy Commendation Medals (one with "V"); two Air Medals (both with "V"); four Strike Flight Air Medals; Navy Achievement Medal.

Editors' introduction: Astronaut Christopher J. "Gus" Loria gave this keynote address to members of the Iwo Jima Veterans and Family Association attending the All Forces Banquet on the 57th anniversary of the raising of the American flag on Mt. Suribachi during the Battle of Iwo Jima. In speaking to the men who had fought in the battle, Loria praised their courage and contributions, envisioning that "love of freedom and country which is the source of our nation's character, its dreams, and its greatest achievements." The speech was prepared by Kathleen Colgan, Ph.D., and Christopher J. "Gus" Loria, and typed by Dannia Hayes.

Christopher J. "Gus" Loria's speech: Thank you for that very kind introduction.

It is a tremendous honor and great privilege for me to be here today.

And perhaps it is because I am a U.S. Marine that I am especially proud to be with you today. As some of you know, I come from a family with a strong Marine tradition.

---

1. Delivered on February 23, 2002, at Wichita Falls, TX. Reprinted with permission of Christopher J. "Gus" Loria.

My father enlisted at 16 years of age and served as a Marine in both World War II and the Korean War.

My uncle Larry, another Marine, served with you on Iwo Jima.

My brother is a Marine who served in Bosnia, and I served in Desert Storm.

In fact, it is impossible for me to express adequately to you the depth of the regard I feel towards, or the respect I hold for, each of you . . . each of you veterans and survivors of the Battle of Iwo Jima.

Your courage, valor, and grit made "February of 1945" legendary in the annals of American warfare. . . .

Your determination and patriotism under fire have come to represent the highest standard of valor exercised in the defense of American freedom. . . .

And not only for Americans, but to the world.

For every man who set foot on Iwo Jima is a hero.

If you Iwo Jima veterans, in your modesty, ever doubt me, consider the soul-stirring effect of what was, even in 1945, that internationally recognized picture of six Americans raising the American flag atop Mt. Suribachi.

For more than 50 years, that image of Americans hoisting our country's flag into an eternal sky embodies the indomitable spirit of the American love of freedom and country . . .

A love of freedom and country which is a source of our nation's character, its dreams, and its greatest achievements. . . .

In military history, the story of Iwo Jima is told with reverent voices and sober tones.

In our country's history, the words "Iwo Jima" resonate a spirit of heroic vitality and patriotism of the same epic proportions as do the words "Bunker Hill" . . . "Gettysburg" . . . "Normandy."

For Iwo Jima was a battle which changed the course of history.

Prior to the capture of Iwo Jima, the Japanese used the island as a base from which to launch their kamikaze attacks and to attack U.S. bombers.[1]

But, once the Americans took Iwo Jima, United States fighter aircraft could use the island's air strips to protect United States bombers flying from Saipan and Tinian. Iwo Jima also then became an emergency landing site . . . a safe haven . . . for crippled American bombers returning from their war missions.[2]

It is estimated that the capture of Iwo Jima eventually saved the lives of more than 30,000 American airmen when more than 2400 disabled B-29s were able to make emergency landings on the island.[3]

But, as all of you too well know, the first capture of native Japanese soil by Americans during World War II was a grueling struggle charged with all the horrors of war.

Though Iwo Jima was less than eight square miles, the enemy had built over three miles of island tunnels . . . a maze harboring ammunition, food, water, and suicidal enemy troops.[4]

As many of you remember, the Marines had requested 13 days of prelanding bombardment, but commitments made to MacArthur's campaign in Luzon made that request impossible to meet.[5]

As a consequence, the three-day Naval bombardment of the island prior to the invasion was far short of what was required.

To compound the dangers, Japanese strength on the island had been underestimated by as much as 70 percent . . . and potential American casualties had been underestimated by as much as 80 percent.[6]

But despite heavy and continuous enemy fire, you fought for the island inch by inch, yard by yard.

On the morning of February 23, and after bitter and exhausting fighting, a patrol led by Lt. Harold Schreir placed a small American flag atop Mt. Suribachi.

A much larger American flag from a landing ship tank was raised later. . . . It was that flag-raising event which was captured in Joe

---

Your memories have resurrected for me the courage and spirit of great American heroes.

Rosenthal's famous photograph.

Confident military planners had predicted Iwo Jima could be secured in five days. They were a little "off the mark." Final capture actually took some six weeks. . . .[7]

At the cost of 6,821 American lives.[8]

Today, I've had the opportunity to meet with a number of you. It has been my privilege to relive the history of the fight for Iwo Jima through your stories. . . .

Your memories have resurrected for me the courage and spirit of great American heroes . . . the heroes who saved not only America, but the world, from the mad and obsessive tyrannies of the 20th century. . . .

And through your stories, your memories have also resurrected for me the courage and spirit of you as young Americans . . .

Young Americans determined to fight for, and defend, our nation's . . . indeed, civilization's . . . highest ideals.

Many of you were, after all, just kids . . . kids from Brooklyn and Detroit and Memphis . . . from Houston . . . Seattle . . . Rhode Island, California and Montana . . .

Young men now far from the hometowns where you had played baseball, studied . . . and dreamed of futures to be lived . . . achievements to be realized.

Young men now thrust upon the distant shore of a Pacific Island some 650 miles south of Tokyo . . . your unshaven faces suddenly black with the grime of a distant volcanic beach.[9]

Young men . . .

Young men who did not start this war . . . but who succeeded in ending it. . . .

Preserving our nation and its principles of freedom and justice has demanded a special kind of American heroism . . . a heroism born of a belief in enduring values, personal responsibility . . . the love of liberty . . . and a trust in God.

Heroism which recognized values and principles greater than the self . . .

Heroism like that once exercised at places like Valley Forge . . . and at Iwo Jima.

Today, we remember a time, more than 50 years ago, when American Marines, under heavy gunfire, bravely scrambled across coarse black sand on a gray beach in the northwestern Pacific Ocean.

Years later . . . back home . . . America was a place where once again . . . children went to school without fear . . . fathers played Saturday morning football with their kids in the backyard . . . and families hurriedly dressed for Sunday morning church services.

Because of your sacrifices . . .

America was a place where, once again, farmers could plow the land in peace, and factory workers could share lunch under the bright noon sun . . . A place where ranchers still drove cattle across western plains . . . and California sunsets, of brilliant red and gold, graced the end of a free nation's day.

Because of your sacrifices . . .

America was a place where knowledge merged with compassion to develop new medicines and seek new cures . . . Where talent and creativity inspired great books, great art, great music . . . a love of beauty and goodness. . . .

America was a place where, once again, its people were known worldwide for their courageous commitment to liberty, their adventurous drive towards achievement . . . and their great spirit of generosity.

Once again, we remembered the America which was forged from a frontier territory . . . a vast landscape upon which the dreams of many nations, and the ideals of many peoples, could, in the spirit of freedom, suddenly find possibility . . . a nation so great as to be unparallel in human history.

America was a place where, once again, dreams were limited only by the scope of imagination. . . .

And, prompted by our country's own flag, America was a place which began extending its spirit of freedom to a pursuit of the stars . . . A Pursuit of the Stars where reside the Dreams of Tomorrow . . .

A Pursuit of the Stars which is a tribute to the men and women . . . like you . . . who have made that reach possible.

It is now more than 50 years later . . . more than 50 years since Iwo Jima . . .

And more than 50 years later, tonight, our nation is, once again, at war.

The enemy is a new one . . . but like the old one, it is an enemy which threatens the future . . . the very existence . . . of the civilized world.

It is not a war we asked for, but it is a war we will end.

As you embodied the Brotherhood that is our Corps . . . on September 11, we witnessed the brotherhood of our countrymen and women.

Once again, our peace and tranquility were trespassed by insane zealots, modern-day kamikazes that attempted to rip apart the fabric of our souls and country.

What they never envisioned—because they never knew us—was the terrible awakening they have again wrought.

We blinked our eyes in collective disbelief at what we were witnessing. Then, as we opened our eyes, we were a Nation United.

A Nation fully aware that war had been declared and delivered to our very doorsteps.

A Nation United against petty tyrants . . . Tyrants without a vision or plan for progress.

On September 11, our nation witnessed something you and I already knew. We witnessed that it is the common men and women all across America that are our greatest strength.

Simple men and women who rushed to help others . . . People of faith, people who were sons and daughters, fathers and mothers.

It was Americans aboard United Flight 93 that banded together to try and regain control of their aircraft. They succeeded in preventing the terrorists from striking another target, but in doing so they perished in a Pennsylvania field.

Our nation has learned that we have quite the commander in chief in President Bush. His clarity of purpose, courage, and ability to speak directly are connecting with the American people.

His goals are simply stated, and will not lend themselves to interpretation or dilution.

"We want Bin Laden, dead or alive . . . and you are either with us or against us."

Those are words and objectives this Marine understands!

I am not a historian, but I see many similarities between President Bush and President Theodore Roosevelt.

Both men seem to be foreign-policy realists. Both men are men of strong morals and character. Both men believe that our foreign policy should be governed by the clear-eyed pursuit of national interests.

Our commander in chief is proving he has the resolve, the strength, and the wisdom to lead this fight.

Militarily, he is ensuring that our combat men and women have all the assets required to achieve their missions.

Domestically, to reduce our dependence on Middle Eastern oil, he is pushing for exploration offshore and on the Arctic National Wildlife Refuge. These two areas alone could free us from Middle East oil dependence for the next thirty to forty years!

And, because energy still fuels the U.S. economy, it is estimated that over 1.5M jobs would be created as a result.

Strategically, President Bush has called for the Missile-Defense program to be revitalized and pursued. We will *not* be held hostage by threats and weapons of mass destruction

We will protect our Homeland.

We will protect our homes.

We will protect our families.

Our nation has watched the Herculean efforts at the World Trade Center since September 11.

With tears in our eyes and pride in our hearts, we have contemplated the image of determined young Americans raising our country's flag against an eternal sky . . .

An image, once again captured in a photograph . . . an image of young American firefighters raising our country's flag not on the hill of a strategic Pacific island . . . but, raising our country's flag, this time, over the burnt wreckage . . . on the ravaged grounds of *our* World Trade Center.

We recall your legacy of unrelenting perseverance and generosity . . . your commitment to human dignity . . . to the principles of liberty and justice.

And at that moment, once again, the world remembered Iwo Jima. . . .

We remembered the lessons you taught us there by the example of your own valiant patriotism . . . your immeasurable capacity for courage and determination.

We recall your legacy of unrelenting perseverance and generosity . . . your commitment to human dignity . . . to the principles of liberty and justice. . . .

From you, we learned about responsibility . . . and what has been called "our privilege to fight Freedom's fight."[10]

We are not naive. . . . The oceans no longer protect us. . . . The threats against our country are legitimate and potentially catastrophic.

But, like you were, we are determined.

Like you were, we are resolved.

We have but one choice . . .

As you once had but one choice.

The dangers ahead will be overcome.

The evil, we will vanquish.

We have the leadership in our president and in our admirals and Generals.

We have the tools.

We have the courage and determination because we are your sons and daughters.

Like you did, we will reflect Honor, Valor and Courage on our families, services, and on this great nation.

Thank you all.

It has been my very great honor to be here tonight.

May God bless you all.

Notes

1. Clark Reynolds, *The Fast Carriers: The Forging of an Air Navy* (Annapolis, MD.: Naval Institute, Press, 1992) and Richard Newcomb, *Iwo Jima* (New York: Holt, Rinehard and Winston, 1965), in "The Battle of Iwo Jima," at *History at USD, http://history.acusd.edu/gen/WW2Timeline/LUTZ/iwo.html*, p. 1.

2. Iwo Jima article, Worldbook Online (America Edition), *http://www.cssvc.worldbook.compuserve.com*.

3. "Battle for Iwo Jima—World War II, February 19 to March 16, 1945: Historical Facts and Figures," at Webtravels: Northeast Connecticut's Online Resource, *http://www. webtravels.com/iwojima/battle.htm*, p. 1.

4. Reynolds and Newcomb, in "The Battle of Iwo Jima" at *History at USD, http://history.acusd.edu/gen/WW2Timeline/LUTZ/iwo.html, p. 1*.

5. Ibid., p. 5.

6. Ibid.

7. "War in the Pacific: Iwo Jima," *Cruising Cyberlinks in Space, http://www. geocities.com/stu_hill/IwoJima.htm*, p. 2.

8. "Eyewitness: Voices of the 20th Century," *EyeWitness: History Through the Eyes of Those Who Lived It. http://www. ibiscom.com/voiwo.htm*, p. 2.

9. Partly inspired by Ernie Pyle in "They are just guys from Broadway and Main Street," *New York World Telegram*, May 3, 5, 1953, reprinted in *A Treasury of Great Reporting*, 2d ed. Louis L. Snyder and Richard B. Morris (New York: Simon and Schuster, 1949), p. 620.

10. George W. Bush, The President's State of the Union Address, January 29, 2002.

Maria College Commencement[2]

Mary O. Donohue

Lieutenant Governor, New York, 1999– ; born Rensselaer County, NY; B.Edn., College of New Rochelle, 1968; M.S. in education, Russell Sage College, Troy, NY, 1973; J.D., Albany Law School of Union University, 1980; teacher, elementary and junior high school, Rensselaer and Albany County school districts, 1969–78; intern, U.S. Attorney's Office, Albany, NY, 1980–83; associate attorney, O'Connell & Aronowitz, P.C., Albany, NY, 1983–88; private law practice, Troy, NY, 1988–92; assistant county attorney, Rensselaer, 1990–92; elected Rensselaer County's first female District Attorney, 1992–96; Rensselaer County's first female State Supreme Court Justice, 3rd Judicial District, 1996–98; chair, Governor's Task Force on School Violence, 1999; chair, Quality Communities Interagency Task Force, 2000; currently chairs Governor's Task Force on Small Business.

Editors' introduction: Lieutenant Governor Mary O. Donohue spoke to faculty, administrators, and graduating seniors and their guests at commencement. Maria College of New York is a private, Catholic institution offering associate's degrees with a curriculum grounded in the humanities. Founded by the Sisters of Mercy, it draws upon the Judeo-Christian tradition to instill in its graduates respect for the dignity of each person and the ability to transform learned skills into caring service. Lieutenant Governor Donohue said her concern was in "doing what we can to raise what I will call the 'common denominator of character,' the base level of virtue upon which our society rests."

Mary O. Donohue's speech: President Fitzgerald, trustees, faculty, family members, distinguished guests, graduates. . . .

I want to thank you for giving me the opportunity to speak to you on this special day. It is always a great honor to be asked to participate in such events. And, I am especially pleased to have the opportunity to address the graduates of Maria College, no longer the Capital District's "best-kept secret."

In preparation of my remarks to you today, I reread a favorite speech of mine delivered by Vice President Teddy Roosevelt in 1901. So rather than discuss the importance of the graduating class of 2002 to our region's hospitals, schools, and businesses, indeed to all the citizens of the Capital District, and remark on what the future might hold for you, I would instead like to discuss a subtopic of

---

2. Delivered on May 19, 2002, at Albany, NY.

Roosevelt's speech that was not only of great interest to Roosevelt, but which has renewed importance to our entire country in this "the 21st century." The issue is character education.

As a mother of two, I cannot begin a speech about character education without a special word of thanks to the parents who have not only been your life source, but very often the example and inspiration from which you developed your values, your character. In the year 2000, my eldest daughter, Sara, graduated from Fordham and went to work for a publishing company in Manhattan. Like the day she left for college, it was a time of mixed emotions for me. More than anything else, I was proud of her accomplishments. All the hard work she invested in her studies was finally paying off (though I still had many years of tuition payments still to pay off). While I was nervous about her going to school in New York City and staying in the city to begin her professional career, I took comfort in the fact that I did the best that I could to teach her the values that I learned as a child. I come from a loving, close-knit family, where my mother and father stressed individual responsibility and brought up my brothers, my sister and me in a way that forged within us a sense of discipline, a strong work ethic, the principles of personal responsibility and accountability, and a commitment to our community. The power of the individual, which was instilled in me from a very young age, has been the guiding principle of my life; it has enabled me to reach all of my goals and dreams, except that of winning the U.S. Open golf championship. I have been a teacher, lawyer, district attorney, a Supreme Court justice, and lieutenant governor for the last four years (and with your help, the next four as well). But the most important job and title that I will ever hold is that of mom. I need not tell you that raising children today is no easier than it was for our parents. So to the parents of our graduates, congratulations. I was going to say congratulations on a job well done, but the job is never done, is it? We never stop being parents, and never stop (much to the consternation of my two children) advising our children what they should do. Though not your parent, I would be remiss in my duties as your keynote speaker if I didn't offer some advice.

While Teddy Roosevelt certainly has been one of the foremost modern political proponents of "character education," he is but one of a long line of philosophers and leaders who recognized the critical importance that personal character plays in the lives of nations and cultures.

Long a foundation of Christian morality, the "seven virtues" of prudence, temperance, fortitude, justice, faith, hope, and charity have parallels in other cultures and religions as well. Throughout history, every successful culture has identified similar virtues that are essential to its survival and well-being. Virtues provide a road map for individuals to achieve excellence within themselves and for their community. In the United States, a pluralistic society like no other, the virtues of Christianity and other faiths combine to offer a common framework from which we can all strive to achieve our collective and individual goals.

The ancient philosophers Socrates, Plato and Aristotle, the Apostle Paul, St. Thomas Aquinas, and others all developed philosophies of moral behavior based on the concept of virtue. Given the universal nature of virtuous behavior, why shouldn't we teach our children the elements of good character? Can't we all agree that courage, honesty, respect, discipline, and self-control, just to name a few, are important character traits that we wish all persons possessed?

In his speech, Roosevelt remarked that

> In this country we rightly pride ourselves upon our system of widespread popular education. We most emphatically do right to pride ourselves upon it. It is not merely of inestimable advantage to us, it lies at the root of our power of self-government. But it is not sufficient in itself. We must cultivate the mind; but it is not enough only to cultivate the mind. With education of the mind must go the spiritual teaching which will make us turn the trained intellect to good account. A man whose intellect has been educated, while at the same time his moral education has been neglected, is only the more dangerous to the community because of the exceptional additional power which he has acquired. Surely what I am saying needs no proof; surely the mere statement of it is enough, that education must be education of the heart and conscience no less than of the mind.
>
> It is an admirable thing, a most necessary thing, to have a sound body. It is an even better thing to have a sound mind. But infinitely better than either is it to have that, for the lack of which neither sound mind nor a sound body can atone—character. Character is in the long run the decisive factor in the life of individuals and of nations alike.
>
> Sometimes, in rightly putting the stress that we do upon intelligence, we forget the fact that there is something that counts more. It is a good thing to be clever, to be able and smart; but it is a better thing to have the qualities that find their expression in the Decalogue and the Golden Rule. It is a good and necessary thing to be intelligent; it is a better thing to be straight and decent and fearless.

On the moral education of children, Roosevelt asked us

> to think of your neighbors, of the people you know. Don't you, each one of you, know some man . . . who gives life an unhealthy turn for children by trying to spare them in the present the very things which would train them to do strong work in the future? Such conduct is not kindness. It is shortsightedness and selfishness; it means merely that the man or woman shrinks from the little inconveniences, to himself or herself, of making the child fit itself to be a good and strong man or woman hereafter. There should be the deepest and truest love for their children in the hearts of all fathers and mothers. Without such love there is nothing but black despair for the family; but the

love must respect both itself and the one beloved. It is not true love to invite future disaster by weak indulgence for the moment.

What is true affection for a boy? To bring him up so that nothing rough ever touches him, and at twenty-one turn him out into the world with a moral nature that turns black and blue in great bruises at the least shock from any one of the forces of evil with which he is bound to come in contact? Is that kindness? Indeed, it is not. Bring up your boys with both love and wisdom; and turn them out as men, strong-limbed, clear-eyed, stout-hearted, clean-minded, able to hold their own in this great world of work and strife and ceaseless effort.

While Roosevelt's advice might be likened by some as a glorified "spare the rod, spoil the child" philosophy, this view, I believe, is misguided and does not do justice to the depth of Roosevelt's concern for children and the multifaceted approach to their education that he espoused. True it might be that Roosevelt's boyhood struggle with illness and his initial weakness was an inspiration and motivating force in his life, but one need only look at this quote in the context of the larger speech I have excerpted for you to fully understand his challenge to parents and to the society at large. It seems clear that Roosevelt must have agreed with Plutarch, who said that "character is habit long continued." It also seems clear to me that we have forgotten Roosevelt's admonition that education must be education of the heart and conscience no less than of the mind.

Could the challenge facing us today, our "crisis in character," if you will, be any greater? Could the need for character education be any more apparent? The increasing frequency of crimes committed by our young people, like the Columbine High School shootings and the recent Midwest mailbox pipe bombings, are becoming all too common, so tragically common, in fact, that much of the "shock value" of such events has been lost. But it's not only these extreme cases that are all too common, but also the small transgressions, the lesser crimes, and the small breaches of unwritten societal rules, when committed en masse, that have contributed to this crisis.

Now I can't stand here and tell you all the forces in our culture that have contributed to this degradation of, this crisis in character, or what are the origins of this problem. But I'm sure that we can all agree that our movies, television, music, even the news must contribute to this erosion of character. You can't bombard a developing child or adolescent with constant images of violence and crime, whether on the news or the silver screen, without numbing an immature conscience. Now I didn't come here today to discuss the challenge of balancing free speech rights against societal interests in maintaining order. However relevant to my comments today, I'll leave that for another time. Instead, my focus is the critical need for character education, both at home and in our schools. If we do not discuss the questions, "What makes up a strong character?" and "How should we teach values to our children?," shouldn't we expect a continuation of these Hollywoodesque crimes?

Yet, I remain ever hopeful. We still see frequent examples of heroism that inspire confidence in the character of our citizens. We need look no further than the terrorist attacks on 9/11 and the response of our firefighters, police officers and emergency service personnel. But beyond the selfless sacrifices of these heroes were thousands more average New Yorkers, as well as citizens of other states, who performed small acts of kindness, sacrifice, and bravery in service to their nation. Whether they donated their time to a local charitable organization, their efforts to provide logistical support to those involved in the cleanup of the World Trade Center or Pentagon sites, their money to a victims fund, or their expertise to provide counseling services to those affected, all such acts, though not the stuff of legend, have been indispensable to our spiritual and economic renewal. These are the everyday examples of character that truly provide our society's firm foundation.

Although they came at a time of great need and in calamitous circumstances, I am not worried whether we will be capable of such displays of great courage and sacrifice in the future. My chief concern is not in the preparation of our youth to be war heroes or decorated firefighters or police officers. Because of the heroic origins of our country, I firmly believe we will always have an ample supply of great men and women who will rise from obscurity to do great deeds and inspire a nation. My concern is doing what we can to raise what I will call the "common denominator of character," the base level of virtue upon which our society rests. The common denominator of character are those decisions that we face and those choices that we make each and every day. Do we treat other people fairly and honestly, do we exercise self-restraint in the face of the world's temptations, do we exercise prudence and ask the difficult questions of ourselves, and do we act with courage in the face of fear and danger? And, perhaps most significantly, do we provide a living example of character in how we live our lives for all to see. Do we teach our children the difference between honesty and deceit, fairness and injustice, when enough is too much, the difference between wisdom and imprudence, bravery and cowardice. This is our nation's greatest challenge as we enter the new millennium.

But what can we do to promote the development of character in our children? Do we merely enforce our laws more strictly? No, I don't believe that is the only answer. As Judge Learned Hand, an Albany native, once said, we cannot "rest our hopes too much upon constitutions, upon laws and upon courts. These are false hopes: believe me, these are false hopes. Liberty lies in the hearts of men and women; when it dies there, no constitution, no law, no court can save it." Because Governor Pataki and I fervently believe in the power of the individual and in the limited effectiveness of government-imposed solutions, this challenge falls upon you, our new graduates, and all my fellow citizens, to touch the lives of others, most especially the lives of your children. However, because this problem is so far-reaching and multifaceted, and so critical to our survival as a nation, we must attack it from every angle and with every resource available to us.

In the last few decades, Maria College has added evening and weekend colleges, demonstrating that education is not a "sometime thing," but an "all-the-time thing." So too is the formation of one's character. Surely, one's character is grounded in our youth and education at the feet of our parents, in our houses of worship and in all of life's lessons, but it cannot end there. The stakes are too high and the circumstances too grave to permit "part-time" character education. Because character is much easier kept than recovered, it requires constant tending, no different than a business or a hospital patient or a child in school.

As a former teacher, I recognize the influence that schools can

---

[Character] requires constant tending, no different than a business or a hospital patient or a child in school.

---

have on our children. Because of this experience, the governor asked me to chair his Task Force on School Violence, which made recommendations that were incorporated into a law that required the State Education Department to develop a K–12 curriculum in civility, citizenship, and character education. The curriculum will include instruction on the principles of honesty, tolerance, personal responsibility, respect for others, observance of laws and rules, courtesy, dignity, and other traits which will enhance the quality of students' experiences in and contributions to the community (note the similarity to the seven virtues).

While academic success may vary from student to student, being good citizens and giving back to your community are activities that all teenagers and young adults can do. This should not be something we hope or wish to happen, but something we should expect from each and every student. This new law provides the critical requirement that our schools provide a complete education to our children and provides the necessary expectations of our children that they be civil, good citizens, and that they behave according to commonly held societal standards.

Over a decade ago, Senator Daniel Patrick Moynihan famously warned that our nation was "defining deviancy down." By this phrase he meant that unacceptable behavior was being redefined to exempt previously stigmatized conduct, because the amount of deviant behavior in American society had increased beyond recognizable levels. To preserve our nation, we must reverse this trend. We must instead champion courageous conduct and elevate ethical expectations.

Our continued societal silence in the face of this erosion of ethical expectations could be the death of our nation. But looking out at you graduates, your parents, your children, and your families, I am confident and hopeful more than ever that we are pointed in the right direction. Maria College certainly has a rich history. However recent its founding, its mission to instill in its graduates respect for the dignity of each person and the ability to transform learned skills into caring service is rooted in the timeless Christian tradition. Yet Maria is a modern institution as well, ever changing, adapting a curriculum grounded in the humanities while teaching a skill set that makes its graduates fully marketable in today's varied economy. You are also an ethnically and racially diverse group of men, women, day, evening, and weekend students, graduates of other institutions, and were often fully employed in the "real world" while attending Maria. Some of you will further your education at other colleges and universities, others will continue in your vocation with greater knowledge and new skills, and others still will begin your career anew. Regardless of your path, you are all particularly well suited to meet not only the challenges of the "real world," but to meet the challenge that I elucidated today. Regarding the first challenge, many of you have already participated in the "real world" while attending Maria at the same time, so you know that it is no more difficult and no more demanding than this world that you are leaving today. Indeed, you may find the "real world" easier to navigate now that you no longer will have day, evening and/or weekend classes.

You are also well suited to meet the second challenge, to implement the lessons of your own youth and the education of your adult life to influence the moral development of children and of all the people you will meet.

Let me leave you with this final thought. The great Supreme Court Justice Benjamin Cardozo once said, "The heroic hours of the life do not announce their presence by drum and trumpet, challenging us to be true to ourselves by appeals to the martial spirit that keeps the blood at heat. Some little, unassuming, unobtrusive choice presents itself before us slyly and craftily, glib and insinuating, in the modest garb of innocence. . . . Then it is that you will be summoned to show the courage of adventurous youth."

As Cardozo recognized, you graduates may never be called to rescue someone from a burning building, or to bravely charge an enemy position, but if you are virtuous in your thought and action on a daily basis, you will be a hero to your children and to all who know you. Your routine small acts of courage, and honesty, and self-discipline, and prudence, and charity, while individually of little significance to society, are of great significance to society when performed on a collective basis by each of you, each and every day. If you do this, you will have fulfilled the responsibilities which accompany the liberty that is your birthright as a citizen and your obligations to the succeeding generations.

Congratulations to one and all. Thank you for this opportunity and God bless you.

Of Faith and Citizenship: My American Jihad[3]

Zayed Muhammed Yasin

Associate, Center for Health Interventions Research, run jointly by the Johns Hopkins School of Public Health and the Aga Khan Health Services, Gilgit, Pakistan, 2002– ; born April 20, 1980; Scituate High School, MA, 1998; A.B. in biomedical engineering, Harvard College, 2002; Fulbright Scholar; former president, Harvard Islamic Society; Harvard Friends of the Red Cross.

Editors' introduction: Zayed Muhammed Yasin, a graduating student, delivered this address at Harvard University commencement. Because of the death and destruction caused by Muslim extremists on September 11, some who found the idea of an "American jihad" repugnant distributed flyers in opposition to the speech, and one e-mailed a death threat. Others, however, said Harvard was the ideal setting in which to advocate strong convictions. Mr. Yasin's speech received considerable applause at the time and extensive international media coverage. In the address, he explained that "jihad . . . is the determination to do right." Mr. Yasin wrote to the editors, "I wanted to send the message that there is no contradiction between being Muslim and being American—that the two are . . . complementary. When the title of my speech was announced, a group of Harvard students launched a movement to have me removed as commencement speaker, trying to smear me as a terrorist, an anti-Semite, and a hate-monger. . . . I feel the majority of people were ready and willing to listen to my message, and that we were able to reopen a dialogue on relations between Islam and the Western world. I received messages of support from across the world, from Jews, Hindus, Christians, pagans, and Muslims."

Zayed Muhammed Yasin's speech: I am one of you. But I am also one of "them." What do I mean? When I am told that this is a world at war, a war between the great civilizations and religions of the earth, I don't know whether to laugh or cry. "What about me?" I ask. As a practicing Muslim and a registered voter in the Commonwealth of Massachusetts, am I, through the combination of my faith and my citizenship, an inherent contradiction?

---

3. Delivered on June 6, 2002, at Cambridge, MA. Reprinted with permission of Zayed Muhammed Yasin.

I think not. Both the Qur'an and the Constitution teach ideals of peace, justice and compassion, ideals that command my love and my belief. Each of these texts, one the heart of my religion, the other that of my country, demand a constant struggle to do what is right.

I choose the word *struggle* very deliberately, for its connotations of turmoil and tribulation, both internal and external. The word for struggle in Arabic, in the language of my faith, is *jihad*. It is a word that has been corrupted and misinterpreted, both by those who do and do not claim to be Muslims, and we saw last fall, to our great national and personal loss, the results of this corruption. Jihad, in its truest and purest form, the form to which all Muslims aspire, is the determination to do right, to do justice even against your own interests. It is an individual struggle for personal moral behavior. Especially today, it is a struggle that exists on many levels: self-purification and awareness, public service and social justice. On a global scale, it is a struggle involving people of all ages, colors, and creeds, for control of the Big Decisions: not only who controls what piece of land, but more importantly who gets medicine, who can eat.

So where is our jihad, where is our struggle as we move on from Harvard's sheltering walls? Worthy adversaries are innumerable. We can turn our struggle to the war against oppression, poverty, disease. . . . But before looking outward, we must first look inward. Before deciding what we are against, we must decide what we are for. The only way to define the inner moral force that drives our struggle is to learn through action—to get our hands dirty. To strive to see the world as it sees itself, testing the boundaries of what we think we know, and how we know it. To combine our academic search for truth with a sense of empathy for our fellow humanity—to seek Veritas in Humanitas.

On one level it's simple: everyone wants the same things that we do. The true American Dream is a universal dream, and it is more than a set of materialistic aspirations. It is the power and opportunity to shape one's own life: to house and feed a family, with security and dignity, and to practice your faith in peace. This is our American Struggle, our American Jihad.

As a Muslim, and as an American, I am commanded to stand up for the protection of life and liberty, to serve the poor and the weak, to celebrate the diversity of humankind. There is no contradiction. Not for me, and not for anyone, of any combination of faith, culture and nationality, who believes in a community of the human spirit.

Some of this is a mantra that has been spoken at myriad graduations. Worth repeating, perhaps, but nothing new. What is new was taught us by last fall's tragedy and carnage. The status quo will not hold, and we have no choice but to engage more closely the troubles of this world. We are in a privileged position to shape a more just, peaceful, and honorable global society.

So I ask again: where is our jihad, our struggle? Whether on our way to an investment bank in New York, or to Sierra Leone to work with orphans, Harvard graduates have a responsibility to leave their mark on the world. So let us struggle, and let us make our mark. And as we do, I hope and pray that, for the sake of our children, our grandchildren, and those who take our seats in the years to come, we will be the change we seek in this world.

Acceptance of the 14th Annual Philadelphia Liberty Medal[4]

Colin L. Powell

U.S. Secretary of State, 2001– ; born New York City, April 5, 1937, and raised in South Bronx; graduated Morris High School, New York City, 1954; B.S. in geology, City College of New York, 1958; M.B.A., George Washington University, 1971; U.S. army, 1958–93, including two tours in Vietnam (1962–63 and 1968–69); assistant to the president for national security affairs, 1987–89; promoted to rank of four-star general, 1989; chairman, Joint Chiefs of Staff, 1989–93, overseeing Operation Desert Storm in the 1991 Persian Gulf war; chairman, America's Promise–The Alliance for Youth, 1993–2001; author, My American Journey, *1995; two Presidential Medals of Freedom; President's Citizens Medal; Congressional Gold Medal; Secretary of State Distinguished Service Medal; Secretary of Energy Distinguished Service Medal; honorary degrees from several universities and colleges, including Yeshiva University; Purple Heart, Bronze Star, and Legion of Merit Award.*

Editors' introduction: Sponsored by "We the People 2000," an organization composed of civic and business leaders, the Philadelphia Liberty Medal and its $100,000 honorarium are presented each year on the 4th of July at Philadelphia's Independence Hall to honor an individual or organization from anywhere in the world that has demonstrated "leadership and vision in pursuit of liberty of conscience or freedom from oppression, ignorance or deprivation." Upon receiving the Philadelphia Liberty Medal, and recalling how the United States was "savagely attacked" on September 11 "on our own soil," Secretary Powell proclaimed that "we showed the world that this nation and this people has a spine of steel, a gallant heart, and a fierce love of liberty."

Colin L. Powell's speech: My special thanks to the Philadelphia Police and Fire Fifes and Drums for their salute to America's armed forces. (Applause.)

Good morning, ladies and gentlemen, and thank you, Mayor Street, Mrs. Street, Governor and Mrs. Schweiker, for your presence here this morning, and all the other distinguished ladies and

---

4. Delivered on July 4, 2002, at Independence Hall, Philadelphia, PA.

gentlemen up on the platform, the wonderful performers that we have heard. But a special thanks to all of you for being here on this very, very warm morning.

We are joined around the nation by millions and millions of our fellow citizens in every town, in every city, all across this great country. The terrorists thought that they could keep us from celebrating the Fourth of July. They were wrong. We are here and we will remain. (Applause.)

I want to express my deep appreciation to Chairman Meyerson and the International Selection Commission and Greater Philadelphia First for giving me this very high honor. Alma and I are very, very pleased to be with you and to receive this honor. To receive the Philadelphia Liberty Medal here at Independence Hall on the Fourth of July, it just doesn't get any better. (Applause.)

The 13 previous recipients of the Philadelphia Liberty Medal, from Lech Walesa to Kofi Annan, have done so much to extend the blessings of liberty, prosperity and peace to people all across the world. It

---

> *I gratefully accept the Liberty Medal, not as a reward for any service I have rendered, but as a symbol of the service I yet owe to our wonderful country.*

---

is both exhilarating and humbling for me to be numbered among so many of my personal heroes.

I gratefully accept the Liberty Medal, not as a reward for any service I have rendered, but as a symbol of the service I yet owe to our wonderful country. Thomas Jefferson said that there is a debt of service due from every man to his country, proportioned to the bounties which nature and fortune have measured to him.

I have received so much from this country, I feel that debt very heavily. But don't we all? Don't we all feel the same obligation, as lucky Americans, to give back to this country as much as it has given to us, and more? (Applause.)

Being an American citizen is a privilege, whether you're a tenth-generation mainline Philadelphian or a child of immigrants, as I am. Citizenship means more than a conferral of rights through the accident of birth or the act of naturalization; citizenship brings with it the most solemn obligations—an obligation to uphold and defend the values of freedom, justice, and democracy that make Americans, in all of our diversity, one nation—and yes, one nation under God, indivisible. (Applause.) An obligation to share these universal values that make our country liberty's lamp unto the world.

Much has happened since we gathered last year to mark the Fourth of July. We were savagely attacked on our own soil. We endured a great national trauma. And we have emerged from it with new strength and a deeper sense of who we are as a people, and who we are as a nation. We showed the world that this nation and this people has a spine of steel, a gallant heart, and a fierce love of liberty. And our enemies now know without doubt that we will not rest until they have been defeated and brought to justice— each and every one of them. (Applause.)

Yes, September 11 brought us back to the fundamentals, the same fundamentals that have defined our nation since its birth, the fundamentals captured in Thomas Jefferson's timeless cadences and the Declaration of Independence. The words are now so familiar that even when they are so beautifully read, as they were by these wonderful young people a few moments ago, we sometimes hear these words without lingering over their meaning.

I don't know how many times I've read the Declaration of Independence. I'm 65 years old, yet every time I read those words I am inspired once again by the magic that took place in this place some 226 years ago during those warm summer days, as those men assembled here and argued with each other, and found compromises, and disagreed and came into agreement, and finally gave us

---

September 11 brought us back to the fundamentals, the same fundamentals that have defined our nation since its birth.

---

these words—famous words, famous words that I have heard repeated by Lech Walesa and Kofi Annan and Nelson Mandela, and so many others, as words that inspire not only us, but others all over the world.

The most famous of these words we all know by heart: We hold these truths to be self-evident, that all men are created equal. Thirteen words for the 13 colonies. Thirteen words that, 226 years later, still throw the light of hope into the darkest corners of tyranny and oppression. Thirteen words conveying truths that need no explanation or analysis or debate. They're not facts; they're truths. They're self-evident. We don't need any explanation. We don't need consultants to come tell us what these truths mean and what they are all about. They are self-evident. They are not subject to dispute.

The truth that all are endowed by their Creator with certain unalienable rights. These are rights granted by no king, by no congress, by no legislature, by no president. They are rights granted to us by a benevolent God, a birthright from God. And they are unalienable, meaning no one can take them away, and that these rights simply are life, liberty, and the pursuit of happiness.

There are many other rights that were not mentioned by the signers of the Declaration, but these rights they did mention: God granted us life, God intended us to have liberty, and God expected us to pursue happiness. Everyone knows these lines oh, so well.

But it's the next line of the Declaration that I really love. It says that "To secure these rights, governments are instituted among men, deriving their just powers from the consent of the governed."

No definition of democracy has ever improved upon those words. In a democracy, the people have the power, not the government, and any power that the people agree to lend their government is to be used solely for securing the rights given to people in the Declaration and then in the Constitution.

And the Declaration says "secure the rights." Not protect them. Secure them. If people do not yet have them, the government's responsibility is to secure them, get them, and give all people in the nation these rights, these God-given rights to life, liberty, and the pursuit of happiness.

By choosing those words, "secure those rights," Jefferson gave us a glimpse of his vision for the future. Because when he wrote about equality and unalienable rights, he knew that those rights didn't apply to everyone—not at that time, not in this place. They didn't apply to women. They didn't apply to people who owned no land. They didn't apply to black people. They surely didn't apply to the slaves that Jefferson had on his plantation at Monticello.

But his words come back to inspire every succeeding generation of Americans to secure these rights for all. And how fitting it is, how especially fitting it is for me, a black secretary of state, to stand next to a black mayor on this day, on this place. Two hundred and twenty-six years ago we would have been seen as nothing but property, and now look what that vision has brought us to—a nation of strength and diversity. (Applause.)

We stand here today because Jefferson penned those words, and then he and the others assembled here were willing to sign away everything, everything they had, to bring those words to life. As Jefferson did in his time, so too must we recognize that America is not yet perfect. If we would be faithful to that Declaration and we would be faithful to our legacy, we must recognize there is still more to be done.

We all know that there are still injustices in this marvelous country of ours. We know that there are still bigots. We know that there is still poverty. We know that all of our children don't yet have the same opportunity for a quality education. We know that our cities aren't all gleaming alabaster undimmed by human tears.

But what gives us hope and faith in the future is that we also know that our system of government, by the people, is designed to correct injustices and make ours an ever more perfect union.

And our obligation as patriots is to constantly work to reach the goal that was set for us here on that day 226 years ago. Each of us has the duty to stand up not only for our rights, but for the rights of all of our fellow citizens, and to help secure the blessings of liberty for all.

And it is no less our responsibility as citizens of the world's greatest democracy to ensure that our country, this great country of ours, remains a force for freedom all around the world. After all, unalienable rights were given to all humankind. They belong to every man, woman and child on this earth. People all over the world, as I've discovered even more forcefully in my year and a half as secretary of state, want the same things that Americans want for their children: respect for their human rights, living in democracies, a better life for themselves and their children, a real say in the future of their country. They want increasingly the consent of the governed as their political model.

As Abraham Lincoln said in 1861 on this very spot as he was on his way to Washington for his inauguration, "Liberty was given not alone to the people of this country, but to the world, and for all time."

So just as we must always stand up for our own rights and the rights of our fellow citizens, Americans must also stand with courageous men and women all around the world who seek to secure the rights of their fellow citizens, just as we stood in solidarity with Liberty Medal recipients like Nelson Mandela and Vaclev Havel and Kim Dae Jung and Oscar Arias, who sacrificed for the freedom of their own people.

Americans must also stand with courageous men and women all around the world who seek to secure the rights of their fellow citizens.

And so since 1776, we Americans have known what we value and what we stand for: human liberty and the rights of humankind. And as to the matter of what we are made of, the Declaration of Independence speaks to that as well. The answer can be found in the very last sentence, right above the 56 signatures. The signers pledged their lives, their fortunes and their sacred honor to one another and to the cause of freedom. Theirs was not just a parchment pledge. It wasn't a rhetorical flourish. The founders knew by affixing their signatures to the Declaration, they could be signing their own death warrants. The signatories of the Declaration put it all on the line, not just for their own futures and fortunes, but for those of their wives and children. They were prepared to risk for what they believed in, and they did it for all the generations that would follow.

Indeed, our nation has been blessed with patriots in every generation, who have been willing to place their sacred honor in the service of their fellow citizens, and give their all for freedom. You often hear about the greatest generation. The truth is there is greatness in every generation.

We saw a great generation again on September 11, when ordinary Americans of every conceivable background and walk of life performed extraordinary acts of heroism, compassion and decency. You saw it in our firemen. You saw it in our policemen. You saw it in all those who stepped forward to help somebody in need in New

York, in Washington, in Pennsylvania. You saw it with the outpouring of support and patriotism, with the financial support that came forward to help those of our fellow citizens in need. We did not hesitate. We saw our duty as human beings and as citizens, and we did it. And we can be very proud indeed, that in the darkest hours of our national pain and grief, we remain true to our democratic values of tolerance and justice.

Under President Bush's leadership, we chose the path of principled action. We did not lash out in a blind rage. President Bush spoke from the very core of our national character when he stood before us, and all the world, and made it clear that the terrorists are our enemies, not people of any particular faith or ethnicity.

And in the months since last September, just as they have done at times of national trials in every generation since the days of George Washington, courageous young Americans have selflessly answered their nation's call to service, this time in the war against terrorism. Today, as I speak, in Afghanistan and all around the world, our military forces, our intelligence officers, our diplomats, are serving on the frontiers of freedom. They are serving for us. (Applause.)

And standing with them and with us in the great global coalition against terrorism are men and women from every continent, every creed, every culture, every region, every race, and every religion. For if in the world today there is a common threat to life, liberty and the pursuit of happiness, it is terrorism.

And in the years ahead, very few of us sitting here will be called upon to sacrifice our lives or our liberty for the rights that we hold dear. But all of us, the old and the young, the high and the humble, can seek out ways in our own life, in our own community, to serve the cause of freedom. Each of us can devote some of our time and talent and resources to the well-being of our community, to spread happiness throughout our community, to serve others in our community, to show that we are a people united, and none of us can be happy if there is any one of our fellow citizens who is in need, and we could do something about that need.

So in this time of service, President Bush has called upon each of us to fight the war on terrorism by devoting at least two years of our lifetime to public service at home or abroad. One of the main paths to public service is the United States of America Freedom Corps, which the president recently created. The Freedom Corps channels contributions of service in three important directions: to the new Citizen Corps, dedicated to homeland security; to the well-established Senior Corps and AmeriCorps, with their impressive community-based reforms; and to the Peace Corps, which for over four decades has embodied America's commitment to constructing a better future for all people.

There are so many good causes, so many needs to be met. Five years ago, right here at Independence Hall, I was very proud to stand and help to launch a crusade to help our children. We call it America's Promise, the Alliance for Youth. And the citizen volunteers involved in America's Promise are dedicated to building the character and confidence of all of our youngsters; that the people of our country are its greatest strength, and our children are its greatest hope. Through Freedom Corps, America's Promise, places of worship, community centers, charities, international organizations, through whatever means, each and every one of us can find ways to serve someone other than ourselves, something bigger than ourselves.

This is also part of the legacy created here 226 years ago. You do not need to join the military or work in government to perform public service, but I certainly applaud both. But everybody can make the time to serve on a school board, volunteer at a local shelter, mentor a kid who needs someone to care. We can take a stand for tolerance whenever we encounter prejudice. We can honor the service of others and teach our children to do the same. We can lend support to refugees fleeing foreign tyrants. We can express our unity with those around the world who work in freedom's name.

And so on this Fourth of July, in this beautiful place, in this precious moment, my red, white and blue message to you is this: It is up to every one of us to make the words of the Declaration of Independence speak to the men, women and children of our time. It is up to each of us to make America beautiful, to ensure that our country remains the land of liberty and opportunity. It is for us to keep the American Dream alive for our children and for our children's children. And it is for America, the Land of the Free and the Home of the Brave, to help freedom ring across the globe, unto all the peoples thereof. That is our solemn obligation, and we will not fail.

So on this wonderful day, may God bless you and your families on this special Fourth of July, and may God bless America. Thank you very much.

Flight 93 Patriots: Our Heroes, Our Family[5]

Mark Schweiker

Governor, Pennsylvania, 2001–02; born Levittown, PA, January 31, 1953; graduate of Bishop Egan High School; B.S., Bloomsburg University, 1975; M.A. in administration, Rider University, 1983; positions with Merrill Lynch, McGraw Hill, and his own management consulting firm; Middletown Township Supervisor, 1979; Bucks County commissioner, 1987–94; lieutenant governor, 1994–2000; chairman, Board of Pardons, Pennsylvania, 1995–2001; Alumnus of the Year, Bloomsburg University, 1990; Nature Conservancy Award, 1993; Commitment to Excellence in Local Government Award, Economy League, 1998.

Editors' introduction: Governor Mark Schweiker spoke at the memorial ceremony in remembrance of the 40 victims of Flight 93 who attempted to overcome their hijackers, causing the plane to crash into a field in Shanksville, PA, rather than a government building in Washington, D.C. (the terrorists' apparent intended target). As he stood on the field where the crash had occurred, Governor Schweiker praised the "patriots" aboard the plane, insisting that "Americans will always rise to the challenge" and "fight for freedom."

Mark Schweiker's speech: Here in Pennsylvania, today is truly a day of remembrance and deep reflection.

We remember brave firefighters who climbed the steps of a crumbling World Trade Center to save lives though they most certainly knew it would cost them their own.

We remember courageous Americans who ignored searing heat and flame to save those caught inside the Pentagon.

And here, in Shanksville, Pennsylvania, we remember heroes who unselfishly gave their lives so that others may live.

Now, one year later, as we reflect on their sacrifice, I can't help but feel humbled at the incredible courage shown by ordinary Americans that day.

When many of us awoke on September 11, America was a country at peace. Times were good. We hadn't known war in quite some time.

---

5. Delivered on September 11, 2002, at Shanksville, PA.

Then, just like that, our peace was shattered by cowards who sought to destroy our way of life. They thought we were weak. They thought we would simply stand aside.

Early on the morning of September 11, in the skies above us, they got their answer.

Americans will always rise to the challenge.

Americans will always fight for freedom.

And Americans will never surrender our way of life.

Today, we stand on a battlefield.

It is unlike other battlefields in our nation's history because that day America's first defenders weren't battle tested.

They weren't even armed.

They were ordinary Americans who were off to work or to visit family.

And in an instant, they became one of the most heralded military units in our nation's rich history.

Some say that America's war against terror really began when our armed forces landed in Afghanistan last October.

But we know better. Those of us here today know better.

Their heroics are so incredibly pure—their sacrifice so enduring.

It was here that freedom took its first stand.

And that's why we come here together today to remember heroes who made the ultimate sacrifice.

They decided their fate wasn't in the hands of terrorists.

It was in their own.

Their heroics are so incredibly pure—their sacrifice so enduring.

It calls to mind something a great American ally, Winston Churchill, once said: "Never in the field of human conflict was so much owed by so many to so few."

And this country will make good on that debt.

You know, a year ago, I came here mournfully at witnessing such great personal loss and the sad reality that there was precious little we could do. I was overcome by emotion because everything felt so painfully final.

But I was wrong. I was wrong because finality means something has reached an end.

But as I stand here, today, I continue to feel the indomitable spirit of America's Flight 93 patriots. I feel it in my heart. And I see it in your eyes.

Make no mistake, they are more than remembered!

They are with us. They are forceful. And they are proud.

Thank you.

Arlington National Cemetery Funeral Service for the Unidentified Victims of the Attack on the Pentagon[6]

Donald H. Rumsfeld

U.S. Secretary of Defense, 2001– ; born Chicago, IL, 1932; A.B., Princeton University, 1954; aviator, U.S. Navy, 1954–57; with A. G. Becker & Co., investment banking firm, 1960–62; U.S. House of Representatives, IL, 1962–69; director, Office of Economic Opportunity, assistant to President Richard Nixon, and member of president's cabinet, 1969–70; counsellor to President Nixon, director of the Economic Stabilization Program, and member of president's cabinet, 1971–72; U.S. Ambassador to North Atlantic Treaty Organization (NATO), 1973–74; White House chief of staff and member of President Gerald Ford's cabinet, 1974–75; U.S. Secretary of Defense, 1975–77; CEO, president, and then chair, G. D. Searle & Co., pharmaceutical company, 1977–85; chair and CEO, General Instrument Corporation, 1990–93; awarded Presidential Medal of Freedom, 1977; honorary degrees from several colleges and universities.

Editors' introduction: About a month after the terrorists' attacks on the United States, as military advisor to President George W. Bush, Secretary of Defense Donald H. Rumsfeld orchestrated the nation's and their allies' assault upon the Taliban entrenched in Afghanistan. One year later, Secretary Rumsfeld expressed his condolences to family and friends of the victims of the attack upon the Pentagon, as well as military personnel, and members of the administration, urging them to "celebrate" the lives of the fallen, who were lost "in a struggle dedicated to the eternal truth of freedom and the human spirit."

Donald H. Rumsfeld's speech: I am grateful to be here, with you, to convey my condolences and the condolences of the Nation for the sudden and grievous loss you suffered on September 11 of last year.

Those we honor today died here at home—not on a faraway battlefield. They died within view of this cemetery.

Yet they did die on a battlefield—and that battlefield tells us a great deal about the war we are in—the first war of the 21st century.

---

6. Delivered on September 12, 2002, at Arlington National Cemetery.

Their attackers said they died because they were Americans.

Put another way: They died because they were part of a nation that believes in freedom. They died because they lived according to a generous creed of "life, liberty, and the pursuit of happiness"—and not the twisted views of those who use a noble religion to try to mask their will to power.

We also know that those we honor here today died because of an institution that is a symbol of this generous creed and way of life. A symbol of military power, to be sure, but of power used to right wrong, to do good, to help achieve a more perfect day when nations might live in peace.

But until that time comes, the events of September 11 remind us that the forces of freedom are locked in a new type of struggle with those who oppose all that our freedom represents. As President Bush stated, our task is to provide the response to aggression and terror, to lift the dark threat of violence from our people and our future.

We have no other choice—the advance of human freedom now depends on it.

While there is nothing any of us can do to bring those loved ones

---

They died because they lived according to a generous creed of "life, liberty, and the pursuit of happiness."

---

back, we can celebrate who they were, how they lived their lives, and remember how their lives were lost—in a struggle dedicated to the eternal truth of freedom and the human spirit.

All this is important to remember. But those of you here today, who have lost loved ones, know that sometimes this too is hard.

When this ceremony is over, you may look again at the memorial, note the names that are special to you, take a final moment—have a last word, or look, or prayer. Then turn and leave this place, feeling again the emptiness, thinking again of a "tomorrow and tomorrow and tomorrow" of an irreplaceable, seemingly endless loss.

And you might say again, what so many times this year you may have said to yourselves . . . that we can be grateful for the time we had with them, that we must trust in a loving God who holds them close and affords them now the greatest of peace and joy.

You might say to yourselves they would have wanted us to remember that life goes on, and that we must live each day for them, as for ourselves. You may remind yourselves that the memories, so hurtful now, will one day turn beautiful and bring solace and comfort.

All this is hard. But all this is true.

Your grief is great. Your love is stronger.

A love seen so many times this last year. A love of who they were—your family members and friends; and, yes, your fellow Americans.

Everywhere I have gone the families of those we honor and remember today have said, "Do not forget." The president and the American people and our young men and women in uniform have heard you.

And so, today, we honor the 184 patriots who died at the Pentagon last September 11. We remember, with special love, the five whose remains were not recovered, and their families and friends who were denied the peace that comes with placing loved ones in their final place of rest.

This day these five join the unknown of wars past, even as we pursue the war that is still unfolding.

Known and unknown, those resting here were bound in brotherhood by their heritage.

Soldier and civilian alike, they were dedicated to the cause of freedom.

Young and old, their lives—and their deaths—gave birth to a new pride and patriotism that has rekindled the flame of freedom across our land.

They will be remembered. We will not forget.

Know that your country shares your sorrow; mourns your loss, and prays that God will comfort you.

May God grant them, and you, his loving peace.

III. Immigration

U.S. Asylum Policy

Reforms Needed in Current System[1]

Dan Stein

Executive Director, Federation for American Immigration Reform (FAIR), 1988– ; born Washington, D.C., March 9, 1955; B.A., Indiana University, 1977; J.D., Catholic University of America, Washington, D.C., 1984; U.S. District Court, Washington, D.C., 1985; U.S. Court of Appeals (D.C. circuit), 1987; U.S. Tax Court, 1987; staff member, select committee on narcotics abuse and control, U.S. House of Representatives, Washington, D.C., 1977–81; private practice, Washington, D.C., 1984–89; executive director, Immigration Reform Law Institute, Washington, D.C., 1986–88; member, advisory board, Social Contract, Petosky, MI, 1990– ; appears often on radio and television programs, including 60 Minutes, 20/20, Nightline, Today, Face the Nation, Crossfire, *and the* NewsHour with Jim Lehrer; *has testified before Congress more than 50 times.*

Editors' introduction: Since 1979, the Federation for American Immigration Reform (FAIR) has worked to halt illegal immigration and establish immigration policies based on the national need, a stable U.S. population size, and the country's overall domestic priorities. FAIR advocates reduced immigration into the United States. Executive Director Dan Stein, an attorney who has worked for nearly 21 years in the field of immigration law and law reform, told some 300 professional lobbyists, congressional staff members, and members of the Immigration Subcommittee of the Senate Judiciary Committee that "it is unfair to the American people to ask them to embrace a policy that attempts to right every wrong and rectify every misfortune, wherever it occurs, no matter who is responsible by bringing the victims into the United States."

---

1. Delivered on May 3, 2001, at Washington, D.C. Reprinted with permission of Dan Stein.

Dan Stein's testimony:

Introduction

Thank you, Mr. Chairman, for the opportunity to present the views of the Federation for American Immigration Reform (FAIR) on the important issue of asylum policy and problems with regard to implementation of the law as it exists today. I am Dan Stein, FAIR's executive director.

FAIR is a national, nonprofit organization of 70,000 concerned citizens nationwide promoting better immigration controls and a return to a moderate level of legal immigration to insure that today's policies serve the current and future best interests of the American people. FAIR does not receive any federal grants, contracts or subcontracts.

FAIR stands by these principles:

- Illegal immigration can and must be substantially reduced by humane measures that are consistent with our democratic ideals; immigration should not be permitted to undermine opportunities for America's poor and disadvantaged to improve their wages and working conditions.

- Our immigration laws must be fairly and effectively enforced; there should be no favoritism toward or discrimination against a person on the basis of race, religion, or ethnicity.

- All immigration should come within a single, stable ceiling which is periodically reviewed on the basis of reasoned, explicit population goals for the U.S.

- Three criteria should guide the selection of immigrants: our fair share of refugees for resettlement, our national manpower policy, and concerns for the maintenance of intact nuclear families.

- The United States should not contribute to a brain drain that entices away the skilled and talented who are desperately needed in their homelands; we should meet our need for skilled professionals by training and retraining our own.

- The United States should make greater efforts to encourage population size stability, economic development, and alleviation of poverty worldwide and especially in countries of great out migration.

- The era of mass international migration as a solution to national problems has come to an end; problems of poverty and overpopulation must be vigorously confronted where people live, rather than postponing their solution by either the exportation or importation of masses of people.

• We should determine our own immigration and population policy broadly and democratically, as a sovereign right and responsibility of our nation.

Mr. Chairman, the American people are extremely hospitable to immigrants and refugees, and our nation's record of generosity and compassion to people in need of special protection from war, anarchy, or natural disaster is exemplary. We have maintained a very munificent refugee resettlement pattern over the years, even though many of the people we have taken in are not considered true refugees by the United Nations High Commissioner for Refugees. The problem comes when the policies established become unrealistically broad or unintended avenues for abuse.

Mr. Chairman, FAIR suggests these principles in asylum policy:

1. Asylum policy should work to provide temporary protection here for persons to work for positive change back home. The goal is to strike a balance between providing protection for those who need it while encouraging people to—where possible—stay home to work for positive change.

2. Asylum policy should be integrated with refugee policy to create a single, unitary statutory scheme. Asylum standards should not create incentives for persons to "get within U.S. jurisdiction first" with the expectation of preferred treatment over similarly situated persons overseas.

3. Because asylum grants allow an alien to line-jump in front of millions of other people, the grant must be made with care, consistent with the statutory scheme. The management of asylum policy must take into account the enormous worldwide migration pressure, the long waiting lists and backlogs, and the incentives that exist to gain residency through false claims. Someone wiser than I speculated "if only refugees are admitted then everyone will become a refugee."

4. Other than for countries of first asylum, the grant should be restored to its original purpose: to provide temporary protection for persons here legally who, as a result of unforeseeable, changed circumstances can no longer return home. Certain evidentiary presumptions are appropriate in certain cases where a claimant is from a particular religious or social group and we possess very little home country information that would allow verification of claims. Asylum is to be a temporary status; it is to allow persons to work here for positive political change back home.

5. Asylum should not be viewed as an alternative to regular immigration.

6. Asylees should not be subject to preferred procedural and legal standards that give an advantage to the would-be asylum-seeker to get to the U.S. in order to make the claim. The "credible fear" prescreening standard for summary return should remain in the law and be actually used by the government.

7. Asylum seekers should be expected to make a claim for protection at the first available opportunity in the first country of refuge. Asylum claimants should not forum shop or otherwise be allowed to pick and choose where they make their claim-passing through several safe-haven nations before getting to the U.S.

8. The legal standards for asylum must be consistent with our international obligations. There should be some "State Action" at the core of the claim of persecution. The newly evolving standard that allows claims to be made on the basis of an alleged absence of state protection for entire classes of "social groups" is fraught with peril as unmanageable and an invitation to fraud.

9. The definition of "membership in a social group" must be defined narrowly enough that it retains some standard beyond the subjective parameters of an imaginative immigration bar.

10. As a practical matter, under our current system, adjudicating asylum claims often involves allegations of abuse that took place tens of thousands of miles away; objective evidence may be entirely lacking and the entire claim may rest on a subjective judgment of the asylum officer. Where the procedural, legal or evidentiary standards become unworkable or an invitation to fraud, it is up to Congress to intervene to reassert the proper standards to insure a manageable program.

Background of the Mid-1990s Asylum Reform

Our generosity and compassion must be reserved for those who are truly deserving of it. That is the reason that there was widespread resentment at the revelations in the middle of the 1990s that the nation's asylum policy had become a major loophole for gaining illegal residence in the United States. So many foreign travelers were arriving in New York and other airports without entry documents and requesting asylum, that the INS had largely shut down efforts to decide the legitimacy of the asylum claims and was waiving the asylum claimants into the country, issuing them work permits and filing away their asylum applications to gather dust. So notorious was the practice that awareness of the loophole spread beyond the alien smuggling rings, and the backlog of pending asylum cases rose into the hundreds of thousands. It appeared to be so easy to get a green card by filing an asylum application that the practice even spread to "green card" fixers in the United States who began enticing Mexicans who were here illegally to begin filing asylum applications.

As Senator Kennedy commented in the June 13, 1993, *Washington Post*, "The asylum system has broken down, and it's up to Congress and the administration to fix it." According to former INS Commissioner Doris Meissner, "The problem we have faced in recent years [she told the March 30, 1994, *Washington Post*] is that people with no legitimate claim to asylum are applying in record numbers, some brought by smugglers, some using fake documents, and some overstaying the visas granted to them as visitors."

Against this background of fraudulent use of the asylum system, abusing the generosity and compassion of the American people, the Clinton administration and the Republican-led Congress finally acted in 1995 to reestablish the integrity of the asylum process and reassure the American public that only people who truly feared persecution were able to gain the nation's protection. The administration acted first, trying to forestall a change in the law. Those changes in the screening system included an enlarged Asylum Corps, halting the automatic issuance of a work permit to new asylum applicants, and an accelerated processing of asylum applications. On July 9, 1995, Commissioner Meissner told the *Post*, "After years in which fraudulent asylum claims were routinely used as a backdoor way to enter the United States, the Immigration and Naturalization Service finally has sufficient staff and resources to stop the abuse and ensure that legitimate asylum-seekers no longer pay the price for those who seek to misuse the system."

These measures were supplemented by Congress in 1996 to add new expedited removal procedures, but the protection against removing someone who feared persecution if returned to his homeland was protected by requiring a screening of all asylum claims by a member of the Asylum Corps. A recent example of the operation of this procedure was demonstrated when a surge of Colombians began arriving in the United States on transit visas (meaning that they were not documented to enter the United States) and began requesting asylum in an effort to bypass consular screening of Colombian travelers to determine if they were intending immigrants. While it is certainly true that life is difficult in Colombia because of drug-related violence and a breakdown in the government's ability to assure order, most of the arriving Colombians were not targets for persecution. The embassy in Bogata was able to suspend the issuance of transit visas for the U.S.; this kind of thing demonstrates abuse potential. We hope that the Asylum Corps was able to meet this surge in frivolous asylum claims and, as a result, discourage recourse to this attempt to circumvent the U.S. immigration law. But the evidence is clear: if you create the opportunity for a loophole, it will be exploited.

Earlier, in a similar fashion the Asylum Corps was pressed into service screening Cuban and Haitian "rafters" seeking to enter the United States. If the United States had continued to accept anyone who sought an opportunity for a better life, the stream of Cubans and Haitians setting sail for our country would have become enormous, and they would likely have been joined by nationals of countless other countries in the area.

Other provisions adopted in 1996 reduce the ability of immigration lawyers to continue to seek sequential reviews of removal orders until they find a sympathetic judge and to use an asylum claim as a defense against removal if the alien has been living illegally in the United States for more than a year without initiating an asylum claim. These changes were adopted to redress the imbalance in favor of the asylum applicant at the expense of the American public.

Asylum Reform Judged Largely Successful

The asylum reform effort of the mid-1990s has been largely successful. The number of frivolous asylum claims have dropped off sharply. From a total of 127,000 claims in FY'93, the level in FY'99 was about 32,000. However, there are still problems. Even with careful prescreening of asylum applicants by trained asylum officers, a large majority of asylum claimants who present a convincing enough claim to get referred to an Immigration Judge are still found meritless. The disapproval rate in FY'99 for claims before Immigration Judges was 62 percent. There is no guarantee that people who get asylum are in fact *bona fide* asylees.

> *The asylum process is still being used as a backdoor route for gaining illegal residence in the United States.*

Proof that the asylum process is still being used as a backdoor route for gaining illegal residence in the United States is the fact that the number of asylum applications is on the upswing again. From the 32,000 in FY'99, the number jumped by about 28 percent in FY'00 to nearly 41,000.

In addition, the INS has no system in place to assure that the denied asylum applicants ever leave the United States. There is every reason to believe that these persons who have been trying to take advantage of the generosity of the American people stay on in the country illegally and hope to gain legal residence by enactment of another amnesty for illegal aliens. We should remember the warning of Barbara Jordan, former member of the House Judiciary Committee and chairman of the Commission on Immigration Reform. She said in testimony in the House on February 24, 1995, "for the system to be credible, people actually have to be deported at the end of the process."

Mr. Chairman, I recognize that immigration lawyers are unhappy with the current state of the asylum screening process, because some asylum applicants at ports of entry may be sent back home without ever gaining access to the services of a U.S. immigration lawyer. If the purpose of the asylum provisions of the immigration law were intended to maximize the number of persons gaining permanent residence in the United States, that concern might have some logic. However, that is not the purpose of the asylum provision. The reason that asylum was created was to deal with people who would qualify for refugee status if they were abroad, but who were temporarily located in this country. It is clear today that most of the persons being accorded asylum in the United States would not be granted refugee status to the United States if they were outside of this country. Because asylum has proven to be a backdoor route to residence in the United States, policymakers have a responsibility to the American people to minimize the possibility that it is abused.

The Shift in Legal Standards: Who Qualifies?

Mr. Chairman, last December the nation learned from an INS leak that Adelaide Abankwah, a poster child for granting asylum to prevent female circumcision (or genital mutilation), was an imposter. (See *Abankwah* v. *INS*, 185 F.3d 22 2nd Cir. 1999.) In fact, she had assumed the identity of another woman, had invented a story that her mother was the queen of a tribe in Ghana and she was due to succeed to that position which would lead to the genital cutting ceremony. She succeeded in posing as an entirely different person throughout the entirety of the case—all the way through appellate review.

What this case highlighted (in addition to a judicial willingness to second-guess matters committed firmly by law to agency discretion) is that asylum procedure allows people to destroy identity documents during the trip over and fabricate stories out of whole cloth. Although the credible-fear procedure was supposed to prevent this, the current asylum system does not insure that the INS even gets a "positive ID" on the alien. It does not allow us to take into account behavior by the alien before arrival—in committing calculated fraud and forum shopping—when determining the credibility of a claim. Limitations of resources prevent the State Department in the home country from individually investigating the claims of individual asylum claimants in the U.S.

The invitation for false claims is compounded by the now unmanageably broad definitions of who is an asylee. The problems presented by broader and broader definitions of who can get asylum is sending this country into new and uncharted waters, especially over the question of who qualifies for a claim based upon membership in a particular social group. The asylum standard codified in U.S. immigration law in 1980 was based on the internationally accepted refugee definition. Whether a person had been persecuted or had a well-founded fear of persecution if repatriated could be evaluated reasonably objectively when the criteria turned on the person's race, religion, nationality, or political opinion. Congress judged in 1980 on the basis of past experience that the maximum number of asylum claimants in a year would not reach 5,000, so they set that as a ceiling. However, experience has taught us what we should already have known: "if you build a new avenue for admission, they will come." By 1990, more than 15,000 approved asylum applicants were waiting in a backlog, and Congress doubled the annual ceiling.

Today, we are facing a replay of the 1990 situation. Again there is a backlog of approved asylum claims in excess of the quota for three years. Legislation has been introduced in the House to again increase the ceiling (H.R. 1560). Why has the number of asylum applicants been increasing? Is it because persecution is becoming more widespread? I don't think that is the explanation. In our view, it is more likely because of a systemic problem and because of the stretching in practice of the scope of eligibility for asylum coverage.

Part of the explanation for the increasing number of asylum claimants is due to a prevailing culture in the INS that creates a much greater onus on an asylum officer or an immigration judge who denies an asylum application than if the application is approved. That appears to explain approval of the fraudulent Abankwah case. The INS said all along that it had doubts about the *bona fides* of her asylum claim, but extensive interest by the press and politicians in the case apparently overcame the INS professionals' good judgment.

Another part of the explanation involves legislative and judicial expansion of asylum coverage. The congressional action occurred with the addition to the asylum definition of China's family planning policy as a form of political persecution by Section 601 of the 1996 Illegal Immigration Reform and Immigrant Responsibility Act (IIRAIRA).

FAIR expressed its concern that this change in the law would be another loophole phenomenon, i.e., that it would lead to an increase in fraudulent Chinese asylum applicants. We have been proven correct. In FY'96 there were 1,509 Chinese asylum applications. In FY'2000 there were 5,541 Chinese applications. There would have been even more except the United States began intercepting Chinese smuggling ships and diverting them to ports in neighboring countries where the smuggled Chinese could not gain entry making asylum based on claims of fear of family planning persecution. In these cases, the neighboring countries brought in representatives from the UN High Commissioner for Refugees and the International Organization for Migration to screen the Chinese for possibly valid asylum claims and found only a miniscule number of possibly valid claimants. If the same Chinese had succeeded in arriving in the United States, the 1996 provision in our law would likely have led to large numbers receiving asylum and few if any removals. That has been the experience with a surge of asylum claims from Chinese illegal entrants as coached by the Chinese snakehead smuggling rings. So-called "one child per family" claims were also asserted after the fact on behalf of the still detained smuggled Chinese from the *Golden Venture*.

Increasingly over the past several years, asylum has been granted to people claiming to fear generalized social customs or conditions, such as female circumcision, and even social ostracism based on sexual orientation, disease or disability. While these practices are at best inconsistent with Western notions of decency and at worst reprehensible, they hardly fit the intended definition of political persecution as contemplated by the Geneva Convention or our other international obligations. The expansive nature of asylum grants over the past several years have moved us from the murky area of rendering judgments about the actions of foreign governments to the even murkier area of judging social and cultural practices that are at odds with our own. Asylum law has deviated from cases where there is direct State Action in perpetrating persecution to the hazy area of a government's alleged generalized failure to provide certain protections for marginalized groups.

If the United States has sometimes been viewed as the world's policeman, these recent expansions of political asylum are moving us toward the role of trying to be the international nanny—of a

---

*These recent expansions of political asylum
are moving us toward the role of trying to
be the international nanny.*

---

nation trying to insure that no person encounters the vexations of life's misfortunes. How can the United States monitor what is taking place in every village square and in every bedroom around the world?

Virtually everyone who is subjected to any injustice, whether perpetrated by a government, social group, or even a father or an aunt, can seek asylum protection by the United States—even if there is no plausible reason to explain why this particular alien is here making the claim in this particular country at this particular time. And, the most troubling aspect of this trend is that increasingly there are no objective criteria to assist the asylum officers and immigration judges in evaluating these claims in order to be able to limit asylum grants to truly meritorious cases. Despite the lessons learned in the early 1990s, there is still very little "discipline in the system" to insure that claims without merit are not approved. If advocates are concerned about claims with merit being denied (and there's little evidence of that fact), what about the problem of meritless claims being granted? Isn't that a problem, too?

As if this were not already a difficult enough situation, and one that has already fueled more asylum claims than were ever contemplated when the asylum law was adopted, a last gasp effort of the preceding administration bequeathed us a new avenue for asylum claims. Under this parting proposal, women around the world who are battered by their spouses may become eligible to receive residence in this country—and asylum generally now seems to mean de facto permanent residence.[1] We have asked the Bush administration to withdraw these proposed rules. Already, the asylum provision, intended to protect people from persecution by their governments, has been broadened to include a whole range of people who might be subjected to objectionable cultural and social practices.

It is unfair to the American people to ask them to embrace a policy that attempts to right every wrong and rectify every misfortune, wherever it occurs, no matter who is responsible by bringing the victims into the United States for permanent residence and giving them instant access to welfare programs, housing assistance, and other taxpayer-supported public assistance programs that are available only to the neediest Americans.

Moreover, unlike political persecution, which can be assessed objectively, rendering judgments about cultural and social practices is highly subjective. It forces the United States into a position of passing judgment on social practices and cultural mores in every society on Earth. If ostracism due to sexual orientation is grounds for asylum, how is a line to be drawn to exclude asylum claims from women who in Islamic societies are required to wear veils, or denied the right to drive a car or work outside the home? At that point asylum ceases to be a mechanism to protect the persecuted, and becomes a process of imposing our values on others or using the asylum law to obtain "legitimacy" for some international cause.

In a world of 6 billion people, most of whom live under political systems and cultures that leave a lot to be desired, real world conditions mean we must be selective in granting asylum protection. Political asylum must not become social asylum, or it will destroy our ability to help anyone. One test: try to apply the asylum standard contemplated to international refugee resettlement screening. If the standard produces refugee eligibility for tens or hundreds of millions of people, then the standards is probably not tenable.

FAIR's Recommendations

Mr. Chairman, as I have outlined above, the gains in control over asylum abuse adopted beginning in 1995 are again beginning to weaken as a deterrent to fraudulent claims. Part of this, as I noted, is a culture in the INS bureaucracy that makes it more difficult to deny an asylum claim than to approve it. Another part of the problem is the process over the past few years of expanding the scope of eligibility for asylum. That not only complicates the asylum adjudication process, it attracts additional claimants.

Now we are faced once again with a backlog of approved asylum claims as in 1990. The so-called ABC backlog has been dealt with—even though most of those claimants were never able to perfect asylum claims.[2] The question is what is an appropriate policy response. Another increase in the asylum admissions ceiling is not the solution. Fair opposes that approach and believes that the American people would be ill served by that measure. The solution to the mounting immigration pressure cannot always be to raise numbers.

The objective we should be striving to achieve is continued assured protection for asylum applicants who fear persecution from governments or from organized nongovernmental elements that are oppressing people with the tacit backing of their government, while discouraging the abuse of the American people's hospitality and compassion. We believe that three reforms would serve that purpose.

The first of the reforms would decouple the grant of asylum from permanent residence. International practice demonstrates that there is no standard requiring us to grant permanent residence to asylees. There is no reason that a *bona fide* asylum applicant can

---

When the fear of persecution is no longer valid, the asylees should be required to return home.

---

not be admitted as a nonimmigrant with the right to work in the United States. That status should not be adjusted to permanent residence until after a minimum of five years. There is no reason that a person who has shown the resourcefulness to get to the U.S. to ask for asylum should be accorded welfare benefits and other public assistance that should be reserved to our most needy citizens. As international circumstances change, the asylum status should be periodically reviewed to determine whether the original circumstances that led to the asylum grant have been reversed. In that case, when the fear of persecution is no longer valid, the asylees should be required to return home. Similarly, an asylum grantee should face a presumption that a fear of persecution no longer exists if he or she travels back to the home country.

The advantage of the adoption of this reform is that it would discourage the still sizable number of asylum applicants who see asylum as a way to permanent residence in the United States, even if their main objective is not the public assistance that comes with a grant of asylum.

The second reform proposal is an amendment to the refugee and asylee definition to delete the reference to "membership in a particular social group." This change would preserve the scope of asylum protection for the traditional range of persecution, i.e., for race, religion, nationality, and political opinion, while ending the expansion of asylum claims into areas of social policy never intended by the framers of the law. Asylum claimants should be judged by the same standards as persons screened as refugees overseas.

The third proposed reform is to put an end to the quasi-asylum status of Cubans who arrive illegally in this country. The Cuban Adjustment Act is an anachronism of the Cold War that treats all Cubans as if they were fleeing persecution. In our current practice, we recognize that is not the case any longer. Those Cubans who are intercepted attempting to enter the United States illegally are given the opportunity to request asylum and are given a hearing if they present a convincing case that they have been persecuted or will be persecuted if they are returned to Cuba. However, most of the intercepted Cubans fail this test and are returned to Cuba, where follow-up programs have convincingly demonstrated they are not subjected to persecution. If the Cuban Adjustment Act is abolished, Cubans will be put on an equal footing with Haitians and all others who arrive illegally in the United States and seek to stay. They will have to present an asylum claim, and if they are not entitled to that protection, they will be removed.

Even if this reform were not inherently logical in its own right (which it clearly is), it is essential to restoring the even-handedness and fairness of our asylum policy. It will assure persons from other countries—who today are denied the opportunity to stay in the United States accorded only to the Cubans—that our policy is not discriminatory against them.

Conclusion

The context in which we make these recommendations is the overall rise in immigration to a level never contemplated by the legislators who created the current system of immigration in 1965. From moderate levels of immigration between a quarter of a million to a third of a million admissions per year during most of the past century, immigration today is averaging closer to 1 million admissions per year, and it is well above that level when illegal residents are included. That massive influx is clear from the 2000 Census numbers. The net increase of over 10 million immigrants during the 1990s demonstrates a trend that also drives the rapid increase in the overall population of the country. FAIR, like the U.S. Commission on Immigration Reform, is concerned that the preservation of a welcoming climate for new immigrants will be difficult unless the level of immigration is scaled back to a more moderate level.

Legitimate, merits-based refugee and asylee admissions deserve our highest priority and attention. They should get first priority in admissions. However, as long as there is no real definable national interest or objective governing our immigration policy, we will continue to be unable to make tradeoffs in order to reallocate priorities. Therefore, asylum policy, too, must be looked at critically as part of any effort to scale back the level of immigration. As I noted above, FAIR thinks that asylum claims can be reduced without any jeopardy to the policy of protecting persons who fall within generally accepted international norms for asylum. We urge on behalf of our members and the American public in general that the pressure from advocates for improper widening of the admissions criteria for asylum applicants be resisted, and further reform of the asylum process be adopted in order to assure continued public understanding and support of this program which, when it is properly administered, is a necessary humanitarian program.

Notes

1. See also *Aguirre-Cervantes* v. *INS*, No. 99-70861, 2001 WL 274698 (9th Cir. Mar. 21, 2001). In this case, the Mexican government was held to be unable or unwilling to provide adequate civil remedies and protective facilities for battered spouses, and the family was the social group involved—where one member (the father) was abusing another member (the daughter).

2. The ABC backlog illustrates the need for speed in asylum adjudications. Backlogs among claimants inside the U.S. will soon obtain the equities to insist that their right to remain be determined on factors other than the merits of the asylum claim itself.

Immigration Reform[2]

Linda Chavez-Thompson

Executive Vice President, AFL-CIO, 1995– ; born Lubbock, TX, August 1, 1944; secretary, American Federation of State, County, and Municipal Employees (AFSCME), Austin, TX, 1967–71; international representative, AFSCME, San Antonio, TX, 1971–73; AFSCME Local 2399, San Antonio, 1973–95; national vice president, the Labor Council for Latin American Advancement, AFL-CIO, 1986– ; vice president, AFSCME, 1988–96; vice president, AFL-CIO, 1993–95; president, InterAmerican Regional Organization of Workers (ORIT), 2001; former vice chair, President's Committee on the Employment of People with Disabilities; on boards of the United Way of America, the Democratic National Committee, the Council on Competitiveness, the Labor Heritage Foundation, and the Institute for Woman's Policy Research; chair, National Committee on Pay Equity.

Editors' introduction: Ms. Linda Chavez-Thompson is the first person to hold the post of AFL-CIO executive vice president, and the first person of color to be elected to one of the federation's three highest offices. While working with AFSCME for nearly three decades, she steered that union to a number of successes in a seven-state district traditionally hostile to unions—Arizona, Colorado, Nevada, New Mexico, Oklahoma, Texas, and Utah. While speaking at the annual convention of Hotel Employees and Restaurant Employees (HERE), Ms. Chavez-Thompson insisted that the "system" should be changed to "recognize the undocumented workers across our land—acknowledge all they do to help keep our economy and our society running—and *give them the rights they deserve.*"

Linda Chavez-Thompson's speech: I'm delighted to be here.
What a terrific group you are!
You know, this is almost like a family reunion for me.
I see so many good friends here.
We've marched together—struggled together—dreamed together.
I'd like to start out by paying tribute to one of the finest, most effective, most idealistic union activists of this generation, whom I'm proud to have as my friend . . . your president, John Wilhelm.

2. Delivered on July 18, 2001, at Los Angeles, CA. Reprinted with permission of Linda Chavez-Thompson.

Everything I say here today about immigration and the union movement—all of the values, all of the policies, all of the ideals—have been influenced by Brother Wilhelm.

As the head of the AFL-CIO Executive Council's Committee on Immigration Policy, John has led the union movement to a new approach towards immigrant workers that is more just, and fair, and decent.

> ## *Immigrants are the history of the union movement.*

Believe me, HERE—and the entire union movement—are lucky to have a leader of such high quality as John.

I also want to pay tribute to some real heroes of mine . . . all the women and men who are here from Locals 11 in L.A. and 814 in Santa Monica.

They organized—they mobilized—and they helped bring out tens of thousands of our sisters and brothers at the sports arena for the AFL-CIO immigration forum last year.

I've never seen anything like it before.

It was the biggest rally for immigrant workers in American history.

The place was packed—in fact, the crowd spilled over to outside the arena . . . and Locals 11 and 814 deserve a lot of credit for that terrific success.

Next, I want to pay tribute to the other speakers at this forum . . . including Cardinal Mahony, who has spoken out for many years for working people's freedom to organize into unions. I know that you also heard from Jorge Castenada, who is helping to reshape Mexico's foreign policy and building new bridges between our two lands.

I'm here to talk about how the union movement looks at immigration issues.

Immigration is the very core of who we are as a movement.

Just look at the executive officers of the AFL-CIO.

John Sweeney is the son of immigrants from County Antrim, Ireland . . . Rich Trumka is from a family of Polish and Italian miners . . . and I am the daughter of Mexican-American sharecroppers. Immigrants are the history of the union movement . . . but too often in the past, our movement hasn't fully embraced new immigrants.

Today, we in the AFL-CIO have a new policy that recognizes that all immigrants are not only our history . . . but also our *future*—our soul and our spirit.

The AFL-CIO supports a fair and just system of immigration . . . and we support fairness and justice for all of America's immigrants.

That's exactly why we insist that all immigrants have the right to good wages . . . decent benefits . . . protection from unsafe and unhealthy workplaces . . . freedom from discrimination . . . and the freedom to choose a union.

But the sad fact is that today . . . for both the 5 to 6 million undocumented immigrants and the 20 million who are documented . . . there is too little justice and too little fairness.

There are lots of examples of this.

For one thing, every day when immigrants go to work, millions of them are rewarded with low wages—violations of their rights—insults—discrimination.

And time after time, we see employers try to divide us from our sisters and brothers.

They try to pit immigrants against nonimmigrants, documented against undocumented . . . to take advantage of the most vulnerable among us, and to drive down the wages and working conditions for us all.

Another example of what's wrong is the government's system of employer sanctions.

Back in 1985, the AFL-CIO took a position in favor of employer sanctions for hiring undocumented workers.

Well, 16 years have passed . . . and we know without a doubt that employer sanctions are a failure.

In fact, the system is so crazy that even while it's called "employer sanctions" . . . it's often the *employers* themselves who are in control.

They can manipulate the system to retaliate against workers who assert their rights.

It's time to scrap the current system . . . to replace it with a new and different enforcement system that's fair, and practical, and just . . . and also to recognize the undocumented workers across our land—acknowledge all they do to help keep our economy and our society running—and *give them the rights they deserve*.

How do we make those principles real?

The answer has three main parts.

The AFL-CIO Executive Council set them out in a resolution last year . . . a resolution that was put together under John Wilhelm's leadership . . . and the Council supported it unanimously.

First, we need a new legalization program . . . one that provides permanent legal status for all of those undocumented workers and their families who have been working hard and contributing so much to their communities.

Second, we need to ensure that all working people—whether they were born here or elsewhere, whether they're documented or undocumented—can have equal rights on the job.

It means the right to a minimum wage—a safe workplace—wage and hour protections . . . and it means the freedom to choose a voice in the workplace—the freedom to organize into unions.

It's only fair and right to make sure that all workers have the basic protections that every worker needs and deserves.

So that's the second part of the solution.

The third part is to throw the INS's I-9 enforcement system on the trash heap, which is exactly where it belongs . . . and replace it with a new system of enforcement that's fair and just—one that focuses on employers, not workers.

We need to target those employers who recruit undocumented workers from abroad so they can exploit them . . . and we need strong criminal penalties against employers who abuse workers' immigration status to trample on their rights.

We in the AFL-CIO believe that these three parts are the center of the solution. For us in the union movement, that is our agenda—that is our battle cry—and that is our poetry.

We're working in every way we can and everywhere we can . . . in Congress, in state capitals, in the workplace, in our neighborhoods . . . to help immigrant workers build a better life.

I want to invite you to join that effort.

Talk to your sisters and brothers in your local union—tell them how important this effort is—share what you know about the fight for justice for immigrant workers.

We in the AFL-CIO start off with one basic idea. We are on the side of working people everywhere . . . whether their families came here 400 years ago on a slave ship or the Mayflower . . . or 100 years ago through Ellis Island . . . or last year across the Mexican border.

That's our moral standard.

In the past, the union movement has fought for a better life for Irish and Italian and Slovak workers—for African-Americans and Asian-Americans and Latinos—for working women, and lesbians and gays, and workers with disabilities.

I promise you here and now that we're fighting for *exactly* the same thing—for *exactly* the same reasons—for this generation of immigrants in the workplace.

We embrace them—we welcome them—and we're determined to struggle until the morning when they have the same rights and the better life that many of the rest of us now enjoy.

Together, we can all help make the land we love into the land we know it can be.

Together, we can all create a community where justice is finally done.

Thank you very much.

Immigration and Civil Rights in the Wake of September 11[3]

Mark Krikorian

Executive Director, Center for Immigration Studies, 1995– ; bachelor's degree, Georgetown University; master's degree, Fletcher School of Law and Diplomacy; former editor at the Winchester Star *(VA), as well as editor of a publication on electronic marketing and of the monthly newsletter of the Federation for American Immigration Reform; frequently testifies before Congress; published articles in* the Washington Post, New York Times, Commentary, National Review, *and elsewhere; appeared on* National Public Radio, CNN, 60 Minutes, Nightline, *the* NewsHour with Jim Lehrer, *and many other television and radio programs.*

Editors' introduction: Executive Director Mark Krikorian spoke at a program on "Briefing on Boundaries of Justice, Immigration Policies Post–September 11," sponsored by the U.S. Commission on Civil Rights and attended by community organizations, legal scholars and experts, and government officials. The Center for Immigration Studies is an independent, nonpartisan, nonprofit organization devoted to research and policy analysis of the economic, social, demographic, and fiscal impacts of immigration on the United States. The Center supports policies that give first concern to the broad national interest, seeking fewer immigrants but a warmer welcome for those admitted. With the "atrocities" perpetrated by the September 11 hijackers in mind, Mr. Krikorian warned that "control over immigration is fundamental to national sovereignty." At the same time, he continued, "we still should seek to create a climate welcoming to those immigrants we do admit."

Mark Krikorian's statement:

> Immigration is not a right guaranteed by the U.S. Constitution to everyone and anyone in the world who wishes to come to the United States. It is a privilege granted by the people of the United States to those whom we choose to admit.

> *—Barbara Jordan, August 12, 1995*

Thank you for the opportunity to participate in this briefing on immigration and civil rights in the wake of the September 11 jihadist atrocities. We are faced with two questions relating to civil liber-

---

3. Delivered on October 12, 2001, at Washington, D.C. Reprinted with permission of Mark Krikorian.

ties: First, Is immigration a civil right? And second, What is the best way to create an environment respectful of immigrants living among us?

Immigration Is Not a Civil Right

Article I, Section 8, Clause 4 of the Constitution grants Congress the power to establish a "uniform Rule of Naturalization." From this has developed the "plenary power doctrine," which holds that Congress has complete authority over immigration matters. The Supreme Court has said that "over no conceivable subject" is federal power greater than it is over immigration. As a consequence, as the Court has said elsewhere, "In the exercise of its broad power over naturalization and immigration, Congress regularly makes rules that would be unacceptable if applied to citizens."

This is as it should be, since control over immigration is fundamental to national sovereignty. If "We the People of the United States" have ordained and established the Constitution, then we by definition retain the power to determine who is, and is not, a member of the American people. Thus, the decision to admit or exclude foreign citizens is a matter solely in the hands of the elected representatives of the people, and anyone from abroad who is admitted to travel or live among us does so as a guest, remaining here at our pleasure, until such time as we agree to permit him to become a member of our people. In effect, foreign citizens, even if they are here illegally, enjoy the human rights endowed to them by God, but they remain here at our discretion and the specifics of their due process rights are determined by Congress.

The decision to admit or exclude foreign citizens is a matter solely in the hands of the elected representatives of the people.

This is relevant in assessing many of the measures to tighten immigration control recommended in the wake of the September 11 attacks. All 19 hijackers were, after all, foreign citizens, as are many of those detained as possible accomplices or witnesses. This was also the case with the conspirators in the first World Trade Center attack, the 1993 CIA assassinations, and the foiled bomb plots in New York in 1995 and in Washington State in 1999. Foreign citizens, or naturalized immigrants, are almost certain to be responsible for the next attack, whether it comes in the next few days, as the FBI has warned, or farther in the future.

To begin at the first step in the process of coming to the United States, there is likely to be special scrutiny applied to visa applicants from Muslim countries and even to people of Middle Eastern birth who now hold other citizenship. Whether or not ethnic or religious profiling is an appropriate tool in the government's dealings with American citizens, there are no civil rights implications of such profiling of foreign citizens overseas. The United States government may refuse entry to any foreign citizen, for any reason, at any time. It is precisely to preserve this irreducible element of national sovereignty that repeated attempts to subject visa refusals to review have been rebuffed by Congress.

One of the grounds for exclusion may well be expanded as a result of the jihadist attacks, one that would not be unacceptable if applied to citizens but clearly permitted, indeed mandated, when applied to non-citizens abroad. Current law makes it extremely difficult to turn down a visa applicant because of his "beliefs, statements, or associations, if such beliefs, statements, or associations would be lawful within the United States." To keep out a terrorist sympathizer, who publicly cheers the murder of Americans but who, as far as we know, hasn't yet raised money for terrorist groups or planned out their assaults, the secretary of state must personally make the decision and then report each individual instance to four congressional committees. It is imperative that visa officers be given a freer hand in excluding enemies of America, even if their hatred for us would be constitutionally protected if articulated by citizens. The First Amendment does not apply to foreigners abroad.

Fingerprinting of visa applicants is another change likely in the wake of the attacks. Ideally, foreign visitors and students and work-

---

It is imperative that visa officers be given a freer hand in excluding enemies of America.

---

ers would have their fingerprints digitally scanned when applying for their visas, scanned again when entering the country, and again upon departure. Again, despite claims to the contrary, there are no civil rights implications of this security measure; this would simply be one of the conditions of being a guest in the United States.

The next stage in coming to the United States is at the border. Here, a tool to prevent the penetration of our system by terrorists and others has already been implemented. Although many have claimed that there are civil rights consequences to the procedure known as "expedited exclusion," enacted in the 1996 immigration law, there are no such consequences. That provision sought to end asylum abuses through the expedited exclusion of false asylum claimants at airports; when a person who has arrived in the United States with no documents or forged documents claims asylum, the initial plausibility of his claim may be judged by the immigration officer, to be reviewed by his supervisor if the officer makes a negative determination, and the alien may then be prevented from entering the United States and pursuing an asylum claim. Again, this is part of Congress's plenary power over immigration and there are no civil rights consequences of this policy.

And, finally, within the country, non-citizens do have rights, more if they are permanent residents, and thus candidate-members of the American people, and fewer if they are "nonimmigrants," i.e., on some sort of temporary visa. One change in the treatment of non-immigrants that is almost certain to be implemented in the wake of September 11 is the tracking of foreign students. Under a pilot program mandated by the 1996 immigration law, about two dozen colleges are participating in a program that requires the schools to update the INS on a quarterly basis about the academic status, address, field of study, etc., of all foreign students. This program was set to expand to all schools accepting foreign students over the next several years, but will now be sped up. Many foreign students and university spokesmen have complained about this as "unfair" or "discriminatory," using civil rights language to express their displeasure. But of course, as I have discussed, these students are here purely as guests in our house, and we are entitled to place whatever conditions we deem appropriate on their stay.

The same is true regarding the registration of lawful permanent residents. In 1940, as a security measure to try to prevent our enemies from infiltrating spies and saboteurs in immigrant communities, Congress required registration of all legal immigrants, which included a requirement that each alien notify the INS annually of his whereabouts. This notification requirement was discontinued in 1981, and shouldn't be revived in that form—members of terrorist sleeper cells cannot be expected to dutifully send in their addresses. However, a computerized system to verify the employment eligibility of new hires (pilots for which were mandated by the 1996 immigration law) could be a very effective tool in tracking the whereabouts of non-citizen legal immigrants and would, in effect, serve as a registration program for most resident aliens.

Deportation policy is another area where some have warned that measures recently passed or now proposed would have civil rights implications. The problem with this view is that deportation is not punishment—only non-citizens may be deported, and they are either here as our guests or as illegal aliens, and may be removed at any time so long as lawful procedures are followed. In the Supreme Court's 1999 ruling in *Reno* v. *American-Arab Anti-Discrimination Committee*, for instance, the free speech rights of, in this case, illegal aliens were sharply, and appropriately limited in the context of deportation proceedings. In the wake of September 11, it is possible that further limitations on speech and affiliation will be imposed on non-citizens, entirely appropriate limitations in such a national emergency.

The 1996 antiterrorism and immigration laws also allowed the use of classified evidence in deportation proceedings of suspected terrorists. Virtually all of the tiny number of cases using secret evidence have involved Arabs and/or Muslims, a result which has given rise to civil rights complaints. There has even been legislation to require that such classified evidence be disclosed, which would compromise intelligence sources and methods. Though little has been heard about this since September 11, complaints based on civil rights concerns will eventually resurface. Again, deportation is not punishment—immigration proceedings are administrative, not criminal, and their purpose, according to the Supreme Court, is to "provide a streamlined determination of eligibility to remain in this country, nothing more." Thus, as the FBI general counsel noted in testimony last year, "the full range of rights guaranteed a criminal defendant, including the Sixth Amendment's right to confrontation of evidence, are not applicable in immigration proceedings."

Even the deportation provision in the original version of the administration's antiterrorism package would not have had any civil rights consequences. That provision, since dropped, would have allowed deportation of persons certified as having terrorist ties without the presentation of any evidence at all. This is admittedly an emergency measure, but it would have been entirely appropriate, and may yet be implemented, as further terrorist attacks take place. Any ability accorded the alien to appeal deportation decisions is an act of grace on the part of the American people, rather than a right possessed by the alien. The courts thus have a role in ensuring that the alien is accorded due process of law, but the content of the law regarding removal of aliens is not a proper object of constitutional review.

Given that coming to America is a privilege and not a right, we still should seek to create a climate welcoming to those immigrants we do admit.

It would be unfortunate if, in our effort to prevent another 6,000 American deaths—or 60,000 or 600,000—we were inadvertently to deport some foreign citizens who pose no threat to us. But their presence here is a privilege we grant, not a right they have exercised, and we may withdraw that privilege for any reason.

Detention is another matter. Although INS rules allowing longer detention for illegal aliens before instituting proceedings are simple common sense, indefinite denial of liberty is disturbing, as the Supreme Court concluded in the *Zadvyas* v. *Davis* case. Even noncitizens possess the natural rights of life, liberty, and property, and the situation of those colloquially called "lifers"—deportable aliens whose countries of citizenship will not accept them back—is untenable. Only those deemed by the INS to be a threat to others should be kept in detention, while the federal government should seek political solutions to coerce, if necessary, the sending countries to take back their criminal citizens. There are some instances, however, where this simply won't happen, since the people finding themselves in this situation are almost always refugees fleeing communist or other despotic regimes hostile to the United States.

To Maintain a Pro-Immigrant Climate, We Need Lower Levels of Immigration

Given that coming to America is a privilege and not a right, we still should seek to create a climate welcoming to those immigrants we do admit. In other words, although we have the right, and the duty, to regulate immigration to the benefit of the American people, it is desirable as a policy matter that the climate we create for immigrants is as welcoming as possible. How may we accomplish this?

The United States admits between 700,000 and 900,000 legal immigrants per year, plus millions of long-term and short-term visitors (tourists, business travelers, students, workers et al.). What's more, it is much easier for immigrants to become citizens in our country than in virtually any other—last year alone, almost 900,000 people began the year as foreigners and ended it as Americans.

The result is that today there are about 31 million foreign-born people in the United States, more than 60 percent of them noncitizens. This is the largest wave of immigration in the nation's history, surpassing the period at the turn of the last century, and with no end in sight. This high level of immigration has a variety of economic, fiscal, social, demographic and political costs and benefits, which are not appropriate subjects for this briefing. But it is appropriate to ask how this unprecedented flow of newcomers affects the treatment of immigrants and the nature of their welcome.

Unfortunately, there is an inverse relationship between the level of immigration and the hospitality accorded newcomers. In other words, more immigration results in harsher treatment for the immigrants. We have seen this process over the past generation as immigration has steadily increased in tandem with restrictions on immigrants. Political responses to this increasing immigration began in 1994 with the overwhelming passage by Californians of Proposition 187, which sought to deny certain government services to illegal aliens, and continued through 1996, with the passage of laws aimed at terrorism, immigration, and welfare. Although all of these changes were within our power as a people to make and raise no legitimate constitutional concerns, some were unfortunately anti-immigrant, such as the sweeping welfare eligibility bans for legal immigrants or the retroactivity of the expanded definition of deportable offenses. Even the many elements of those laws which were positive were made necessary by high immigration—such as expedited exclusion or the rules making immigrant sponsorship agreements legally enforceable.

This contradiction is not merely a function of ethnic animus or fear of the other, though I have no doubt they play a role. Even in the absence of our darker impulses, mass immigration necessitates more restrictive treatment of immigrants. For instance, the presence of a large and continually increasing number of poor people forces us to set priorities regarding social spending, whereas a small number of immigrants, even if they made relatively heavy use of welfare, would not force such choices. Also, the rapid population growth driven mainly by high immigration fuels the growth in government regulation of all aspects of life, whereas lower population density necessitates less government regulation of society.

More immigration also means more immigrant criminals, whatever the general crime rate among immigrants, and this requires more restrictive rules governing noncitizen criminals, whereas a lower level of immigration would not give rise to the need for such special rules.

Therefore, we cannot have pro-immigrant policy of high immigration, however much many on the left seek it. What we have now is an anti-immigrant policy of high immigration, crafted mainly by the libertarian wing of the Republican Party, and especially by Spencer Abraham, formerly a senator and now secretary of energy.

There are two other policy options. One is an anti-immigrant policy of low immigration. There are people who actually support this, but their number is small and their political impact is infinitesimal. The other option is a pro-immigrant policy of low immigration, one that admits fewer immigrants but extends a warmer welcome to those who are admitted. This is the only way in the real world to cultivate a pro-immigrant policy that would defuse many of the civil rights concerns, valid or not, surrounding our treatment of noncitizens.

Statement at SEIU Immigration Press Conference[4]

Wade Henderson

Executive Director, Leadership Conference on Civil Rights (LCCR), 1996– ; graduate, Howard University and Rutgers University School of Law; counsel to Leadership Conference Education Fund (LCEF), 1969– ; first Joseph L. Rauh Jr. Professor of Public Interest Law, David A. Clarke School of Law, University of the District of Columbia; Washington bureau director, National Association for the Advancement of Colored People (NAACP); associate director, national office of the American Civil Liberties Union; executive director, Council on Legal Education Opportunity (CLEO); assistant dean and director, Minority Student Program, Rutgers University School of Law; author, numerous articles on civil rights and public policy issues; awards from several civil rights organizations.

Editors' introduction: The Service Employees International Union (SEIU) sponsored a press conference urging the U.S. Congress to renew efforts to push a pro-immigrant legislative agenda. Present were some 90 persons, including activists from labor, business, and immigration and civil rights communities. It was moderated by SEIU Executive Vice President Eliseo Medina. The LCCR is the nation's premiere civil and human rights coalition. As executive director of that organization, Mr. Henderson asserted that, "in the wake of September 11, . . . no public policy issue has been affected more than immigration."

Wade Henderson's statement: Good morning. My name is Wade Henderson, executive director of the Leadership Conference on Civil Rights—the nation's oldest, largest and most diverse civil rights coalition.

In the wake of September 11, it is clear that no public policy issue has been affected more than immigration. To the civil rights community, this is unfortunate—as our country has a tragic history of reacting in times of crisis by placing the blame on groups of people that we do not consider to be fully American. And when we look at some of the actions being taken by our attorney general, and at the rhetoric being hurled about in Congress, we are again seeing too

---

4. Delivered on April 11, 2002, at Washington, D.C., in Sheraton Four Points Hotel, 11:30 A.M. Reprinted with permission of Wade Henderson.

much of the same type of patterns that eventually led to shameful incidents like the Palmer raids and Japanese internment.

It is certainly true that our immigration policies that touch on national security may need to be reexamined. But amidst the calls to tighten our borders, I would urge that the very least we can do is ensure that our nation's immigration policies still demonstrate a genuine respect for the rights of immigrants who are already here, and who are doing their best to make positive contributions.

First, we need to leave no doubt that our institutions and our basic notions of due process exist to protect everyone, not just citizens. Even before September 11, and particularly since 1996, our immigration policies have been sending out exactly the wrong message. The message has been that the rights of noncitizens are not all that important—that they can be denied a meaningful day in court, they can be locked away for months or even years with fewer rights than even convicted criminals, and in many cases they cannot even turn to the federal courts for help. The civil rights community believes it is essential that we restore due process to immigration law because history has proven, time and time again, that if the civil rights of one group are undermined, everyone else becomes vulnerable as well.

Second, our immigration policies need to reaffirm one of our greatest traditions—that of rewarding people who are here and who are trying hard to contribute to our economy, our culture, and our communities. While we certainly need to do all we reasonably can to enforce our immigration laws, we should never lose sight of the fact that they are only one of many ways in which we pursue our bottom line: doing what is in the best interests of our country in the long run. When it becomes so overwhelmingly clear that we have particular groups of people in our country who are helping us pursue those best interests, we have little to lose and so much to gain by shaping our policies in a way that encourages them. And by this, I am not only talking about undocumented workers. There are also groups of people whom we once welcomed in a more official sense. For example, while we welcomed thousands of Liberians into our country, with the idea of providing them a temporary safe haven, so many of them have become so much a part of America that it only makes sense—for them, and their American families, but also for us as a whole—that we recognize it and allow them to stay.

I would just close by asking Congress and the Administration to show their commitment to respecting the rights and the contributions of our nation's immigrants. It is even more important now, post-9/11, when our worst fears make doing this more difficult than ever and when we are more tempted than usual to turn our backs on them. Protecting civil rights is never supposed to be easy; it ultimately means standing up for the least popular and most feared groups among us. But in the end, this means that our immigration policies, the way we treat noncitizens in this country now, will be the real yardstick by which we measure our nation's commitment to upholding the civil rights of everyone.

Remarks on the National Security Entry-Exit Registration System[5]

John Ashcroft

U.S. Attorney General, 2001– ; born Chicago, IL, May 9, 1942; raised in Springfield, MO, where he attended public schools; graduated with honors, Yale University, 1964; J.D., University of Chicago, 1967; taught business law, Southwest Missouri State University at Springfield, 1967–72; auditor, Missouri, 1973–75; assistant attorney general, Missouri, 1975–77; attorney general, Missouri, 1977–84; governor, Missouri, 1985–92; chair, Education Commission of the States, 1987–88; chair, National Governors Association, 1991–92; attorney, Suelthaus and Kaplan P.C., 1993– 94; United States Senate (R), 1995–2001; U.S. Senate Judiciary Committee; chair, U.S. Senate Constitution Subcommittee; co-authored with wife Janet It's the Law *(1979) and* College Law for Business, *7th–11th editions; authored* Lessons from a Father to His Son *(1998).*

Editors' introduction: The September 11 attacks prompted national debate about what changes should be made to policies governing immigration. Concerned that current regulations and enforcement do not adequately track persons into and out of the United States, particularly individuals who pose potential national security risks, the Department of Justice proposed changes to the Entry-Exit Registration System mandated by Congress. In supporting the changes, Attorney General John Ashcroft told some 95 reporters, representatives of special interest groups, and Justice Department staff that, under the new rules, when authorities "encounter an alien of national security concern," that person can be arrested, a policy which the American Immigration Lawyers Association objected would "subject individuals . . . to a lengthy and complicated procedure that will not make us safer."

John Ashcroft's speech: I want to thank Commissioner Jim Ziglar for his assistance and for being with me today.

On September 11, the American definition of national security was changed forever. A band of men entered our country under false pretenses in order to plan and execute a murderous act of war. Some entered the country several years in advance; others

---

5. Delivered on June 6, 2002, at the U.S. Department of Justice headquarters, Washington, D.C.

entered several months in advance. Once inside the United States, they were easily able to avoid contact with immigration authorities and violate the terms of their visas with impunity.

In this new war, our enemy's platoons infiltrate our borders, quietly blending in with visiting tourists, students, and workers. They move unnoticed through our cities, neighborhoods, and public spaces. They wear no uniforms. Their camouflage is not forest green, but rather it is the color of common street clothing. Their tactics rely on evading recognition at the border and escaping detection within the United States. Their terrorist mission is to defeat America, destroy our values and kill innocent people.

The vulnerabilities of our immigration system became starkly clear on September 11. About a quarter-century ago, the United States stopped asking international visitors to register periodically with immigration authorities, and stopped keeping track of our visitors' activities and whereabouts. This is in contrast to the practice of European nations, most of which have rigorous registration systems. Consequently, we have been unable to determine if foreign visitors follow their stated plans while guests in our country or even if they overstay the legal limit of their visas.

The vulnerabilities of our immigration system became starkly clear on September 11.

Accordingly, today I am announcing the National Security Entry-Exit Registration System. This system will expand substantially America's scrutiny of those foreign visitors who may pose a national security concern and enter our country. And it will provide a vital line of defense in the war against terrorism.

The responsibility to establish the National Security Entry-Exit Registration System is already contained in U.S. law. Some of the provisions date to the 1950s; others were added by Congress in the 1990s. Congress has mandated that, by 2005, the Department of Justice build an entry-exit system that tracks virtually all of the 35 million foreign visitors who come to the United States annually. This entry-exit registration system is the crucial first phase in that endeavor and will track approximately 100,000 visitors in the first year.

There are three components to this initiative: first—fingerprinting and photographing at the border; second—periodic registration of aliens who stay in the United States thirty days or more; and third—exit controls that will help the Immigration and Naturalization Service to remove those aliens who overstay their visas.

We will evaluate individual visitors for the risk of involvement in terrorist activity and impose these requirements on visitors who fall into categories of elevated national security concern. The Immigration and Naturalization Service and the State Department will work together to identify these individuals at or prior to entry. The criteria that are used to identify such visitors will be continually updated to reflect our evolving intelligence on terrorist threats.

The first component of the system is fingerprinting and photographing at the border. It is critically important that we stop known or suspected terrorists from entering the country. Fingerprints are essential to that enterprise. Terrorists and wanted criminals often attempt to enter the country using assumed names and false passports. But fingerprints do not lie.

With new technologies, we are able to perform a quick fingerprint check at the border that takes only three minutes to complete. We have already deployed systems at a limited number of ports of entry that can scan a person's fingerprints and compare the prints to vast databases of known criminals and terrorists. The early results of this pilot program are extremely promising: we are receiving an average of 67 hits per week, and 1,400 wanted criminals have been arrested in the past five months as they have attempted to enter the country.

Under the National Security Entry-Exit Registration System, we will run the fingerprints of entering aliens against a database of thousands of known terrorists. The operations of the U.S. military in Afghanistan have allowed us to expand that database considerably.

By running the fingerprints of entering aliens against these prints, we will be able to stop terrorists from entering the country. In addition, we will run the fingerprints of incoming visitors against a database of wanted criminals. And finally, we will be able to stop terrorists from entering the United States a second time under a different name using forged documents.

Terrorists and wanted criminals often attempt to enter the country using assumed names and false passports. But fingerprints do not lie.

We have the technological capacity to do this, and now we have a sizable database of fingerprints of known terrorists. We need to deploy this technology as soon as possible to protect American lives.

The second component of the system is periodic registration. This will only apply to those individuals of elevated national security concern who stay in the country for more than 30 days. They will have to register at an INS office and simply verify that they are doing what they said they came to America to do and living where they said they would live. Such registration will be required at the 30-day point, and every 12 months after the date of entry. Aliens already in the United States who fall into categories of elevated national security concern will be asked to come in and register as well.

Our European allies have been using such registration systems for decades. For example, long-term visitors to France must register within 7 days of arrival, every 12 months thereafter, and whenever they change their address. This is a well-established way of making sure that visitors do not try to disappear into society, and that they stick to their stated plans while in the country.

The third component of the National Security Entry-Exit Registration System is establishing a system of exit controls, so that we know who leaves on time and who does not. This is a critical part of the system. Which brings me to a critical aspect of the system: arresting those individuals who attempt to evade the registration requirements or who attempt to stay in the country beyond their permitted time.

When aliens violate these rules, we will place their photographs, fingerprints, and information in the National Crime Information Center (or NCIC) system. The nation's 650,000 police officers check this system regularly in the course of traffic stops and routine encounters.

When federal, state and local law enforcement officers encounter an alien of national security concern who has been listed on the NCIC for violating immigration law, federal law permits them to arrest that individual and transfer him to the custody of the INS.

The Justice Department's Office of Legal Counsel has concluded that this narrow, limited mission that we are asking state and local police to undertake voluntarily—arresting aliens who have violated criminal provisions of Immigration and Nationality Act or civil provisions that render an alien deportable, and who are listed on the NCIC—is within the inherent authority of the states. The Department of Justice has no plans to seek additional support from state and local law enforcement in enforcing our nation's immigration laws, beyond our narrow antiterrorism mission.

We are an open country that welcomes the people of the world to visit our blessed land. We will continue to greet our international neighbors with good will. Asking some visitors to verify their activities while they are here is fully consistent with that outlook. To meet our responsibility to protect American lives in the future, we take the steps that I have outlined today.

Thank you.

IV. Labor and the Economy

State of the Workforce[1]

Elaine L. Chao

U.S. Secretary of Labor, 2001– ; born China; graduated Dartmouth College, 1974; B.A., Mt. Holyoke College, 1975; M.B.A., Harvard University, 1979; studied at Massachusetts Institute Technology, 1979; White House Fellow, 1983–84; department administrator, Maritime Administration, 1986–88; chair, Federal Maritime Commission, 1988–89; deputy secretary, U.S. Department of Transportation, 1989–91; director, Peace Corps, 1991–92; associate, Gulf Oil Corporation, 1978; senior lending officer, Citibank, 1979–83; vice president, Syndications, BankAmerica Capital Markets Group, 1984–86; president and CEO, United Way of America, 1992–96; first Asian-American woman appointed to a president's cabinet; recipient of 15 honorary doctoral degrees, including Villanova University, 1989, Sacred Heart University, 1991, and Niagara University, 1992; distinguished scholar, Heritage Foundation; Outstanding Young Achiever, National Council of Women, 1986; one of ten Outstanding Young Women of America, 1987; Outstanding Alumni Award, Harvard Business School, 1993.

Editors' introduction: Secretary of Labor Elaine L. Chao addressed the Council for Excellence in Government, a nonpartisan, nonprofit organization founded in 1983 that works to improve government performance at all levels. To achieve their goals, the Council—whose members have leadership experience in government and the private sector—acts as a convener, catalyst, and communicator. Secretary Chao told the Council that the task of the U.S. Department of Labor "is to anticipate change and prepare the workforce to meet it."

Elaine Chao's speech: Thank you for inviting me here today.

On this Labor Day weekend, we pay tribute to the generations of men and women who built this great land—and have given us the highest standard of living and the greatest production the world has ever known.

The first Labor Day celebration was in 1882 in New York City. History suggests that it was a member of the Brotherhood of Carpenters and Joiners who started this tradition, a man named Peter J. McGuire—the first to propose a day to honor "those who from rude nature have delved and carved all the grandeur we behold."

---

1. Delivered on August 30, 2001, at Washington, D.C.

I have often turned to the Carpenters and Joiners' current president, Doug McCarron, for advice. We have a good working relationship. And I am pleased to have Chris Heinz representing the union today. Thank you, Chris, for being here.

Ladies and gentlemen, in 2001, the state of the workforce is strong, skilled, and safe.

But we still have work to do.

At the Council for Excellence in Government, you call the changing times "the next American Revolution." You call it E-Government. It is a work*force* in transition: work*places* transformed overnight from physical plants and offices to mobile packages of 21st century technology and work *trends* that tell us old notions of the workforce cannot meet the needs and expectations of a new generation of workers.

Today, America's working people are embracing changes no one could have imagined even a decade ago. They're rewriting the rules. They are challenging the status quo and daring government to match its pace to theirs.

> *The American workforce is stronger, safer, and more skilled than any generation before it.*

The result? A workforce that isn't just responding to "the next American Revolution"—but leading it. The American workforce is stronger, safer, and more skilled than any generation before it.

But challenges remain. There are tremors on the economic landscape. Manufacturing is struggling. Dot-coms are scaling back. The sluggish economy needs a jumpstart.

President George W. Bush is responding. He's cut taxes, reduced the debt, and expanded markets for American products. He's moved landmark education reforms through the House and Senate, forged a compromise on the Patient's Bill of Rights, and given America the serious energy policy that it needs.

President George W. Bush is improving the lives of America's working families. While others are sitting on the sidelines pointing fingers, President Bush is pointing the way.

And the Department of Labor is responding as well. Our job is to anticipate change and prepare the workforce to meet it. We need to make sure that the policies, programs, and regulations we create support the American workforce. And we need to make sure that they reflect the realities that American workers confront every day when they walk into their stores, offices, and factories.

One of the first things I did after coming to the Department of Labor was call for a Summit on the 21st Century Workforce. Union leaders, business leaders, nonprofit executives, and academics from all across America came to Washington with a single purpose: to focus America's attention on the challenges of the 21st-century workforce. President George W. Bush was there—and so was the chairman of the Federal Reserve, Alan Greenspan.

Let me tell you what we discovered.

First, yesterday's skills will not fuel tomorrow's economy

Today unemployment has a new meaning. Years ago, unemployment meant no jobs. Today, in many cases, unemployment means a disconnect between the new jobs our economy is producing and the current skill levels of Americans in the workforce. The skills gap is too wide for too many Americans.

Many Americans want to work; yet many of the jobs created by the economy go begging because employers cannot find qualified workers. Job training and education are more important than ever—especially for workers in manufacturing jobs and those just starting out.

Just take a look at the earnings gap between college and high-school graduates in this country—in 1979, college graduates made 38 percent more than high school grads. Today, in 2001, college graduates earn 70 percent more.

The unemployment rate for a high school dropout is nearly four times the rate for a college graduate.

In some cases, America's schools have come up short. And in these cases, our young people are the casualties, victims of a system unable to prepare them to reach for the American dream.

President George W. Bush is changing that with efforts like the President's New Freedom Initiative—a program to provide assistive technologies to Americans with disabilities to better enable them to integrate into the workforce and community life. Nearly 2,500 companies are already working to provide assistive technologies to these talented, yet untapped, workers.

Another example is the Department of Labor's Job Corps Kids program—where kids leave the program not just with a trade, but with a high school education as well.

All of this translates into a new pledge to the American workforce. A promise on the part of a new administration and the Department of Labor to leave no child, no worker, no contributing member of our society behind.

Second, America is facing an incredible shrinking workforce

No one needs to tell us that our workforce is growing smaller. Or that the number of retired Americans is increasing.

I call it the incredible shrinking workforce. Another name for it could be a 21st-century labor shortage. The number of people in the labor force ages 25–34 is projected to decline by 2.7 million in the next seven years.

The American workforce needs to keep up, to move faster, to introduce new populations, nontraditional employees into the workforce, and to meet this challenge head-on.

When the nature of work changes, so does the nature of retirement. The American Association of Retired Persons used to have a magazine they called *Modern Maturity*. Now, the same magazine is called *My Generation*.

The largest, most demographically influential generation in America's history will soon be exiting the workforce—with time on their side. They will have years that pensions and retirement plans must fund and years that experts on Social Security predict may test our system in unforgiving ways. Government needs to keep up, to move faster, to build solutions—more generous and secure pensions, more investment options—into the system now.

In the next seven years, the number of people in the labor force ages 45–64 will grow faster than any other age group. And young people are more fluid, less tied down to one job and one career.

Today, the average 32-year-old has already changed jobs nine times. Gone from broke to flush, from worker to manager, from dreamer to company president and back again—in less time that many of us spent on our first apprenticeship.

What we need now is new solutions. We need ways to use technology to guarantee that everyone who wants to work, can work—older workers, workers with disabilities, single moms.

We also need to address help for those who are working harder and longer. Today, only 24 percent of American children have a working father and a stay-at-home mother. We need to help people balance the demands of work and home.

And we can help immigrants. They are the dreamers who came to America—the land of opportunity for a new start and a brighter future. America is welcoming more immigrants into the economy than ever before. Just a few miles outside of Washington, a local Wal-Mart employs workers from over 45 different countries, speaking 100 different languages.

There may just be a sliver of hope in the labor shortage: necessity is going to require us to draw from the pool of untapped workers—those traditionally left out of the workforce. And that is good for the workforce and it is good for America.

Third, workers are safer and healthier

The American workplace has never been safer than it is today. Statistics released less than two weeks ago tell us work fatalities have decreased even while overall employment has grown.

For the first time since the fatality census was initially conducted in 1992, the number of job-related highway deaths—the most frequent accidents—are down and declining. This is evidence that government and industry can work hand-in-hand to create the safest workplaces in the world.

Compliance education is working and can be more effective over time. It is a proactive program that keeps accidents from happening in the first place instead of slapping wrists after the fact. But you can be sure that the Department of Labor will punish those who try to disregard worker health and safety.

But the Department is not resting on these accomplishments. We can do better. For example, workplace fatalities among Hispanic workers are going up. More English language training, more education, more partnerships, and more

> *We can help all workers enjoy a safe and secure retirement.*

outreach to community and faith-based groups are needed. I have asked OSHA to form a task force to reach out and educate Hispanic workers and their families about health and safety.

And we can help all workers enjoy a safe and secure retirement.

At the close of the 20th century, a typical worker received more than 25 percent of their compensation in the form of benefits.

In the past, workers depended on well-defined contribution plans when they retired. Today, workers expect and receive individualized, portable 401(k) plans. And this is just the beginning.

American workers must be given the opportunity to "trade up" on old expectations. That is, to reach beyond the old promise of "a secure retirement" toward new possibilities such as options that include safe, personal retirement accounts in Social Security.

As recently as 1960, there were five workers for every Social Security beneficiary. In 50 years, experts predict that only two workers will pay for every beneficiary. We need new ways of thinking about Social Security. And President Bush has a positive solution.

At the Department of Labor, we are taking a leading role in "the next American Revolution."

One way is through information. As we all know, information is power. And the Department is providing tools for American workers.

We've created a Department of Labor National Call Center to help employees and employers get accurate information without delays.

We've redesigned the DOL Web site, *www.dol.gov,* providing visitors with the best access to DOL's information and services.

We've developed a compliance E-Mail Initiative on our Web page that guarantees a rapid response to every e-mail inquiry from every DOL customer.

And we've initiated E-Laws Advisor—an interactive Web-based compliance initiative.

The Department of Labor is changing with the times.

Labor Day 2001. The state of the workforce is strong, skilled, and safe. Challenges abound. We will meet these challenges if we work together—as one nation, with one focus: to improve the lives of America's working families.

Thank you and may God bless our work.

America's Economy: Rising to Our New Challenges[2]

Thomas Daschle

U.S. Senator from South Dakota, 1987– , and Democratic Majority Leader, U.S. Senate, 2001– ; born Aberdeen, SD, December 9, 1947; B.A. in political science, South Dakota State University, 1969; intelligence officer, Vietnam War, U.S. Air Force Strategic Air Command, 1969–72; chief legislative aide to Senator James Abourezk of South Dakota 1973–77; U.S. House of Representatives, 1983–87; Democratic Minority Leader, U.S. Senate, 1995–2001; member, Agricultural, Nutrition, and Forestry Committee, U.S. Senate; co-chair, Senate Democratic Steering and Coordinating Committee; co-chair, Senate Democratic Technology and Communications Committee; chair, Senate Democratic Conference Committee; co-chair, Senate Democratic Policy Committee; National Commander's Award, Disabled American Veterans, 1980; Legislator of Year Award, Vietnam Veterans of America, 1997; Golden Triangle Award, National Farmer's Union, 1997–98.

Editors' introduction: Senate Majority Leader Thomas Daschle addressed the Center for National Policy, which for two decades has conducted public opinion research. The CNP undertakes technical, substantive, and political analysis to frame options and to formulate policy recommendations regarding the economy, equal opportunity, community studies, and foreign relations. In his speech Senator Daschle, the highest-ranking elected Democrat and a potential presidential candidate in 2004, charged that "Republicans chose exactly the wrong solution" for a sluggish economy—"a huge tax cut." In doing so, Senator Daschle continued, Republicans "discarded the framework of fiscal responsibility." He concluded that "we can restore fiscal integrity, keep America on the cutting edge of technology and help Americans seize the extraordinary opportunities this new global information economy affords."

Thomas Daschle's speech: Thank you, Bob, for those overly generous words. And thank you all for inviting me to join you today. It's quite an honor.

---

2. Delivered on January 4, 2002, at Washington, D.C.

It's also quite an honor to be introduced by Bob Rubin. Bob is a dear friend and someone whose judgment and economic advice I rely upon very heavily. I expect history will record him as one of America's most distinguished secretaries of the Treasury, of the same caliber of another great New Yorker, Alexander Hamilton.

You may remember a cover story in *Time* magazine during the 1997 Asian economic crisis. The story was about how U.S. economic leadership helped prevent that regional crisis from touching off a worldwide recession. The cover showed a picture of Bob Rubin, Alan Greenspan and Larry Summers. The headline called them the Committee to Save the World.

That may be a slight exaggeration, to say that Bob Rubin has saved the world, but it is certainly no exaggeration that he's saved me many times with his wise and patient counsel, and I'm very grateful to him for being here today.

Now, if I could just get him to advise me on my stock portfolio, I'd be in great shape.

(Laughter)

I also want to thank my good friend Leon Panetta. How can anyone go through as many tough budget battles as Leon has and still keep that wonderful laugh, is one of the great mysteries of Washington. He's a role model for all of us. He was a great chairman of the House Budget Committee, a distinguished OMB director and White House chief of staff, and he's doing an outstanding job as chair of the CNP.

And I want to acknowledge, speaking of directors, Mo Steinbrenner's incredible leadership at CNP. Under her direction, the Center for National Policy has become a real force for thoughtful discussion on America's economic and foreign policy. We're all indebted to her for that as well, and I thank her so much for the opportunity to be here today.

As we begin this new year, our nation is engaged in two great battles. One is literally about life and death; and that is our battle against global terrorism.

Our other battle will determine a great deal about how we live, and what kind of future we leave to our children. That's the battle to deal with the economic challenges facing our nation—both short-term and long-term.

In the first battle, the battle against terrorism, President Bush and his national security team are doing a superb job. They've united our nation, and virtually the entire world, in defense of freedom and civilization. They deserve our support, and our praise.

Our men and women in uniform have been nothing short of heroic. They took on an assignment that some said was un-winnable, and they're winning. Not only are they bringing justice to the killers, they're helping to bring the people of Afghanistan their first real chance for peace in nearly a quarter-century. They are making our world safer, and making us all very proud. Next week, I'm going to be visiting some of our troops stationed in Central Asia, and I'm looking forward to it.

When it comes to our second battle, our economic battle, I think most Americans would probably agree that the news hasn't been so good lately. But there's no reason we can't win both of our battles. Americans are the most productive, most innovative workers in the world. We have the most advanced technologies. We are the people who pioneer new ideas and break new ground.

If we can root out a network of terrorists half a world away, we can solve the problems in our own economy. After all, unlike the war on terrorism, the economic battle is a battle we have fought many times before, and won.

The way we've won it has always been the same: by keeping our fiscal house in order, and by relying on comprehensive plans to keep our economy growing.

Today, I would like to make a case for a return to fiscal responsibility, and a comprehensive, new plan for economic growth.

If we can root out a network of terrorists half a world away, we can solve the problems in our own economy too.

We don't have to look back too far to see a template. A decade ago, our economy was shrinking, as we struggled to emerge from a recession. We were running record annual budget deficits, with no end in sight. From 1980 to 1992, our national debt had quadrupled.

Some people feared we'd never get out of that fiscal hole. But we did. And we did it the old-fashioned way. In 1993, we made a decision: No more living beyond our means. No more borrow-and-spend and piling up mountains of debts to leave to our children and grandchildren. From that point on, we decided, everything we did had to fit into a new framework of fiscal discipline.

Fiscal discipline lowered our long-term interest rates and increased business confidence . . . which helped spark new investment . . . which produced strong economic growth . . . which lowered the deficits even more . . . which reduced long-term interest rates even further . . . which created more jobs and stronger economic growth.

By embracing fiscal discipline, investing in people and technology, and opening up new markets abroad, we helped lay a foundation for a new growth economy. Over the next eight years, we achieved broad-based economic growth. Businesses boomed and people benefitted. Corporate profits rose, and so did family incomes—and not just at the top. We created more millionaires and billionaires in the '90s than at any time in our nation's history, while creating a boom that raised family incomes across the board.

More companies were started—more people went to college—and more Americans owned their own homes in the last decade than ever before in our nation's history. At this time last year, unemployment, inflation and long-term interest rates were all lower than they'd been in a generation. We'd disproved the old idea that you can't have low unemployment and low inflation at the same time.

While we were laying the foundation for a prosperous future, we were also paying off the mistakes of the past.

In 1993, our economy was saddled with a record $290 billion deficit, and that deficit was projected to grow substantially for years. By 2000, not only was the deficit gone, we had a record $236 billion surplus—and that surplus was expected to increase dramatically for years.

We'd also paid down more than $400 billion of the trillions of dollars in debt the federal government had run up during the 1980s and early '90s, and were on a path to pay off the full debt. For the first time in years, the challenge of the Baby Boomers retirement, while still formidable, no longer seemed insurmountable.

For the first time in a generation, both our short-term, and our long-term, economic positions appeared strong.

Then, the inevitable happened: our economy started to cool. By last March, we now know, the expansion was officially over and a recession had begun. Every economic boom eventually slows down. When that happens, the question is not who is to blame, but what do we do to get the economy growing again? How we answer that question is critical, because it will determine—to a large extent—how deep the recession will be, how long it will last, and how strong the recovery will be.

Unfortunately, last spring, Republicans chose exactly the wrong solution. They made a huge tax cut their number one priority—ahead of everything else—and discarded the framework of fiscal responsibility. They said their tax cut cost 1.3 trillion dollars. It is actually $1.7 trillion when you include interest costs. And many experts believe the true costs are even more dramatic. The IMF, for instance, estimates the cost of the tax cut at $2.5 trillion—nearly a trillion dollars more than advertised.

Supporters of the tax cut said the surplus was so massive and so certain that we could have a huge tax cut, increase spending on education and the military, and provide prescription drug coverage. We could protect the Social Security surplus, pay off the entire federal debt in a decade, and still have enough money left over to get us through any unforeseen disasters.

What we got instead was the most dramatic fiscal deterioration in our nation's history.

Instead of the record surpluses we expected, the President's own budget director now says the federal government will run deficits until at least 2004. Instead of continuing to pay down the debt, the president's treasury secretary sent Congress a letter just after Thanksgiving asking us to approve raising the nation's debt limit.

There are those who say the reason the surplus deteriorated so quickly is the attacks on America and the war against terrorism. Clearly, September 11 was a major blow to our economy. And, to some industries, it's been devastating, especially travel and tourism, which is hugely important to my home state. But September 11th and the war aren't the only reasons the surplus is nearly gone. They're not even the biggest reasons. The biggest reason is the tax cut.

In May, the Congressional Budget Office reported a 10-year budget surplus of $5.6 trillion. By the end of the year, $3.7 trillion was gone. Nearly half of that was a direct result of the tax cut. The tax cut was by far the largest factor.

> *The rapidly disappearing surplus is a key reason long-term interest rates have barely budged.*

The rapidly disappearing surplus is a key reason long-term interest rates have barely budged. This, despite the fact that the Federal Reserve cut the short-term, federal funds rate a record 11 times last year. All together, the Federal Funds Rate dropped nearly 5 percentage points last year. Yet the 10-year Treasury rate ended the year almost exactly where it began.

Investors understand that the dwindling surplus means the federal government may have to borrow money soon or, at the very least, won't be paying down nearly as much of the debt as had been expected. That is keeping long-term interest rates higher than they would have been. And the continued high interest rates and the adverse impact on investor confidence, in turn, leads to less investment, less consumption, more job losses and bigger deficits. That's the hidden tax of the current fiscal policies.

So, not only did the tax cut fail to prevent a recession, as its supporters said it would, it probably made the recession worse. It also put us in an unnecessary fiscal bind at the worst possible time. At a time when we need to fight both a war and a recession—when our nation has urgent needs on all fronts—the tax cut has taken away our flexibility and left us with only two choices—both of them bad. We can shortchange critical needs, such as homeland defense, or we can raid the Social Security surplus—and even run deficits—to pay for these critical needs.

We should not be in this position. A year ago, we had the resources and the flexibility to make virtually any urgent investments we needed. We don't have that flexibility, or those resources today, because Republicans chose ideology over experience. Experience showed that fiscal responsibility works. Ideology dictated tax cuts no matter what the circumstances.

I know a lot of good, fiscally conservative Republicans. South Dakota is a majority-Republican state, and the people in my state are about as hard-working and fiscally conservative as you get. But the Republican agenda in Washington today is being written by a wing of the Republican Party that isn't interested in fiscal discipline. They have one unchanging, unyielding solution that they offer for every problem: tax cuts that go disproportionately to the most affluent.

Democrats see things differently. We support tax cuts that work. But we want to make sure that any tax cuts we pass don't threaten the Social Security or Medicare reserves, crowd out other critical investments, or drive us deeper into debt.

President Bush deserves great praise for the way he is leading our armed forces. He's shown real leadership by setting aside partisan criticism of America's necessary involvement in multilateral military action and "nation building." And he's demonstrated statesmanship by re-engaging in the difficult work of the Middle East peace process, where American engagement is essential.

President Bush is absolutely right to use every tool at our disposal to fight the war on terrorism: diplomatic, military, financial, and humanitarian.

But we also have to use every tool at our disposal, including the right kind of tax cuts, in our battle to strengthen our economy.

America's greatest strength is our resolve and our unity in times of challenge. The world saw that again on September 11 and in the months that followed. If we can come through a tragedy as terrible as that, I have no doubt we can solve the economic challenges facing us, too.

We can restore fiscal integrity, keep America on the cutting edge of technology, and help Americans seize the extraordinary opportunities this new global, information economy affords. We can go back to paying off our debt rather than risk running up the deficit.

The first step is to get our economy back on track by passing a real economic stimulus plan.

In putting together a plan, we talked to business leaders in high tech, manufacturing, finance and other key industries. We consulted with Bob Rubin and Alan Greenspan, two of the chief architects of the economic success of the 1990s. On the basis of those discussions, we proposed a plan designed to increase consumer demand, and spur business investment.

Nearly 2 million Americans lost their jobs last year. New figures out this morning show the unemployment rate in December rose to 5.8 percent—the highest in six years.

We included unemployment and health care benefits for laid-off workers in our plan because, as any objective economist will tell you, it's one of the most effective ways to boost demand and pump money into the economy quickly. It's also the right thing to do.

To spur business investment and job creation, we proposed allowing businesses to write off a larger share of their investments immediately.

Our Republican friends like to describe the economic stimulus debate as a choice between Republican tax cuts and Democratic spending. The fact is, both of our economic stimulus proposals are more than 75 percent tax cuts.

The real difference is our tax cuts will keep people at work and keep the economy growing by stimulating economic activity right now. Their tax cuts have very little to do with sparking an economic recovery.

Sixty percent of their stimulus plan's five-year cost occurs after 2002. It occurs after the administration and most economists believe the recovery will be well on its way. They also want to eliminate the corporate alternative minimum tax. Even if you think that's good economic policy—and I don't—it's not a stimulus.

Let me be clear about what I think needs to be done to stimulate the economy right now: We should move quickly to pass a bill that boosts demand, encourages investments and creates jobs. It should consist entirely of one-year measures that promote economic activity now—when our economy needs it. And it should include nothing that will run up long-term deficits or drive up long-term interest rates. This adheres to the bipartisan principles established last fall.

Today, I am proposing two new ideas to try to get the economic stimulus debate back on track. First, we should pass a new Jobs Creation Tax Credit. This tax cut would be available to every business in America. It says, simply, that if you increase your payroll—if you hire new people, restore hours that have been cut, or give your workers a raise—you'll be reimbursed for all of the extra payroll taxes.

In addition, we know that many companies are deferring investments right now. Providing a robust depreciation bonus gives companies an incentive to make investments now, when the economy needs a boost. So today, I'm also proposing that we allow 40 percent bonus depreciation for the first six months and 20 percent for the next six months.

If you want to know whether this will work, just take a look at what's happened with car sales these last three months. When consumers were told that they'd be able to purchase a car with a zero percent interest rate, they shelved their financial uncertainty and purchased cars in record numbers. We want businesses to do the same thing when it comes to purchasing new equipment and technology.

I hope President Bush and our Republican colleagues will work with us in the spirit of compromise to pass an economic stimulus plan early this year, and put America back to work.

Second, in addition to the predictable costs like Social Security, we now have the new and urgent costs of homeland security.

If people don't feel safe about getting on an airplane, going about their business, and living their lives, our efforts to stimulate the economy won't work. We made a start last year with new airline security measures—emergency assistance to help rebuild New York and the Pentagon—and more funds for antibiotics and vaccines for anthrax and other kinds of bioterrorism. But that's only a small fraction of what we need to do if we're going to better protect against terrorist attacks and the economic damage they cause.

Consider just a few facts:

- Right now, out of every 100 cargo containers that enter U.S. ports each day, two are inspected.

- Canadian intelligence sources estimate that 50 terrorist groups—including al Qaeda and Hamas—operate within their borders. Yet we have only 300 agents working the 100 ports of entry along the 3,000-mile U.S.-Canadian border.

- Russia cannot account for some of its highly enriched uranium, and there have been 14 confirmed cases of trafficking in FISSILE material in that country.

- Our public health system is dangerously under-prepared for the possibility of future biological attacks, like the anthrax attack on my office. Eighty percent of our cities and counties have no bioterror response plan. Some of our nation's best scientists are working in obsolete labs. A couple of years ago, a movie crew that was working on a film called *Outbreak* asked to shoot some scenes at the CDC labs. But the labs were so decrepit, the crew decided no one would believe that America's best public health scientists actually worked there. So they built a set instead.

In addition, we've done practically nothing since September 11 to improve cyber security, rail security or security at America's nuclear and chemical plants. These gaps in our homeland security are unacceptable.

We ought to be pursuing homeland security with as much vigor as we are pursuing the war in Afghanistan.

Take, for example, the way we help protect Russia's nuclear material and know-how. If we're serious about homeland security, we shouldn't be cutting programs that safeguard weapons of mass destruction and that support the experts who know how to make them—we should be expanding them.

The highly successful Nunn-Lugar program should be extended to India and Pakistan. And it should be broadened to keep Russia's biological and chemical weapons material—and know-how—from falling into the wrong hands.

Next week, I plan to visit what is known as the world's largest anthrax burial ground—a site in Uzbekistan where Soviet scientists devised, tested, and then abandoned some of the deadliest biological and chemical weapons imaginable. We are rightly helping the Uzbeks decontaminate that site. But we can and should be doing more to ensure that Russian scientists, and their skills, are not misused.

Democrats worked hard last year to include $15 billion in emergency homeland security investments as part of an economic stimulus measure. When that effort was blocked by the other party, we tried to include the homeland security in the defense appropriations bill. Again, we were prevented from doing so. It has since been reported that Governor Ridge will request $15 billion in homeland security funding at some point this year.

While we welcome this news, we're puzzled by the timing. If Republicans had supported our proposal last month instead of blocking it, that money would already be available. As it stands, the money won't be available now for several months.

Homeland security itself will provide economic stimulus because it will increase confidence and spur spending.

Homeland security itself will provide economic stimulus because it will increase confidence and spur spending. The federal government can't ignore the need for homeland security, and we can't push it off on the states. They're already looking at a combined budget shortfall of at least $40 billion this year.

Today, we ask our Republican friends to work with us to protect Americans from terrorism. The firefighters and police officers and the other heroes are doing their jobs. Let's work together to do ours.

Passing a real economic stimulus plan and strengthening our homeland security are two things we must do now to get our economy back on track, but we can't stop there. We don't just need an economic stimulus plan. We need a comprehensive plan for economic growth.

As part of any plan for economic growth, the third and most important thing we should do is restore long-term fiscal integrity to our budget, so we can bring long-term interest rates down. When interest rates fall by two points, the average family with a $100,000 mortgage saves $2,000 a year. In a real sense, low interest rates are the best possible tax cut. They help families afford college, buy cars, purchase homes and pay off credit card debt.

Monetary policy alone can't bring down long-term interest rates if our long-term budget outlook remains so precarious. We know that. The federal government needs to show the markets that it has not abandoned fiscal discipline, but is still committed to it.

That is why I am asking the President today to submit to Congress not simply a one-year budget proposal, but a long-term plan to restore economic growth. We need a plan to return to fiscal discipline—protect the Social Security and Medicare surpluses in the long-term—and make essential investments in critical areas, including defense, homeland security, and education. It needs to be a real plan—not one that relies on rosy scenarios or accounting gimmicks.

Fourth, we should invest in education, training, and technology to promote job creation and economic growth. One of the keys to our economic success in the 1990s was a productivity revolution driven by information technology. In the last couple of years, the technology sector has gone through a shakeout. Now, it's poised to grow again. It's essential that the federal government continue to be a good partner, so that American tech companies can continue to lead the world.

Again, targeted tax cuts are part of the solution—but only part.

Right now, we're importing hundreds of thousands of workers because our system cannot provide companies with the educated workers they need. Close that gap and everyone benefits: Companies get the skilled workers they need . . . workers get better jobs at better wages . . . and our economy becomes more innovative and productive. Closing that gap will require us to improve our entire system of education and training, so that kids come to school ready to learn and leave college and trade school ready to work.

Before Congress adjourned, we sent the President a new, bipartisan bill to strengthen America's public schools. The "No Child Left Behind Act" continues our bipartisan efforts to increase investment in educational quality. Now we need to build on it.

Schools are getting better. More people are going to college because of steps we took in the '90s to make college more affordable. But there is still a big gap between the skills of Americans who want to work and the skills that many jobs require.

In 1998, we worked together to craft a new training system to better respond to labor market needs. We now need to help that system meet the challenge of rising unemployment by renewing our commitment to training and lifelong learning.

We should also reauthorize our bipartisan welfare reform laws this year to ensure that people who have made the transition from welfare to work can remain in the workforce and not slide back into dependency.

In addition, we should act to make the research and development tax credit permanent—the sooner, the better. Democrats included a permanent R&D tax credit in the tax cut plan we offered last year, but Republicans rejected it. Obviously, this is an expensive proposal. But the R&D tax credit is one of the most effective mechanisms to encourage innovation, increase business investment and keep the economy growing. We should work together to make it permanent.

High-speed, broadband Internet access has become an indispensable tool for businesses, schools, libraries, and hospitals. And access to this service is fast becoming the line between the haves and have-nots in the information age. We should create tax credits, grants, and loans to make broadband service as universal tomorrow as telephone access is today.

Over the past century, federal investments in research have helped split the atom, sequence the genome, invent the microchip, the laser, and the Internet . . . and helped create millions of jobs.

In this century, nanotechnology, robotics, advanced energy technologies like fuel cells and solid state lighting, and biotechnologies like gene therapy, have the potential to do the same. We should double civilian R&D funding, including funding for the National Science Foundation. And we should fully fund the Advanced Technology Program—to speed these innovations to market.

It's critical that the Congress provide funding for a balanced research portfolio. Increasing the NIH budget is important, but it should not be the sole objective of U.S. science and technology policy. Expanded investments in areas such as physics, computer science, mathematics, and electrical engineering, are essential to maintaining America's economic and technological leadership in the 21st century.

Fifth, we must open new markets and help workers who are hurt by trade. No country is better situated to thrive in this global information economy than the United States of America. That is why I support fast track and intend to bring it up for a vote in the full Senate early this year. In the Finance Committee, we passed a bill that addresses critical labor and environmental issues.

Our society as a whole benefits from greater trade and globalization. But we need to recognize that not everyone benefits. Some workers are displaced. We can't afford to leave those people behind—for their sake, or ours. We need everyone's skills and contributions.

That is why, as part of our consideration of fast track, Senate Democrats are proposing to expand trade adjustment assistance.

We believe that we should expand assistance to all workers who are hurt by global production shifts. That includes people who work for the suppliers and contractors of trade-affected companies. It also includes farmers.

We should help these workers learn the new skills they need to earn a living. We should help them maintain health insurance while they're unemployed. And help protect against wage loss when they become reemployed.

Expanded trade will provide billions and billions of dollars in economic growth for the United States. Certainly, we can dedicate a small fraction of this gain to those Americans who are harmed. It is the right thing to do, and frankly, it will be impossible to build a broad consensus for expanded trade unless we do it right.

Sixth, we need a balanced national energy plan.

We've seen in the last year that energy security is related to economic security and national security. We need an energy plan that truly moves us towards energy independence. Democrats have a plan that reduces our dependence on foreign oil, balances production and conservation, and creates hundreds of thousands of jobs in the process.

The administration has been pushing an energy plan that is based mainly on opening sensitive wilderness areas to oil drilling. Just as tax cuts are not a panacea for the economy, oil drilling is not the only solution to our dependence on foreign oil.

Our plan includes production—like an incentive to build a natural gas pipeline to bring 35 trillion cubic feet of natural gas from Alaska to the lower 48 states. But production alone isn't the answer. Our plan includes provisions to improve the supply and distribution of traditional energy resources like oil and gas, improve the efficiency of America's electrical transmission system, and invest in clean coal technologies.

We're committed to developing new energy technologies that will increase energy independence, and help us tap the estimated $1 trillion market for energy conservation and alternative energy development.

Seventh, and finally, we need to get serious about retirement security.

Expanded trade will provide billions and billions of dollars in economic growth for the United States.

Social Security and Medicare may be the most successful government programs in history. Together, they have lifted millions of seniors out of poverty. They reflect our values, by guaranteeing, after a lifetime of work, a retirement with dignity. But now, the very programs that so strengthen our nation, and our economy, are in danger of being undermined themselves.

During the crippling deficits of the '80s, the government was forced to use the Social Security and Medicare surpluses to pay other bills. Fortunately, because the Baby Boomers were a long way from retirement, we had time to recover from that mistake. If we repeat that mistake with the first of the 76 million Baby Boomers just eight years from retirement, we will be creating a fiscal time bomb.

The administration's handpicked Social Security Commission has recommended three options. Two would require drastic cuts in benefits and large infusions of cash from outside the system to keep it solvent. The third would do nothing but allow money to be siphoned away from the system.

I support private accounts to supplement—not replace—Social Security. But to create private accounts with revenues that drain Social Security will only hasten the day when the system becomes insolvent. We don't have to choose between private accounts and a healthy Social Security system. We need both, and we can have both. What we cannot afford is to weaken this vital program at the time when America needs it most.

Democrats and Republicans need to work together to find a better way. And we should all be able to agree on a starting point: we need to restore the fiscal discipline and growth economy that did so much to extend the solvency of the Social Security system in the 1990s.

In the battle to defeat terrorism, President Bush has shown real bipartisan leadership, and we Democrats have embraced him and his efforts. The president came to Congress, told us what he needed and why, and we gave it to him.

We immediately passed a measure authorizing the use of force against al Qaeda and other members of the global terrorist network.

We passed the USA PATRIOT Act, giving the federal government powerful new weapons to prevent terrorism and prosecute terrorists.

We passed an emergency spending bill to help communities devastated on September 11 begin to rebuild, and to give the Pentagon the initial installment it would need to fight the war on terrorism.

We passed an airline security bill.

I believe, in this new year, we can summon that same spirit when it comes to our economy.

By returning to fiscal discipline and putting partisanship aside for the good of our nation, we can craft a plan that leads us back to fiscal integrity and that promotes economic growth and opportunity for all Americans. What this moment calls for is experience, not ideology—cooperation, not conflict. America faces new challenges in the new economy, there is no question about that. But if there is one thing America has learned about itself in the last four months, it is that, united, there is nothing we cannot do. And when it comes to helping one another, there is nothing we will not do.

With that understanding as our guide, and that spirit as our inspiration, I look forward to beginning our work anew.

Thank you all very, very much.

Remarks Before the Economic Club of New York[3]

Harvey L. Pitt

Chair, U.S. Securities and Exchange Commission (SEC), 2001–02; born Brooklyn, NY, February 13, 1945; B.A., City University of New York, 1965; J.D. with honors, St. John's University School of Law, 1968; staff attorney, SEC, 1968; legal assistant to SEC Commissioner Francis M. Wheat, 1969; special counsel, office of the general counsel, SEC, 1970–72; editor, SEC's Institutional Investor Study Report, *1972–73; chief counsel, Division of Market Regulation, SEC, 1972–73; executive assistant to SEC Chairman Ray Garrett, Jr., 1973–75; general counsel, SEC, 1975–78; managing partner, Fried, Frank, Harris, Shriver & Jacobson, Washington, DC, 1978– 89, Co-Chair, full firm, 1997–2001; founding trustee and president, the SEC Historical Society; adjunct professor, George Washington University National Law Center, 1974–82, Georgetown University Law Center, 1976–84, and University of Pennsylvania School of Law, 1983–84; Learned Hand Award, Institute for Human Relations, 1988; honorary doctorate in law, St. John's University School of Law, 2002.*

Editors' introduction: The primary mission of the Securities and Exchange Commission, of which Harvey L. Pitt is chair, is to protect investors and maintain the integrity of the securities markets. With the stock market in steep decline and corporate executives being investigated and indicted for fraud, Chairman Pitt addressed members of the Economic Club of New York. He asserted that "serious jail time is called for by serious financial crime" and outlined action the SEC was taking "to restore faith in our markets."

Harvey L. Pitt's speech: Good evening.

I offer heartfelt thanks to Dick Grasso, and not just for his kind introduction. Long before becoming SEC Chairman, I knew what a special leader Dick was. But, in the aftermath of 9/11, observing him in action from a front row seat, I now fully appreciate Dick's unique strengths and leadership. And this is certainly a time in which our markets demand strong leadership. Dick, thank you.

Since I arrived, the Commission has confronted not one, but four, crises—9/11, the implosion of Enron, the demise of Andersen, and now the concomitant investor crisis of confidence. The problems

---

we've inherited reflect the irrational exuberance of the '90s and the longest sustained bull market in history. Alas, sometimes the main thing bull markets give us is a lot of bull!

WorldCom's announced $4 billion restatement puts a sharper point on all the concerns we have been expressing—that our system has had serious dysfunctional aspects for quite some time. It leads me to offer you a simple message this evening, from the movie *Network*, a message in which I encourage you all to join: "I'm mad as hell, and I'm not going to take it anymore." What happened at WorldCom—and we do not yet know all that happened at World-Com—is an outrage. What we also know we're looking at isn't a mistake, it's a fraud.

The Commission is actively investigating the events related to WorldCom's appalling disclosures. To inform the market, we've ordered the company to file under oath, before the opening of the market this coming Monday morning, a detailed report of all the specifics, including the relevant circumstances that led to the

---

The problems we've inherited reflect the irrational exuberance of the '90s and the longest sustained bull market in history.

---

restatements. We will make that public as soon as we get it. By the way, this is the third time in history that we have invoked this authority, all within the last few months.

I've uttered the old adage that we are doomed to repeat history if we don't learn from it. Or, as my mother used to say, "Fool me once, shame on you. Fool me twice, shame on me." As a result, we also have filed a fraud suit against WorldCom in federal district court here in New York seeking the appointment of a corporate monitor to ensure WorldCom does not destroy any documents or information related to the SEC's pending investigation, and to assure no asset dissipation occurs to any affiliates, or current or former officers, directors or employees from the company while it is in the process of restating its financial statements.

These actions underscore the active role the SEC has played and will continue to play in uncovering wrongdoing, and correcting it. We are fully partnered with the Department of Justice and U.S. Attorneys across the country to ensure that where conduct warrants criminal prosecution, justice will not only be swift, it will be maximized. Serious jail time is called for by serious financial crime. We have to await the outcome of our inquiries, but I am pushing our staff to complete its review as rapidly as is humanly possible, so that any violations are sternly and quickly redressed.

During my 10 months as chairman, it has become increasingly clear that the problems that keep surfacing now are deeper than any one person or any one company and have been festering for years. Our free markets have generated unparalleled growth, jobs, innovation and prosperity. But the bubble that inflated in the last years of that run has burst.

The seemingly endless drumbeat of Enron, Global Crossing, Tyco, ImClone, Xerox, Andersen, Adelphia, and now WorldCom has caused investors around the globe to lose confidence in American business, and to question its basic integrity. If that is allowed to persist, a key pillar on which our capital markets are premised will crumble.

Therefore, consistent with the numerous reforms the president has called upon us to implement, we are following his direction and leadership by taking several other immediate steps to restore faith in our markets:

First, as part of our goal of reassuring fraud-weary investors, we plan to require our 1000 largest companies to file a formal certification with us on the accuracy and completeness of their last annual reports. The president has emphasized the need for individual responsibility on the part of CEOs and CFOs, and we are determined to assure investors that the financial statements they presently rely upon are in fact reliable. These certifications will be required to be provided by the time most companies file their next quarterly report—August 15.

Beyond this, I have today renewed my prior request to Congress for more resources to address these crises. Three months ago, as we were facing the twin crises of Enron's collapse and Andersen's demise, I asked the Administration and Congress for immediate additional personnel to help us in our enforcement, accounting and corporate finance activities. We were gratified that rather than have the SEC wait until the next fiscal year to begin hiring 100 additional attorneys, accountants and financial examiners, the administration promptly proposed to give us the money immediately, to enable us to begin the hiring process this year and continue through next year.

Congress indicated its immediate support for that proposal, but the money that we sought then has not yet been approved. It hopefully will be approved any day now, when the administration's supplemental appropriations bill receives final clearance from the House and Senate.

With all the new initiatives we are undertaking, it is clear to me that we need even more resources than those we asked for three months ago. In conversation with OMB Director Daniels this morning, I was assured that he and OMB will work with us, as they have done with our previous request, to assure that we receive the additional personnel we require to do our job appropriately. I am grateful for their support.

Finally, we formally released our proposed reform of the oversight of the accounting profession this morning. While it's out for comment, I intend to talk to government officials, members of Congress, former SEC chairs, individual and institutional investor representatives, academics, and others, to identify and encourage those people who could and should serve on a PAB to come together for that purpose.

Sixty days is a long comment period, and I originally had thought getting a PAB in place by year-end was appropriate. We have been helping Congress on their legislative proposals, and if there is legislation, we will implement it. However, in the event there is no legislation, my hope now is that we can begin implementing our proposals as shortly after the close of the comment period as is possible.

We believe that these steps underscore our commitment to full and fair disclosure by public companies to the American public and America's capital markets. But they are not the only ones we are taking—we have begun, and will continue to propose, an unprecedented number of reforms in the areas of accounting, corporate disclosure and corporate governance.

I have already mentioned our proposed framework for oversight of the accounting profession, and the CEO and CFO certification. In addition, we've been actively assisting FASB in retaining its independence and addressing key issues on a more timely basis and in a way that will better adapt to changing business environments and emphasize overall accuracy. We have been pleased with FASB's responses on these issues.

We've also begun a retooling of disclosure requirements to help ensure that investors have the information they need, when they need it, and can understand it when they receive it. Our initiatives in this area include:

- a proposed rule that requires companies to discuss the effects of their critical accounting policies;

- reminders to companies to disclose off–balance sheet financing arrangements, and about the appropriate use of, and limitations on, pro forma financial information;

- enforcement actions underscoring that technical compliance with GAAP, without more, can still produce insufficient disclosure;

- a proposed rule to require accelerated reporting of insider transactions, including company loans;

- a proposed rule to more than triple the number of items that companies must report currently, and to accelerate those disclosures; and

- a proposed rule to accelerate the deadline for annual reports from 90 to 60 days, and quarterly reports from 45 to 30 days.

Similarly, in partnership with the NYSE and Nasdaq, we're working on the most dramatic and far-reaching changes in corporate governance in decades. And, where corporate leaders abuse the trust of investors to whom they owe fiduciary duties, we are seeking to strip them of corporate offices, salaries, bonuses and stock options.

Again, starting a year ago, in partnership with the NYSE and the NASD, and after months of intensive focus by the House Financial Services Committee, the Commission's staff, and the SROs, we adopted real reforms to minimize and disclose research analysts' conflicts of interest. And our review of those practices is ongoing.

And these steps are only the beginning. We are considering other ways to improve the quality of information investors receive directly from issuers, including requiring disclosure of current trend and evaluative data upon which corporate executives base critical decisions.

We also will propose later this summer, for the first time, that public companies vest in fully independent audit committees the sole authority to hire, fire and retain auditors. These rules will also vest in audit committees, not senior management, sole authority whether, when and how to hire outside auditors to perform nonaudit services. Moreover, we've promised that, by midsummer, we will put out for public comment rules regarding auditor independence that could extend beyond independence rules approved in 2000 that take effect this August.

The recent large restatements of earnings that were misreported over the last several years have caused unacceptable and horrendous losses for large numbers of innocent people; but, the broader damage to investor confidence that these and other recent events have caused, including WorldCom's announced $4 billion restatement, presents a far more serious ongoing problem for our markets—and crisis is not too strong a word for it.

The American investing public has a right to better than it's been receiving, and we all must figure out how we get there, and without further delay. Corporate America, those who serve it, and those who monitor and regulate it, must embrace meaningful reform, and act in concert to restore integrity in our corporations and their leaders: how they're managed, governed, report to public shareholders, and account for themselves. Investor confidence can be rebuilt, but only by our total commitment to broad reform.

We have laid out, and are implementing, a creative and aggressive reform agenda. We can achieve these fundamental reforms, and make no mistake we will. We're counting on your support.

Thank you.

Remarks on the Wall Street Rally[4]

John J. Sweeney

President, AFL-CIO, 1995– ; born Bronx, NY, May 5, 1934; B.A. in economics, Iona College, New Rochelle, NY, 1956; researcher, International Ladies' Garment Workers Union; member, Local 32B (merged with Local 32J in 1977), New York City, 1960– , and president, 1976–80; member, Service Employment International Union (SEIU), 1960– , and President, 1980–95; Vice President, AFL-CIO, and chair, Committee on Health Care and the Organizing and Field Services Committee, 1980–95; coeditor, Family and Work: Bridging the Gap, *1987; coauthor,* Solutions for the New Work Force: Policies for a New Social Contract *(1989) and* America Needs a Raise: Fighting for Economic Security and Social Justice *(1996); David L. Clendenin Award, Workers Defense League of New York 1981; Quirk Award, for work in labor and management relations 1983.*

Editors' introduction: The AFL-CIO is a voluntary federation of 66 autonomous national and international unions. Unions represent 13 million working women and men of every race and ethnicity and from every walk of life. In the AFL-CIO, workers and unions strive to improve the lives of America's working families, bring fairness and dignity to the workplace, and secure social and economic equity in our nation. President John J. Sweeney spoke to some 1,000 Wall Street workers, union members, and the general public at a rally on Wall Street regarding corporate greed. Laid-off Enron and Arthur Anderson workers spoke prior to Mr. Sweeney. Enraged that "corporate greed" at "Enron and WorldCom and Arthur Andersen . . . cost 28,500 workers their jobs and nearly $2 billion dollars in retirement savings," Mr. Sweeney insisted that "when corporate criminals invade our workplaces and our markets to steal our jobs and our savings, we must react every bit as decisively as when thieves enter our homes and try to bring harm to our loved ones."

John J. Sweeney's speech: Brothers and sisters, we're here today to bring the voices of Cara and Diane and Coretta and Debra to Wall Street, to tell their story to the nation—and to demand action on their behalf.

Theirs is a story of Enron and WorldCom and Arthur Andersen, where corporate greed cost 28,500 workers their jobs, and nearly $2 billion dollars in retirement savings.

---

4. Delivered at New York City, on July 30, 2002, at noon. Reprinted with the permission of John J. Sweeney.

But it is also a story of 2 million other workers who've been thrown out of work by failing companies and a struggling economy, a tale of $1.5 trillion dollars drained from worker retirement and savings funds since the collapse of Enron.

And it's an unbelievable story of corporate criminals wrecking the lives and retirement dreams of millions of working families and flaunting their ill-gotten gains in our faces.

As the pages of this story turn, we see Enron CEO Ken Lay paying himself and other executives bonuses of $100 million dollars, even as he cheats thousands of employees and stockholders out of their jobs and their savings.

We witness the sorry spectacle of Gary Winnick, the CEO of Global Crossing, selling off $734 million in stock while urging his employees to buy more, and then using the money to purchase a $92 million dollar mansion in Bel Air.

Our families watch as WorldCom CEO Bernie Ebbers pockets $400 million dollars in loans, and the company dumps 17,000 employees into the streets and dives into bankruptcy without paying their severance.

More than 1,000 companies are forced to admit they cooked their books.

Top name companies like Merrill Lynch, First Boston, Johnson & Johnson, and AOL Time Warner fall under investigation.

The stock market loses $7 trillion dollars in value as the White House drags its feet and Congress refuses to rescind the $1.6-trillion-dollar tax break they gave to the same CEOs who are now stealing us blind.

Brothers and sisters, this isn't the way we do business in America.

Working hard. Playing by the rules. Making new products. Lifting up families and communities. Finding new solutions instead of creating cheap illusions. That's the way we do business in America.

That's how we built the strongest and most competitive economy and the largest middle class in the history of the world.

That's how we made it possible for ordinary people to do extraordinary things—fly in an airplane, drive an automobile, read a book after dark, speed around the world with the push of a button or the click of a mouse.

Nearly 100 years ago, robber barons hijacked our country and our wealth by taking advantage of the legal and regulatory voids created by our change from an agricultural to an industrial economy.

It took years, but we reclaimed our nation by heeding the words of John Adams and generations of patriots and renewed our Republic as a government of laws and not of men.

Now we're faced with 21st century corporate pirates who took advantage of our transition from an industrial to an information economy to kidnap working families and take us back to the past.

They plundered our companies by replacing long-term prosperity with short-run insincerity.

They polluted our capital markets by pumping up prices instead of producing profits.

Then they perverted our government by purchasing every politician money could buy, creating legal black holes where they can enrich themselves out of public sight.

The most cruel irony of all is that today the corporate criminals not only break our laws, they make the laws.

CEOs like Ken Lay and Gary Winnick and Bernie Ebbers aren't businessmen, and they aren't even capitalists—they are thieves and they are stealing our hopes, stealing our dreams and stealing our future.

When corporate criminals invade our workplaces and our markets to steal our jobs and our savings, we must react every bit as decisively as when thieves enter our homes and try to bring harm to our loved ones.

And we must respond just as strongly when co-conspirators of those criminals occupy and take control of our government, our legislative bodies and our regulatory agencies.

> *American workers can depend more on the lottery than on their employers for decency, fairness, and security.*

The sad truth is that American consumers can shop with more assurance of quality and safety at their corner grocery store than American investors can shop for equities in our stock market.

And American workers can depend more on the lottery than on their employers for decency, fairness, and security.

In the wake of our corporate crime wave, Congress passed a much needed corporate accounting bill—but cooked books are just a part of the problem and accounting reform is just part of the solution.

We have to reshape our corporate priorities and put people first.

We have to hold CEOs accountable and put integrity back into the companies they lead.

We have to give shareholders a voice in the companies they own.

And we have to clean up corporate corruption of politics through public financing of congressional election campaigns.

We're not going to restore confidence in the stock market, or renew trust in American business, or bring equity to our economy unless we seize this historic opportunity.

And so we've come here today to announce five new action steps to put a stop to "business as usual."

First, we insist that the Securities and Exchange Commission and all three stock exchanges agree to a single higher standard for publicly-traded corporations.

That standard must require companies to expense and index stock options they give CEOs, or, better yet, ban them outright.

It must prohibit CEOs from selling their company stock while they are in office.

It must outlaw the use of offshore tax havens.

And that standard must give workers and their pension funds the real power to choose corporate directors so we can replace the yes-men and -women and the rubber-stampers with genuinely independent directors.

This afternoon I am meeting with New York Stock Exchange President Dick Grasso and with Henry Paulson, the CEO of Goldman-Sachs, to discuss how we can bring business and labor together to demand and enact these changes.

The New York Stock Exchange has taken positive steps already—but we have to insist on more.

Second, we're demanding that Congress write these standards into law. And we're also going to insist that Congress put workers in the front of the line in bankruptcy proceedings and make genuine pension reform—not just 401(k) protections—its first order of business when it returns from its summer recess.

These things shouldn't require an act of Congress, but they do and Congress should act.

But when it comes to the families victimized by the largest corporate bankruptcy in history, we can't wait for Congress.

And that's why, as our third action step, I'm announcing today that the AFL-CIO will go to court with a suit on behalf of the 17,000 laid-off WorldCom workers to get the severance they are owed—and we will win for them just as we won $34 million dollars for the Enron workers.

But we aren't going to leave corporate accountability and business reform up to the lawmakers and the regulators and the courts alone.

We have more than $6 trillion dollars in workers' pension funds invested in American corporations; it is our country's single largest source of investment dollars.

When it comes to the families victimized by the largest corporate bankruptcy in history, we can't wait for Congress.

We intend to use that power to insist on higher standards of corporate behavior and change "business as usual" on Wall Street.

Company by company, starting with the S&P 100, we will demand corporate accountability through shareholder action, cyber-action, suite action, and street action.

Yesterday, I joined the machinists union at Stanley Works in New Britain, Connecticut, to protest that renegade corporation's plans to reincorporate in Bermuda.

Now Bermuda may be a fine place to vacation—but we all know that it's a code word for corporate corruption and tax evasion—we should not tolerate that and we will not tolerate that.

Tomorrow, we will call on Fidelity Investments in Boston—the biggest mutual fund firm in our country—and make it clear that we will not support funds that prop up companies like Stanley Works that want to take from America, but not give back.

As investors, we will no longer tolerate the greed of short-term speculators or corrupt insiders, and we will not tolerate companies that overcompensate executives, cheat their employees, lie to their shareholders, or cook their books—no excuses, no exceptions.

Fifth and finally, we will demand political accountability by using the influence of 40 million people who live in union households in our country to change the way business is done in Washington.

Our campaign is already underway. During the month of August, the AFL-CIO will be publicly linking corporate criminals with their congressional coconspirators while those members of Congress are home in their districts.

On Labor Day we will launch the most aggressive effort in our history to replace antiworker members of Congress with men and women who reject insiders and special interests and put people first.

And then, on October 19, we will convene a "No More Business As Usual" National Day of Action to educate and energize workers and their families and to motivate them to go to the polls and vote on November 5.

We undertake this campaign to protect workers and retirees, but also to help restore confidence to our markets, trust in our companies, and faith in our employers.

Brothers and sisters, workers' retirement and savings funds own over 20 percent of all the stock in America.

As investors, as employees, as consumers and as stewards of our communities, we must demand standards of basic decency and morality from corporate America.

The same standards of decency that we insist on in our communities.

The same standards of morality we teach our children.

We ask nothing more, and nothing less, of American business.

Thank you and God bless you all and God bless America.

V. Food Safety

S.T.O.P.'s Position on FDA's Prevention Efforts Toward BSE to Date[1]

Janet Abrams and Laurie Girand

Janet Abrams: Senior Director, The Corporate Executive Board Company, Washington, D.C., a firm conducting strategic research and executive education for more than 2000 corporations and government agencies worldwide; born Atlanta, GA, April 24, 1961; B.A. in history, summa cum laude, Harvard College, 1983; M.B.A. with certificate in public management studies, Stanford University, 1987; White House Fellow, 1994; president, White House Fellows Association; chair, White House Foundation; positions in government, business, and nonprofit sector.

Laurie Girand: Co-president, Safe Tables Our Priority (S.T.O.P.), 2001–02; born Boston, MA, March 15, 1961; B.S.E. in electrical engineering and computer science, Princeton University, 1983; M.B.A., Stanford University, 1987; product management and marketing, Apple Computer, 1987–89; director, Product Marketing, SuperMac Technologies, 1989–91; CEO, Beyond Marketing Strategies, 1992–; produce programs manager, S.T.O.P., 1997–2002; board member, S.T.O.P., 2000–2.

Editors' introduction: This speech was written by Co-President Laurie Girand and presented by Senior Director Janet Abrams on behalf of Safe Tables Our Priority (S.T.O.P.), a national coalition of victims of severe foodborne disease, their families and friends, and other concerned individuals. S.T.O.P. was founded in 1993 in the aftermath of a West Coast *E. coli* 0157:H7 outbreak that killed 4 people and sickened 700. Ms. Girand's daughter Anna McGregor was among those taken critically ill from drinking unpasteurized apple juice in the fall of 1996. Ms. Abrams presented this speech at an FDA consumer briefing on BSE (mad cow disease). Attending were FDA officials, policymakers, industry and consumer representatives, and others. Ms. Girand and Ms. Abrams cautioned that the "USDA's and FDA's present precautions are not adequate to prevent transmissible neurologic diseases from gaining a foothold in our country."

---

1. Delivered on April 16, 2001, at Washington, D.C. Reprinted with permission of Janet Abrams and Laurie Girand.

Janet Abrams and Laurie Girand's speech: S.T.O.P.—Safe Tables Our Priority—is a national, nonprofit organization of victims of foodborne illness and many consumers concerned about pathogens in our food supply. S.T.O.P.'s mission is to prevent unnecessary illness and death from foodborne illness. We appreciate the opportunity FDA has offered today for us to submit comments on behalf of past victims of foodborne illness and consumers concerned about TSE.

I am also here today to represent Americans who will die in the future from new variant Creutzfeld Jakob disease. Though we don't know who they are yet, Americans *will die* from this disease, even if they do not become infected on American soil. People who traveled abroad over the last 10 years, people who relocated to Europe for work, or even members of our armed services or diplomatic corps stationed overseas in the 1990s, all represent American populations presently at risk of developing this disease.

I want to remind FDA's representatives as well of the hundreds of thousands of Americans who suffer already from debilitating neurologic disorders that may someday be proven to be caused in a manner similar to new variant Creutzfeld Jakob disease. FDA needs to be mindful that if one neurologic disease can be transmitted in this fashion, others might certainly take advantage of a similar pathway.

S.T.O.P.'s message to you should be clear: USDA's and FDA's present precautions are not adequate to prevent transmissible neurologic diseases from gaining a foothold in our country. FDA's and USDA's delayed action and sporadic, incrementally raised barriers renders the public's health vulerable to this menace. We do not have to wait for TSE to come to the United States. It is already here in sheep and both wild and domestic elk and deer herds. It merely simmers, awaiting an opportunity to jump species barriers and be amplified through mass agribusiness practices and poorly enforced regulations just as other diseases such as *E. coli* O157:H7 and *Salmonella* have already done. It is essential to act aggressively *now*.

We offer several examples of dangerous delays that put industry interests ahead of those of public health and safety in feed, gelatin and dietary supplements.

- In 1988, the UK introduced a ban on feeding ruminant protein to ruminants. This was expanded in 1994 to be a ban on feeding mammalian protein to ruminant species. In 1996, this ban was again expanded to prohibit mammalian meat and mammalian bone meal to all farmed livestock. These rules were again superseded in the year 2000, when the UK instituted a temporary ban through June, 2001 on the feeding of processed animal protein to animals grown for human consumption.

- In contrast, in 1997, the FDA's Center for Veterinary Medicine finalized a rule prohibiting the feeding of mammalian protein to ruminant animals in most cases. This rule, which lagged behind its UK counterpart by three years had already been set aside as too minimal. Following the rule, FDA then proceeded to take more than three years to perform inspections to verify that renderers and feed mills were in compliance. As of March 23, 2001, inspections have revealed that 14% of U.S. renderers do not have a system for preventing commingling. 13% of FDA licensed mills do not have a system to prevent commingling, and 18% of Non FDA licensed mills do not have a system to prevent commingling. For feed, FDA has regulations but does not rapidly enforce them. Instead, reinspection continues and U.S. cattle and consumers continue to serve as guinea pigs.

- Gelatin is a food product typically derived from the long bones and hides of farm mammals including cattle. In 1994, based on very preliminary data, FDA's CFSAN exempted gelatin from the USDA ban on importing bovine materials from countries known to have BSE. In 1997, based on new data, FDA reversed its 1994 decision and developed guidelines for industry. FDA merely suggests that gelatin manufacturers should avoid using inputs from BSE herds, though they might still source gelatin inputs from BSE countries. It is unconscionable that there are still no regulations on prohibiting bovine materials from identified or suspect countries to be used in gelatin, a product used to create candy and jello for children.

- In 1992 and 1994, CFSAN wrote letters to some manufacturers of dietary supplements, that included bovine body parts such as the adrenal and pituitary glands. These letters advised that the manufacturers investigate the sources of their materials and not use materials from BSE countries, as identified by APHIS. The number of countries with insufficient surveillance for BSE has risen considerably since 1992 when FDA first wrote letters, and yet FDA still does not have rules prohibiting the use of bovine and ovine sourced materials in dietary supplements.

Here is what S.T.O.P. urges the FDA to do:

1. FDA's Center for Veterinary Medicine must immediately finalize rules and enforce the full EU ban on feeding "processed animal protein to animals which are kept, fattened or bred for the production of food." This rule is essential to keeping BSE from gaining a toehold in the U.S. cattle industry.

2. FDA's CFSAN must immediately create a gelatin "sourcing" rule and enforce it. This rule should not pussy-foot around distinctions such as gelatin can be derived from BSE-free herds, when no one is entirely certain if a herd is BSE free. Gelatin raw materials, at a minimum, should be prohibited from any country known to have BSE. The current guidance has existed for almost four years; a regulation is long overdue. Guidelines are insufficient when regulations are not even followed due to lack of enforcement.

3. While FDA's CFSAN works toward regulations prohibiting the use of animal parts in dietary supplements, FDA must immediately implement a rule that dietary supplement manufacturers carry warning labels on their products if those products contain suspect animal parts, and the label must also reveal the country from which they are sourced. FDA must also prepare to implement recalls of such products as new reveal BSE in their herds.

4. FDA must immediately put into place a mandatory, national registration program for manufacturers of dietary supplements, gelatin manufacturers, and dairies. FDA must equip itself with the ability to quickly notify *all* manufacturers potentially affected by TSE. This is merely the first line of defense in a true readiness campaign to act against this disease. Issuing press releases is wholly insufficient for notifying food processors.

5. FDA must ensure that American consumers consuming mammalian meat in restaurants and grocery stores are notified as to the country of origin of that meat. With the list of BSE infected countries or countries with suspect feed practices exploding, consumers deserve to be able to make informed choices about the meat they eat.

6. Lastly, FDA must fully disclose how many American consumers, living in the United States, have been exposed to the risk of BSE, through the combination of delay, insufficient guidance, and inadequate enforcement as well as the misunderstanding of how widespread the problem has been overseas. Americans deserve to know the range of true public health costs associated with delay and incomplete barriers.

If there is only one lesson to be learned from the disastrous consequences of the infection of UK and European farm animals, it is that FDA and USDA must get ahead of the science. As long as U.S. government officials continue to act as though BSE is not here yet, we will have slow and lax regulation and enforcement. The results could be devastating. We ask that FDA erect all formidable barriers to amplification of transmissible neurologic diseases in the year 2001. Without them, you cannot possibly continue to say that the U.S. food supply is among the safest in the world. Instead, we are all sitting ducks.

We thank you for your time.

Behind the Headlines

What Laymen Should Know About Everyday Issues in Science and Health[2]

Gregory Conko

Policy Analyst and Director of Food Safety Policy, Competitive Enterprise Institute, Washington, DC, 1994– ; born Connellsville, PA, June 16, 1970; B.A. in political science and history, American University, Washington, DC, 1992; Research Associate, Capital Research Center, Washington, DC, 1992–93; cofounder and board of directors, AgBioWorld Foundation, Auburn, AL, 2000– ; authored reports and articles in journals, newspapers, and magazines; Principal Investigator for the California Council on Science and Technology's 2002 report Benefits and Risks of Food Biotechnology.

Editors' introduction: The Competitive Enterprise Institute of which Gregory Conko is director is a nonprofit public policy organization dedicated to the principles of free enterprise and limited government. Director Conko spoke at a workshop on understanding everyday issues in science at the 24th Annual International Conference sponsored by the International Association of Culinary Professionals. Attending were some 150 chefs, restauranteurs, cookbook authors, and food industry representatives. Mr. Conko advised that "by overestimating the riskiness of new things, and underestimating the riskiness of old things, you can actually trap yourself—and society—in a world that is unnecessarily dangerous."

Gregory Conko's speech: Every day, we see newspaper headlines about the latest scientific findings. Just in the last few years, we've been deluged with scare stories about everything from allergy drugs to vasectomies causing cancer. And, naturally, many people change their behavior to avoid these newfound demons.

Typically, though, there is very little substance to these reports. But, while our attraction to sensationalism means that scary health reports are bound to get press attention, the bigger problem is that most laymen—journalists included—do not have the basic tools needed to see through the scary headlines and truly under-

---

2. Delivered on April 19, 2002, at San Diego, CA, San Diego Marriott Hotel and Marina, at 11:00 A.M. Reprinted with permission of Gregory Conko.

stand the relevance of basic scientific findings. The end result is that, in the absence of a better understanding of the issues, our innate biases tend to get in the way of making rational decisions.

Take the example of a story made famous a couple of years ago, when a junior high school student named Nathan Zohner surveyed a group of classmates for a school science project. Zohner told them about a chemical called dihydrogen monoxide. It is colorless, odorless, tasteless, and causes thousands of deaths every year. Prolonged exposure to its solid form causes severe tissue damage, exposure to its gaseous form causes severe burns, and it has been found in excised tumors of terminal cancer patients. Of 50 people Nathan surveyed, 43 said that dihydrogen monoxide should be banned, 6 weren't sure what to do, and only one person correctly identified dihydrogen monoxide as plain old water, or H_2O.

Now, the thought of reasonable people wanting to ban water may seem like a bit of an exaggeration. But this story makes two good points:

The scientific method can only prove that things are dangerous. It can never prove them to be safe.

First, it illustrates how even educated laymen will often fall back on a reflexive opposition to things that seem strange or new to them—especially things with complicated chemical names.

And second, it serves as a reminder that nothing—not even clean, pure water—is ever totally safe.

Thus, it is important for laymen to become familiar with some basic scientific concepts, because bad science—or a poor understanding of good science—can cause consumers, policymakers, and businesses to misallocate attention and resources away from where they are needed most and to waste resources on things of little importance.

Unfortunately, the public tends to have unrealistic expectations about what science can deliver. A recent poll in England found that 61 percent of the public expect scientists to provide 100 percent guarantees about the safety of products. But science can not deliver that. The scientific method can only prove that things are dangerous. It can never prove them to be safe.

Let me give you an example. If you wanted to see whether or not a new food additive can be safely used, you would conduct a number of experiments. And your hypothesis that the additive was safe could be proven false by observing a harmful effect. However, if the ingredient wasn't dangerous at all, you could never conduct enough experiments to show that there were no harmful effects under every possible circumstance.

You cannot prove a negative. Internalizing this fact is especially important in the context of interpreting scientific findings and making decisions based upon them.

In addition—for reasons that I'll get into in a moment—it's not always clear that the result of any one experiment is correct. So, making reasonable judgments about scientific reports becomes even more difficult.

Now, the task of giving you all the knowledge you need to adequately judge scientific information is a pretty daunting one—especially given the limited time I have today. So, I want to concentrate on just three things that you should consider when thinking about questions of health and safety: Validity, Context, and Tradeoffs.

- First, Validity—Was the study conducted properly, and are its conclusions generalizable to broader populations? Is it true?

- Next, Context—Any scientific study is just a little snapshot of data. So, what broader ramifications do the findings have for real life situations?

- And finally, Tradeoffs—Since even the safest products are not totally safe, there is no simple solution to any health problem. Be aware that sometimes the cure can be worse than the disease.

Now, let's take a look at each of these in a little more detail.

First, Validity. The best kind of science for determining if something is hazardous or beneficial is the "randomized trial." You set up an experiment, in which you assign subjects at random to a test group or a control group in which every single variable—apart from the one you're testing—is held constant.

But when testing substances that are suspected of being toxic or carcinogenic, including enough people in a randomized trial over a long enough time to be of any use would be extremely slow and hugely expensive. In many cases, you would literally have to test thousands of people over their entire lifetimes to gauge whether the effect was caused by the substance you're testing. Moreover, randomly exposing human subjects to a substance that is suspected of being dangerous would be unethical. So, alternatives must be found. The two primary alternatives are epidemiology and animal experiments.

Epidemiology is the examination of population statistics to see if any differences in lifestyle, diet, or some environmental factor happens to be correlated with a particular disease or disorder. The problem with epidemiology is that it can tell you if two things happen to be correlated with one another. It cannot provide a biological explanation for the coincidence of two data sets, so it cannot prove causation.

In theory, epidemiology can be very useful—but only if you understand its limitations, and if you control for all the other variables. But it is extremely difficult to actually control for all those relevant factors. And where the purported effect is small, it is very difficult to distinguish between an actual relationship and a random difference between populations.

Even epidemiologists admit that random differences often get confused with cause and effect relationships. Michael Thun of the American Cancer Society says, "With epidemiology you can tell a little thing from a big thing. What's very hard to do is tell a little thing from nothing at all."

In most cases, though, the only real alternative is to test substances or behaviors on lab animals. But toxicologists have a saying: "Lab rats are not little people."

Take the example of saccharin, reported in the early 1970s to cause bladder cancer in rats. Scientists pointed out that the cancer developed due to specific biological characteristics that humans don't have. Nevertheless, consumer safety advocates started scaring people about saccharin. Products with saccharin in them had to be labeled. And a useful product that could have helped address the very real problem of obesity was all but forced out of the marketplace.

A few years ago, saccharin was totally vindicated by the UN's World Health Organization when it acknowledged that saccharin really didn't cause cancer in humans—only rats. But that came thirty years too late.

By themselves, neither epidemiology nor animal tests is really conclusive. Epidemiology asks the right questions, but answers them poorly. And in most cases, animal tests answer questions very well, but ask the wrong questions in the first place. In the end, strong conclusions should never be based upon the results of a single study. The best conclusions are drawn only on the basis of multiple studies using a variety of different methodologies that compile a large body of evidence.

Next, let's talk about Context. Given that scientific studies only produce little snapshots of data, even well-established results often have limited applicability outside the laboratory.

For example, another shortcoming of animal tests is that, because normal exposure to most test substances isn't enough to produce a large enough effect to study, toxicologists frequently use what's known as the "maximum tolerable dose" methodology. This is just what it sounds like: the lab animals are fed or injected with the maximum possible amount of the test substance that won't kill them outright. But at such high doses, about half of all substances will eventually cause cancer. So, those results are not remotely related to real-world exposure to the chemicals that are tested.

A good illustration is the scare about dioxin. A couple of years ago, ice cream maker Ben & Jerry's was going to stop using bleached paper for its cartons because chlorine from the bleaching process creates dioxin as a byproduct. According to the Ben & Jerry's advertising, the "only safe level of dioxin exposure is no exposure at all."

That sounds pretty scary, doesn't it? No safe level. But, 500 years ago, the Swiss doctor Philippus Aureolus Paracelsus coined a saying that is still a fundamental principle of toxicology: "It's the dose that makes the poison."

Lots of things are dangerous at very high levels, but totally harmless at lower levels. And many things, like iron, zinc, even arsenic, and other minerals and chemicals are both potentially dangerous and essential for sustaining a healthy body. Paracelsus himself developed a treatment for syphilis that used mercury, which is toxic in high doses.

Arsenic, the source of a big controversy lately because it shows up in drinking water, has been a component in lots of different medicines over the years. In fact, arsenic is a component of some "organic" pesticides, and was one of the primary antifungal agents

---

Lots of things are dangerous at very high levels, but totally harmless at lower levels.

---

used in French vineyards until it was phased out only recently.

And while it is a common reaction among laymen to presume that natural things are generally good and man-made things are generally bad, even synthetic chemicals—like industrial pollutants, pesticides, and dioxin—have safe and dangerous levels.

In her book *Silent Spring*, Rachel Carson wrote, "For the first time in the history of the world, every human being is now subjected to contact with dangerous chemicals, from the moment of conception until death." She prophesied a future where modern synthetic pesticides and other chemicals would cause epidemics of cancer.

But, Rachel Carson was wrong. First, because age-adjusted rates of cancer are falling, not rising. And second, because every human being who ever lived has been exposed to a background dose of potentially dangerous chemicals and has eaten lots of them in every meal since the beginning of time.

You see, plants are essentially little factories—making proteins, micronutrients, and other chemicals. They've evolved over time to produce certain chemicals as a way of fending off insect pests, bacteria, and fungi. There are more than a thousand natural chemicals in coffee. Of the 25 that have been tested, 19 of them have been found to cause cancer in rats. The same can be said about every other plant in the food chain—from apples to zucchinis. A single ounce of potato has about as much carcinogenic potency as the Environmental Protection Agency's "safe level" of dioxin.

According to cancer researcher Bruce Ames at the University of California at Berkeley, 99.99 percent of all pesticides in the human diet occur naturally in plants. And, ounce for ounce, natural pesticides are at least as potent—if not more so—than synthetic ones.

Interestingly enough, plants that are grown organically tend to have even higher total levels of carcinogenic chemicals than plants grown with synthetic pesticides—because the plants produce more of their own chemicals when they're bitten by insects. Don't worry though. I suspect that many of you will be happy to know that Bruce Ames is a friend of noted chef Alice Waters and has been eating at her organic restaurant Chez Panisse since it opened 30 years ago.

I'm not trying to scare you away from organic food. The point I'm trying to make is that the background rate of chemicals in both organic and conventional produce is so small as to be inconsequential.

Now, let's go back to Ben & Jerry's ice cream for a moment and to what I think is a particularly amusing bit of irony. Dioxins are produced any time things with chlorine in them are burned, and even from some natural processes like forest fires and volcanic eruptions. They don't break down easily in the environment. And they tend to accumulate in the fatty tissue of animals over time. Consequently, dioxins exist throughout the food chain, and are present in all dairy and meat products, including Ben & Jerry's ice cream.

A sample of Ben & Jerry's vanilla ice cream tested at an independent lab contained 0.79 parts per trillion of dioxin, or about 200 times more than the "virtually safe dose" of dioxin determined by the EPA. So, if you really believed what Ben & Jerry say about dioxin, you should eat their cartons and throw away the ice cream. But that level of dioxin doesn't make Ben & Jerry's ice cream dangerous. For nearly every chemical it regulates, the Environmental Protection Agency sets safety levels that are so much smaller than the dose that would reasonably be expected to cause any harm.

Permissible levels of most synthetic chemicals are typically one-thousand times lower than what's been determined by scientific research to have no health effect. So, I'm certainly not suggesting that anyone give up Ben & Jerry's ice cream. Except for the fat and the sugar, it's perfectly safe. But this makes a good point about worrying too much about exposure to chemicals.

Most people tend to think, like Rachel Carson did, that pesticides and other pollutants are the leading causes of cancer. But the number one cause of cancer—responsible for over 30 percent of all cases—is poor diet characterized by too many high glycemic carbohydrates and too few fruits and vegetables. Next is cigarette smoking, responsible for about 30 percent of all cancer cases. Pollution and pesticides account for considerably less than 1 percent of all cancers—and those are mostly from heavy air pollutants in large underdeveloped cities like Calcutta and Shanghai.

Of course, one might be tempted to say, "So what if pesticides are less dangerous than I thought? Why should we settle for any exposure at all?" To answer that question, let's move on to the third and last point: Tradeoffs.

As I mentioned at the very beginning of my talk, nothing is ever totally safe—if by safe you mean completely devoid of risk. Remember dihydrogen monoxide? Things are only more or less safer than other things.

The point is that lots of things to which we're totally accustomed have considerable risk associated with them. And in many cases, they're far more dangerous than the new products or practices that could replace them. By overestimating the riskiness of new things, and underestimating the riskiness of old things, you can actually trap yourself—and society—in a world that is unnecessarily dangerous.

Probably the best example of how "erring on the side of caution" can actually lead to lower safety is the Food and Drug Administration's pharmaceutical review process. On the one hand, FDA can approve a product that later turns out to be dangerous. This is the kind of problem we're all familiar with and, consequently, the kind of mistake that FDA tries very hard never to make.

On the other hand, FDA can deny approval to a product that actually is safe and effective—or even just sit on its hands doing nothing. When the FDA fails to approve a drug that could save lives—or waits for a complete assurance of safety—real people stay sick longer, and many of them die. But because regulatory agencies are so intent upon "erring on the side of safety," this type of mistake happens all the time.

Even delaying the approval of things like new food additives, pesticides, and genetically engineered crops can be just as detrimental to public health as putting them on the market too quickly. Pesticides, for example, boost farm productivity by as much as 30 to 40 percent and consequently make the fruits and vegetables that are necessary for a healthy diet much more affordable. Given all the safety factors that are built into the system, banning products that boost farm productivity is usually much riskier than those products are themselves.

In decision making, regulatory agencies generally try to balance the benefits and drawbacks of putting products on the market, in what is called a cost-benefit analysis. One problem is that this sounds like regulators are trying to put money on an equal footing with peoples' lives. But it would be more accurate to describe good regulatory decision making as a risk-risk analysis, where the risks of approval are weighed against the risk of refusal, and a decision is made that leads society in the direction of increased overall safety.

Critics of this approach argue that it's impossible to foresee all potential risks. As an alternative, they advocate what's called the precautionary principle, which many of you may have heard about. The precautionary principle is the belief that, where there is some uncertainty about the safety of new products, regulators should ban or restrict them, even if the risks have not been demonstrated scientifically.

> *In the end, it is risk-risk analysis that is the true "look before you leap" policy.*

It sounds intuitively appealing, doesn't it? Look before you leap, and all that.

But the caveat about risks not being demonstrated scientifically means that any hypothesized risk is enough to keep products from being used. In effect, advocates of the precautionary principle believe that new technologies should be kept off the market until they are proven to have no risk. But, as I discussed earlier, the limitations of science are such that the absence of a danger can never be proven.

Precautionary principle advocates respond that they're just trying to ensure that products aren't rushed onto the market without thinking through all the potential negative effects. But that's exactly what traditional risk analysis does. If what you really want is to see that the potential dangers of a technology or behavior are taken into consideration before adopting it, you don't need anything more than what's already standard procedure for practically every government around the world. In the end, it is risk-risk analysis that is the true "look before you leap" policy.

It might even be said that advocates of the precautionary principle support a "look, but never leap" policy. After all, most of them even support restrictions on products like genetically engineered crops, new generations of pesticides, and even the chlorination of drinking water—all cases where there are reams and reams of scientific evidence indicating no real hazard, and where the products they would replace are demonstrably less safe.

Consider chlorination. In the mid-1980s, environmental activists convinced the Peruvian government to stop chlorinating its drinking water because byproducts of the chlorination process pose a potential cancer risk. Now, on the one hand, Peruvians didn't have to worry about the one in ten million chance of getting cancer from chlorine byproducts. But on the other hand, that decision contributed to the spread of a major cholera epidemic in the early 1990s, which afflicted more than 1.3 million people and killed at least 11,000.

Or consider genetically-engineered plants, which critics call Frankenfood. We hear over and over about how moving genes between organisms could unwittingly introduce toxins or allergens into the food supply. Others are concerned about the possibility that new genes in plants could have negative environmental impacts. Here again, though, fear arises because genetic technology is poorly understood by people who express an unwarranted preference for what they believe is natural.

What skeptics often don't realize is that all types of plant breeding move genes from one organism to another. And even the wholly "natural" process of sexual reproduction gives rise to exactly the same potential risks.

Take tomato breeding as an example. Wild tomatoes can be toxic to human beings. But wild tomatoes generally have better natural resistances to viruses and fungi than food-grade tomatoes. So, it is common for plant breeders to mate standard garden-variety tomato plants with wild relatives in order to move the genes coding for those resistances from the wild plant to the cultivated one.

Unfortunately, the "natural" process of mating the two plants can just as easily transfer the toxin genes into the off-spring as it can transfer the resistance genes. Furthermore, ordinary sexual reproduction can also disrupt the normal functioning of other genes and routinely is used to introduce entirely new genes into the food supply—just like genetic engineering. Yet, no activists or regulators seem to be concerned about an impending Attack of the Conventionally Bred Killer Tomatoes.

Why? Because over the years, plant breeders have developed ways of making sure that potentially harmful products never make it to market.

On the other hand, genetic engineering—or gene splicing—lets plant breeders identify exactly which genes they want to transfer. It lets them isolate those genes from potentially harmful ones and insert the "good" genes into another plant. And then it lets them test to see that all the relevant genes are in normal working order. None of these assurances can be made with conventional breeding, which is why most scientists actually believe genetic engineering to be "safer," not less safe, than conventional methods.

But the expanded range of modifications that can be made with genetic techniques means that agricultural productivity can be improved, farming practices can be changed to have a lighter impact on the environment, and the staple crops grown in less developed nations can be fortified with additional nutrients and made more resistant to special problems that plague tropical regions, like extremes of heat and drought.

A friend and colleague of mine is a plant geneticist at Tuskegee University in Alabama. His research has helped produce a genetically engineered sweet potato variety that has five times the normal level of essential amino acids. And many other scientists at other universities and public sector research labs are working on engineering sweet potatoes for improved virus resistance. Once these varieties clear all the regulatory red tape, they'll be used to help poor farmers in central Africa, for whom sweet potato is the primary source of dietary starch and proteins.

But it could take quite a long time for improved sweet potatoes to ever help anyone. Two years ago, one of the key research facilities in this effort—the lab of Catherine Ives at Michigan State University—was firebombed by anti-biotechnology activists, setting back the entire project by years.

In my opinion, this is the worst manifestation of misunderstood science. It is based on Invalid criticisms of the technology that are too often not placed in the Context of the broader knowledge about plant physiology, and pays no attention whatever to the Tradeoffs involved in giving up the technology. All too often, there are very real, human costs to our failure to consider all these factors when making relevant decisions.

So, I hope I've alerted you to the importance of looking behind the headlines and considering these factors next time you read about a new scientific study. And, hopefully, I've helped you move a little farther down the road toward a better understanding and a better appreciation for science.

Thank you.

Food Safety and Bioterrorism Legislation[3]

John D. Dingell

U.S. Congressman from Michigan (Democrat), 1955– ; born Colorado Springs, CO, July 8, 1926; B.S. in chemistry, 1949, and J.D., 1952, Georgetown University; 2nd lieutenant, infantry, U.S. Army, 1945–46; Park Ranger, U.S. Department of the Interior, 1948–52; assistant prosecuting attorney, Wayne County, MI, 1953–55; member, Migratory Bird Conservation Committee; ranking member, Committee on Energy and Commerce.

Editors' introduction: Congressman John D. Dingell addressed some 350 persons attending the 25th Annual National Food Policy Conference for 2002, sponsored by the Consumer Federation of America (CFA). Since 1968, CFA has supported pro-consumer policy on a variety of issues before Congress, the White House, federal and state regulatory agencies, and the courts. Concerned that the United States lacked the "resources" to inspect food arriving at U.S. ports, in light of threats of bioterrorism, Congressman Dingell insisted that "more inspectors are needed, and they are needed now."

John D. Dingell's speech: Thank you for inviting me to speak today before the 25th Annual National Food Policy Conference sponsored by the Consumer Federation of America. I salute the members of CFA who dedicate themselves to advocating for, and educating consumers on, a wide range of issues, both nationally and at the state level.

This is the largest group of food safety advocates I have ever had the opportunity to address, and for that I want to sincerely thank you. For the past five years I have had the pleasure of working with Carol Tucker Foreman, Caroline Smith DeWaal and other consumer food safety advocates on improving the Food and Drug Administration's inspection and regulation of imported food.

This conference is particularly relevant to the current work of Congress, in particular defending our nation's food supply against threat of terrorist attack. Important work is being done in the House-Senate conference on bioterrorism, and I hope that you will lend your voice to the urgent need for additional resources to improve the safety of our food system.

---

3. Delivered on April 23, 2002, in Washington, D.C., at the National Press Club.

We knew that something as important as strengthening the Nation's food safety system would not be an easy task. But the difference now is that the issue is finally getting attention, from the public, the press, from government, and from both proponents and opponents of strong food safety measures. My hope is that this attention will translate to action.

All the past work done by this great organization of consumer advocates, and by all those represented here today, is now paying off. You have an audience that is listening. Much more will be demanded of you in the future as we fight to keep food safety at the forefront of public attention.

In each of the past two congresses, most of my Democratic colleagues on the Committee on Energy and Commerce have joined me in sponsoring legislation aimed at improving the safety of imported food that Americans eat.

Unfortunately, few others have shared our enthusiasm for acknowledging and taking steps to address the threats to food safety generally, and in particular threats to the safety of imported food.

The bioterrorism legislation is clearly the most important food safety legislation to be considered by the Congress in years.

The legislation I have introduced in this and past Congresses has not received so much as a hearing. Then came September 11, and instantly our vulnerabilities as a Nation were exposed to the alarm of everyone. For the first time, we had a secretary of health and human services say there is a need to take steps to detect the intentional adulteration of food coming into the United States and to prevent entry of food which presents risk of injury to American consumers.

From that came the bioterrorism bills that passed both the House and the Senate. The bioterrorism legislation is clearly the most important food safety legislation to be considered by the Congress in years. It has new money and much needed new authorities for FDA to improve its regulation of imported food. This legislation, for the first time, gives FDA authority to act independently at the border. FDA would no longer need to rely on the Department of the Treasury either for information about food at the border or for the ability to detain shipments it suspects are adulterated.

For those of us who advocate stronger food safety protections, our first and most important challenge is to make sure Congress passes the bioterrorism bill with the strongest possible food safety provisions. Although I am generally pleased with the work the conference is doing, I would be less than candid if I did not say I'm more than a little concerned at how long the conference is taking. And the longer it is before agreement is reached, the more opportunity there is for those who don't want a strong food safety bill to undermine our work.

Furthermore, it should be remembered that the bioterrorism legislation is a big bill. Food safety is only one of several titles in the legislation. While the conference is closer to agreement on food safety than on some other titles of the bill, agreement on the whole bill must be reached before the food safety provisions can be enacted into law.

All who care about food safety should now be making your voices heard. The conferees need to know that you have high expectations for the work they are doing and very long memories should they fail. American consumers have for too long been treated like guinea pigs. A successful bioterrorism conference is critical to defending our food supply.

But, the bioterrorism legislation is only one step in the right direction. Once the bioterrorism legislation becomes law, and I am hopeful it will become law, much will still need to be done on food

---

There are only 150 FDA inspectors to cover the 307 ports of entry where food now enters the U.S.

---

safety. A high priority for all food safety advocates must be building on and sustaining the concern about food safety that last year's horrific events created. Active grassroots support will be needed to maintain the momentum for greater food safety.

This afternoon, I want to give you an overview of my food safety goals in the bioterrorism conference. Before I do, however, it's important to understand what the regulation of imported food looks like today. And I know you will not be surprised that it is not a pretty picture.

As bad as you may believe FDA controls are at the border, the reality is they are much worse than you think. As a result, imported food that is intentionally or unintentionally adulterated is much more likely to end up on America's dinner table than it is to be detected and held at the border. This is true largely because FDA doesn't have enough inspectors at ports of entry, but FDA's own practices and lack of authority make matters worse.

FDA does no testing to prevent adulterated imported food from entering the United States. It should. And when food is actually denied entry it is often brought to another U.S. port and admitted.

FDA's current practice is to tell food importers whether their shipments will be inspected even before the shipment is put on a boat or a plane for delivery to a U.S. port of entry. This must stop.

FDA lacks authority to "trace back" food borne illness beyond the border. Congress must provide that authority.

And FDA often lacks timely information. Consider this: 54 percent of the fresh fruits and vegetables that come into the U.S. enter at either the Canadian or Mexican border. Yet FDA gets no documentation on more than 10 percent of all food imports entering the United States from Mexico or Canada until 10 days after the food arrives in this country. By then, the food very likely has been eaten. That is almost certainly true in the case of fresh fruit and vegetable imports. We must do better.

But the most pressing problem is straightforward—resources. Currently, there are only 150 FDA inspectors to cover the 307 ports of entry where food now enters the U.S. If there is no FDA inspector present when imported food arrives at a U.S. port, that food is allowed into the U.S. and is eaten by American consumers without FDA so much as reviewing its paperwork.

It would take six times the current number of inspectors just to put one FDA inspector at each port on a full-time basis. It is clear that we cannot detect adulterated imported food at the border unless we have inspectors at the border to inspect and examine shipments of food coming into the United States. More inspectors are needed, and they are needed now.

Over the last five years, the volume of food imported into the U.S. has almost doubled, forcing FDA to admit it is "in danger of being overwhelmed by the volume of products reaching U.S. ports." With more imports reaching U.S. ports, FDA's inspection rate for imported food has fallen from eight percent in 1992 to less than one percent last year. At a minimum, FDA needs to be inspecting 10 percent of food imports, and that can only happen if FDA is given greater resources than even the bioterrorism bill envisions.

That's what things look like today, and here are my goals for the bioterrorism conference:

FDA must have the ability to detain food, at the border and elsewhere, on its own authority. And when no inspector is present at a port of entry, FDA needs the ability to order food held until an inspector can be dispatched to the location. Before imported food can be seized now, FDA must first convince the Justice Department to initiate a case on its behalf, and then Justice has to convince a judge that the seizure is warranted. That's unacceptable, and the bioterrorism legislation must give FDA this needed authority.

FDA needs to know in advance when food is going to be presented for importation. At the same time, notice must not be given so far in advance that shippers learn whether their shipments will be inspected even before they are ready for transport to the U.S. Unless FDA receives adequate advance notice that a shipment of food is coming to port, it faces a serious handicap in being able to determine whether that shipment should be detained. FDA needs to know what is being imported, the manufacturer and shipper of the article being imported, and if known, the grower of the article, the country of origin, the country from which the article is shipped, and the anticipated port of entry. Without this basic information submitted sufficiently in advance of the food's arrival, FDA cannot effectively evaluate when a shipment of imported food may present a threat of serious illness or death.

FDA needs to have inspectors present when food comes through a U.S. port of entry. There is no substitute for on-site examination of product and product documentation that can only be performed effectively by a trained, inquisitive, inspection professional. The Administration says it can hire 600 new inspectors with the funds authorized by the bioterrorism legislation. That's a big increase over the 150 FDA inspectors who must now cover 307 ports of entry. But even this sizeable increase in the inspection force will ensure that only one inspector will be on duty at all times at all 307 ports. That's a good start, but it's not enough. And it's not at all clear to me that the 600 new inspectors will actually be hired. We will need to address the adequacy of FDA's inspection force again in the future, and I hope I can count on your support for making sure FDA has the inspectors it needs to do a thorough and effective job at the borders.

FDA also needs to know who it is regulating. Today it does not know this. Sounds like a simple enough proposal, but it has caused much controversy. To remedy this deficiency, both the House and Senate bioterrorism bills provide that every food warehouse, factory, or establishment must register with the FDA and provide its name and address. Access to records gives FDA its best chance of identifying food that is adulterated, intentionally or not. For this reason, a strong recordkeeping and records access provision must be retained in the conference bill.

Other important new powers. I expect the conference bill to provide the ability for FDA to "debar" importers who are convicted of felonies in connection with the importation of food into the U.S. or who repeatedly offer adulterated food for importation. FDA also needs the authority to mark food it does not permit to be imported with a "refused entry" stamp so that if the importer tries to bring a rejected shipment of food through another U.S. port, inspectors can readily identify it as having already been "refused entry." And to make sure food that has been refused entry stays out, such food must be deemed to be adulterated, allowing FDA to bring legal action to stop the food itself.

We must also develop rapid test technologies that will allow inspectors to detect contaminants on imported food right at the border. Currently, inspectors don't even bother to test imported food because it can take up to two weeks to get test results back, and by that time the food has most likely already been eaten by American consumers.

These new authorities and resources that I expect to be included in the bioterrorism bill will be a great start. But in the coming years, more will be needed.

My ongoing goals for food safety include the following:

FDA needs, but does not have, mandatory recall authority. If FDA believes a recall is appropriate today, the only thing it can do is ask the states to use their recall authority to take a particular food article out of commerce. It is very interesting that all but one state has food recall authority, but FDA does not.

FDA needs a user fee to fund the additional cost of inspecting imported food. This would insure a steady revenue stream for much needed inspectors and tests to detect pathogens at the border.

Imported food regulated by the FDA should be labeled to identify its country of origin. American consumers have a right to know whether their food was grown halfway around the world or at the local farm down the street.

FDA needs, but does not have, the ability to file a seizure action without the Department of Justice. The Department of Justice does not always have the same priorities as FDA, and as a result, FDA enforcement suffers along with the safety of our food supply.

If a foreign food firm or foreign government denies FDA the ability to perform an inspection in a foreign country, or if the foreign country does not provide the same level of food safety protection as the U.S., *then FDA should be able to prohibit importation of food from that country*. Either FDA can establish with some certainty the safety of imported food, or it cannot. And if it cannot, the food should not be allowed into the U.S.

These deficiencies, which we were unable to resolve in the bioterrorism bill, must be addressed in the future. The legislation my Democratic colleagues on the Committee on Energy and Commerce and I have introduced contains many of these additional authorities that FDA very much needs. H.R. 3075, the Imported Food Safety Act that so many in this room have supported, needs your help. I urge you to contact your members of Congress and encourage them to cosponsor this important legislation.

The key to being able to do these important things in the future lies right here in this room. You must not let the American people, the Congress, or the administration forget how vulnerable our food supply is. We must not wait for the unthinkable to happen again before we do what is needed to protect the safety of our food, both imported and domestic. Our window of opportunity to do something important is still open. Don't let it close without getting the job done. I pledge my efforts to this cause. Together we can make it happen.

Thank you.

Taking Food Safety to the Next Level[4]

Elsa Murano

Under Secretary for Food Safety, U.S. Department of Agriculture, 2001– ; born Havana, Cuba; B.S. in biological sciences, Florida International University, Miami; M.S. in anaerobic microbiology and Ph.D. in food science and technology, Virginia Polytechnic Institute and State University, Blacksburg, VA; assistant professor of Microbiology, Immunology, and Preventive Medicine, 1990–95, and professor in charge of research programs at Linear Accelerator Facility, 1992–95, Iowa State University, Ames; associate director, 1995–97, and director, 1997–2001, Center for Food Safety, Institute of Food Science and Engineering, Texas A&M University, College Station, 1995–2001; Department of Animal Science Research Advisory Committee and the Food Safety Response Team of the Texas Agriculture Extension Service, Texas A&M, 1997–2001; National Alliance for Food Safety Operations Committee, 1998–2001; chair, Food Safety State Initiative Committee of the Texas Agriculture Experiment Station, Texas A&M, 1999–2001; associate professor, 1995–2000, and professor, 2000–01, Department of Animal Science, Texas A&M; Sadie Hatfield Endowed Professorship in Agriculture, Texas A&M, 2000–01; USDA National Advisory Committee for Meat and Poultry Inspection, 2001.

Editors' introduction: Elsa Murano oversees the policies and programs of the Food Safety and Inspection Service of the U.S. Department of Agriculture. In her address to delegates attending the National Association of Farm Broadcasters Conference, Dr. Murano outlined five goals that she and her colleagues were pursuing "to enhance food safety." Following the speech, she responded to questions and comments from the audience. Dr. Murano discusses Hazard Analysis and Critical Control Point (HACCP), a system implemented in January 2000 by the Federal Safety and Inspection Service (FSIS) of the U.S. Department of Agriculture to improve food safety.

Elsa Murano's speech: Good morning everybody. It's a pleasure to be here to give you a quick update on what we're doing in the food safety mission at USDA.

---

4. Delivered on April 29, 2002, at Washington, D.C.

Last month, my fellow undersecretaries and I testified before the Senate and House Appropriations Committees on USDA's budget request for FY 2003. And I can tell you it was a unique educational experience for me, considering my background as a food safety researcher from academia.

> *We have a strong food safety infrastructure in place today.*

My piece of USDA's budget pie concerns providing $905 million to fund the Food Safety and Inspection Service's inspectors, veterinarians and other food safety officials who safeguard the nation's meat and poultry supply. This is the mission of FSIS, to protect the public's health, and it is a mission that I take very seriously.

When I began this job last fall, I spent some time thinking about how far food safety has come in the last decade. One of the things I realized is that we have a strong food safety infrastructure in place today.

Within the FSIS alone, more than 7,600 inspection personnel verify the safety of the nation's meat, poultry and egg products. In addition to this strong workforce, the implementation of the Pathogen Reduction/HACCP rule in plants of all sizes brought forth significant modernization in the way meat and poultry are processed, with an emphasis on the prevention and control of foodborne hazards.

Well this HACCP-based inspection system has certainly played a vital role in preventing and reducing the overall number of pathogens. Just over a week ago, USDA announced that the prevalence of *Salmonella* in the nation's raw meat and poultry has decreased in comparison to studies conducted prior to the implementation of HACCP.

In only the second year of aggregate data on all sizes of plants, the new data indicate that all categories of product show improvement over baseline studies conducted prior to HACCP implementation.

Perhaps more importantly, this decrease in the prevalence of *Salmonella* in raw meat and poultry from 1998–2001 correlates with the Centers for Disease Control and Prevention's report indicating a decline in human illnesses linked to *Salmonella* during the same time period. The CDC attributes the reductions in illness in part to the implementation of FSIS's pathogen reduction/HACCP rule.

So this is great news indeed about the prevalence of *Salmonella*, and it is an indicator that our food safety system is strong. However, improvements are needed so that HACCP can reach its full potential to take food safety to the next level. Let me talk about two initiatives underway, which are designed to help HACCP become more effective.

Improving the Quality of FSIS's Workforce

First, I'm determined to ensure that FSIS has the best trained, best supervised, and best-motivated force of inspectors. Suffice it to say that I am convinced that HACCP will become even more effective as our inspection workforce continues to become more scientifically focused.

Our new Consumer Safety Officer (CSO) initiative is a step in the right direction. These individuals are highly trained in HACCP and are an essential component of our in-depth review teams. As with most new initiatives, we will monitor the progress of our CSO program and make any necessary adjustments along the way.

New Meat Safety Directives

A second initiative to improve the effectiveness of HACCP was announced one week ago. It consists of new meat safety directives, which are aimed to control pathogens in plants that produce ground beef. If establishments do not employ effective decontamination strategies or do not require their suppliers to do so as part of their HACCP systems, they will be targeted for increased testing for *Salmonella* and *E. coli* O157:H7.

I believe that by increasing our efforts and resources on those establishments where microbial control might be lacking, we will continue to drive down the prevalence of pathogens in raw ground beef.

The Five Goals

As part of our complete effort to enhance food safety, we are vigorously pursuing five goals. Let me take a few minutes to briefly go over these with you.

Goal 1: The first goal is to improve the management of FSIS programs.

Many of the efforts related to improving the management and efficiency of FSIS programs started before I came on board last fall. We are restructuring our district offices and providing more training for our field workforce to maximize efficiency. We are also making sure that communication within FSIS is improved and flows as easily from the top to bottom, as from bottom to top.

Goal 2: The second goal is to improve coordination with sister agencies.

The coordination of food activities is something that we have done in the past, and it has contributed to the strength of our current food safety system. However, we are continuing to seek ways to enhance coordination and cooperation with other agencies to make our food safety net even stronger.

An example of how we are currently improving coordination with sister agencies is our close working relationship with the Food and Drug Administration. FSIS and FDA are examining ways to further leverage both agencies' resources for the maximum public health benefit, especially in dual jurisdiction establishments. One of the initiatives we are working on is the possibility of empowering our inspectors, in emergency situations, to help FDA address threats to the food supply in establishments where we both have jurisdiction, but where FDA is not completely present as we are.

Goal 3: The third goal is to base policy decisions on science.

My background as a food safety researcher has shown me the importance of science and how it should influence policy. Achievement of this goal is essential if we are to make sound decisions in protecting the public's health.

We are accomplishing this several ways, such as through risk assessments, the proper use of performance standards, and engagement with the scientific community for needed data and input into policy making.

Improving upon performance standards is a priority for FSIS, and we have several microbiological performance standards in place today. We believe that performance standards are needed in conjunction with HACCP. They verify the ability of a plant to control contamination through HACCP to ensure that its products are safe.

But what those standards should look like is under debate. As you may know, that is why we have turned to the National Advisory Committee on Microbiological Criteria for Foods and the National Academy of Sciences to get input. Both groups are studying this issue, and their findings and recommendations should be complete by the end of this year.

Goal 4: The fourth goal is to engage in aggressive education programs.

I mean it when I tell you that I want FSIS to be the entity that consumers look to for guidance regarding food safety. I am seeking an aggressive education and risk communications campaign within USDA to ensure that our efforts are recognized, and that consumers have confidence in our system.

As an example of how we are meeting this goal, we are helping to sponsor a food safety education conference on September 18–20, in Orlando, Florida, in cooperation with the Department of Health and

Human Services and the Partnership for Food Safety Education. This conference will provide an opportunity for food safety education and communication leaders from across the country to present and share projects, assess current trends, and plan for the future.

Goal 5: And finally, the fifth goal is to secure our meat, poultry, and egg products supply from intentional harm.

Biosecurity is an issue that is of paramount concern to USDA and to all other organizations involved in food safety. FSIS has a long history of success in dealing with food emergencies, and a strong food safety infrastructure (that I just mentioned).

But even a localized event that does not cause significant harm can greatly undermine consumer confidence nationwide. That is why we have taken a multifaceted approach to biosecurity, which includes both short- and long-term strategies that focus on coordination, prevention, preparedness, as well as rapid response.

One example of how FSIS has been meeting this goal has been through its formation of its own Food Biosecurity Action Team (or F-BAT). The team is comprised of FSIS officials who are coordinating efforts to protect our meat and poultry supply through several initiatives, such as:

- assessing potential vulnerabilities along the farm-to-table continuum;
- strengthening coordination and cooperation with law enforcement agencies;
- enhancing security features at all FSIS laboratories, and increasing their capacity to test for additional food safety hazards and biological agents; and
- developing guidelines for industry on food security and increased plant security, particularly in small and very small plants.

Public Symposium

In supporting these five goals, FSIS is hosting a series of scientific symposia, where leading scientists and other stakeholders will discuss a specific issue of significance. Our first symposium was in January, and it focused on epidemiology.

The next one is titled "Pathogen Reduction: A Scientific Dialogue," and it will be held on May 6–7 right here in Washington at the Georgetown University Conference Center. Leading public health experts from government and academia will meet and generate new ideas for strengthening the effectiveness of HACCP, microbial testing, performance standards, pathogen-reduction interventions, and inspection at this meeting.

This meeting is open to the public, and it promises to be a great opportunity for a frank discussion of various important issues, so I encourage you to make every effort to attend!

In closing, I hope this brief discussion of USDA's food safety mission area has been helpful. I have enjoyed the opportunity to talk to you this morning. Now, in the time remaining, I would like to open up the table for any questions or comments you might have.

VI. Stem Cell Research and Cloning

Keeping the Faith[1]

Carl B. Feldbaum

President, Biotechnology Industry Organization (BIO), Washington, DC, 1993– ; A.B., Princeton University, 1966; LL.B., University of Pennsylvania Law School, 1969; assistant district attorney, Philadelphia, PA, 1970–73; assistant special prosecutor, Watergate Special Prosecution Force, Washington, DC, 1973–75; inspector general for defense intelligence, U.S. Department of Defense, 1976–79; assistant to secretary of energy, U.S. Department of Energy, 1979–80; president, Palomar Corporation, Washington, DC, 1980–87; vice president for planning, System Planning Corporation, Roslyn, VA, 1987–88; administrative assistant and chief of staff to U.S. Senator Arlen Specter, 1988–93; Distinguished Civilian Service Medal, 1979; Christopher Medal for Looking the Tiger in the Eye: Confronting the Nuclear Threat, *designated by the* New York Times *as a notable book of 1988; Best of Biotech 1995, awarded by 140 biotechnology CEOs; APEX '96 Award for Publication Excellence.*

Editors' introduction: BIO is committed to the socially responsible use of biotechnology to save or improve lives, improve the quality and abundance of food, and clean up hazardous wastes. It represents more than 1,000 biotechnology companies, academic institutions, state biotechnology centers, and related organizations in 50 U.S. states and 33 other nations while encouraging discussion of the ethical and social implications of scientific developments in biotechnology research. In that spirit, Mr. Carl B. Feldbaum explained that the "scientific method is not antithetical to religious conviction, and that religious principles can give greater meaning to the work of the scientist." This plenary and welcoming address was presented via videotape to some 3,500 senior international biotech executives, scientists, and international delegates attending the BIO Convention, as a family emergency prevented President Feldbaum from attending in person.

Carl B. Feldbaum's speech: Ladies and gentlemen. Islam has the Qur'an. Christianity has the Gospels. Judaism has the Torah. Now we, many here in this room, have gone up the mountain and come down with what: the map of the human genome.

---

1. Delivered on June 25, 2001, at San Diego, CA, early afternoon. Reprinted with permission of Carl B. Feldbaum.

Well, let me pretend to be your prophet for a few minutes. I have a warning for you: Do not bow down to this. Let's not confuse the profundities of science with the depths of faith. As an industry, and as individuals, we will have to work intimately with both.

Assembled here in San Diego this week are the explorers of our small but expanding universe. Allow me to say that the technology you have achieved is remarkable. The technology you will be talking about this week is astounding, and its intended uses are compassionate. Our temptation is to tell people: "Wait till you see what we have for you! We are going to change your lives for the better. Feel free to show your gratitude any time now."

And somehow: All of them are not entirely grateful. Many are suspicious. Some are even angry.

It's not that folks reject your valuable achievements. And this isn't the stereotyped confrontation between scientists and so-called Luddites. It is, for the most part, a lack of trust and a lack of communication between our industry and people of good faith, many of them people of deep faith. And the costs to our industry and global society will only grow unless we work with these people, to the fullest extent possible.

As president of BIO, I hear their questions. Recently, I've been asked:

- Carl, what is BIO's position on what day of development a human embryo gets a soul?

- Will gene therapy lead to a brave new world of genetically engineered kids who can do advanced calculus by five and run four-minute miles soon thereafter?

- Is it morally right to develop animals so we can mine them for replacement body parts?

- How does biotechnology change our place in the universe—are we usurping God by attempting to improve upon God's creatures?

- And finally, can we trust any human beings with such power?

My talk today is on "Keeping the Faith." I want to cover religion and science, scriptures and the Constitution, revolution and faith—in the next 20 minutes. Am I crazy or what?

Crazy or not, we have no choice but to address these issues. And we will need to keep addressing them long after my 20 minutes are up.

I believe the fundamental truth to keep in mind is this: Science is a method, not a faith, and the two are not mutually exclusive. I do not need to point to the many leading figures in biotechnology who also are firm believers in God and adherents of various religions. They are not hypocrites. They do not keep their faith in a little box for use only on weekends and holidays.

They have come to understand, and I count myself among them, that scientific method is not antithetical to religious conviction, and that religious principles can give greater meaning to the work of the scientist. Albert Einstein put it well when he said, "Science without religion is lame. Religion without science is blind." In any case, I see no point whatsoever in standing on either side of the chasm between science and faith and shouting across: "You're wrong! You've got it all wrong!"

> *Science is a method, not a faith, and the two are not mutually exclusive.*

Let me tell you about a group BIO met with recently in a semi-rural community in Virginia.

Most were Protestant and socially conservative, but on the whole this was a typical group of middle-class American adults, ranging in age from their late twenties to a few in their mid-sixties. They watch TV shows like *Survivor*, *The Sopranos* and *Will & Grace*; they pay the mortgage; a few play golf; most have kids and pets, and some have grandchildren. We asked to meet with them because all of them identified themselves as deeply religious. They attend church regularly and say that God is very important in their lives.

You'll be happy to know that most of them also turned out to have a favorable impression of biotechnology. They associated our industry primarily with advances in medical care and cures for life-threatening diseases. One participant said: "Anything to improve society, to improve medicine, I'm for." A couple of people mentioned that day's FDA approval of a targeted medication for leukemia. So we can see that the tangible achievements of our industry mean more to people than the alarms raised by critics who attempt to portray us as either "godless" or "playing God."

When we asked these people about the insertion of new genes—gene therapy—most were apprehensive but willing to keep an open mind. Several said they didn't want to interfere with "God's plan" and would rather deal with the consequences of disease than try such therapies, but others took no issue with gene therapy. Concerns centered on what some considered eugenic applications: They don't want biotechnology used at IVF clinics to design made-to-order children. Neither do we.

Xenotransplantation—the transfer of cells or organs, hearts, livers or lungs, for example, from one species to another—was considered more acceptable, as a way to deal with our dramatic shortage of organ donors.

There was a discussion about our distinction between reproductive and therapeutic cloning. Even the most accepting people in the group rejected the concept of experiments and therapies that involve destroying embryos. One young mother said: "The embryo is where I draw the line." For the record, BIO opposes the use of cloning technology for reproductive purposes. We believe the safety, ethical, and moral issues require us to draw the line—and to continue our self-imposed moratorium on the implantation of a cloned embryo. At the same time we have urged the Bush administration and Congress to allow the therapeutic cloning of cells, genes, and tissues that do not lead to the birth of a child. This has been a tough distinction to make with many politicians.

And yet, the idea of therapeutic cloning is no longer so alarming to people, despite years of talk from our critics and decades of creepy movies on late-night TV. In our focus group session, Len, a diabetic in his fifties, said: "I don't have any nerves in my feet. I can walk on needles and not feel it. And I have wounds that won't heal. So if they could do something to clone or develop a new pancreas for me, then, yes, I would be for some type of cloning."

Regarding embryonic stem cell research, one of the staunchest opponents in our meeting—a mother in her thirties who said she would never consider stem-cell-based therapy for her own arthritis—said her reservations would go out the window if the health or life of one of her children were at stake. Almost everyone in the group agreed.

Finally, we had an older woman in the group, Janet, who said flatly that all cloning and embryo research were wrong. She recounted how, many years ago, she gave birth to a son who died after only a week from a lung disease. She said that she would not have used a therapy based on stem cells or cloning to save this much loved child, whose birthday she still marks, along with the anniversary of his death. She said: "If they could have changed anything, I still would have let God have His way, but the doctor is not God."

We may never win over Janet. We will never win over Jehovah's Witnesses on blood transfusions, either. It would be foolish and arrogant of us to say that people must abandon the positions dictated by their faith.

A science teacher in a small Missouri town once described to a reporter how she taught evolution, crafting her approach with sensitivity toward religious concerns without shortchanging the science. She told her students a bit about Charles Darwin, who studied to become a minister but was deeply interested in nature. She described the scientific discussions of his time about how plants and animals could change over generations. She talked about what he saw during his five-year voyage on the *Beagle* after he graduated from college, and how he came to the revolutionary idea that natural selection for favorable traits could account, over long periods, for the evolution of new species. She assured these students, these children of strict Christian fundamentalism, that Darwin was not looking to attack anyone's religious beliefs—that he worried about the distress many people felt over the revolutionary nature of his theory.

And when he was vilified, in fact, his greatest anguish came from the pain inflicted on his deeply religious wife. Finally, this teacher described how the discoveries in the decades since *The Origin of Species*—in geology, paleontology, genetics, and other fields—reinforced Darwin's basic premise. The particulars had to be revised, but scientists no longer doubted that Darwin was right.

As for whether these students would accept it as well—that was up to them. The teacher was not going to attack the faith of her friends and neighbors, and she would not look for some way to keep her students from hearing beliefs that conflicted with her science. But she was determined that these children learn about evolution.

Her story brings to mind another small-town science teacher: John Scopes. Why couldn't he have done his job in the obscurity of Dayton, Tennessee—and been forgotten? Because the fundamentalists of his era chose to attack science through the legislature. Science is alive only when it can be taught and discussed, and Tennessee outlawed the teaching of evolution. Scopes agreed to serve as the test case. Never mind that he was convicted—that was guaranteed, and an appeals court threw out his hundred-dollar fine. What mattered was that his spectacular trial crystallized in the public's mind the folly of letting the church dictate to the state and restrain the teaching of science. What is also clear, at least in the United States, is that we can no more impose a complete separation of church and laboratory then we can a complete separation of church and   state.

But when people understand what's at stake, even deeply religious individuals will frequently be on the side of scientific inquiry and discussion, and so will the United States Constitution.

Let me again drop back in time, and say a few words about Galileo's run-in with religion. It's actually quite instructive. Galileo stirred the rage of Pope Urban VII with his 1632 publication of a treatise called the *Dialogue of the Great World Systems, Ptolemaic and Copernican*. The very basic idea—Copernicus's theory that the earth circled the sun, rather than vice versa—was already in circulation and was hardly revolutionary. Galileo's chief offense appears to have been arrogance: Although a devoted Catholic, instead of a dialogue, Galileo initiated a diatribe in which he knew he would have the pleasure—based on science—of trouncing the naysayers. Such pleasures are dearly bought. He ended up under house arrest, and the church banned his so-called *Dialogue* until 1822, almost two centuries later. Now here we are in the middle of our own revolution—an extension of Darwin's, and as profound as Galileo's. We ought to expect a certain amount of opposition and suspicion from defenders of established social and religious doctrines. We can get a taste of that opposition and suspicion right outside this building.

But the world has changed for the better: No one's going to put us under house arrest for our work, as the Vatican did with Galileo. No one in biotech risks being burned at the stake for cloning a sheep or mapping a human chromosome. And it would be inhumane to ban knowledge of our discoveries for even two weeks, much less two centuries, as were Galileo's, because desperately ill patients deserve hope—and knowledge of new therapeutic options.

Instead of all that, we have even people of faith ready to support us, at least to some extent, and discuss their differences with us. For them, keeping the faith includes engaging in the issues of the day and bringing their perspective to bear. When we came down from that mountain with the map of the human genome on a Web site, there were bishops and imams and rabbis celebrating the triumph of human achievement and the prospect of relief to some human suffering.

Just two weeks ago, I met with a group of religious leaders ranging from a Baptist preacher and a Greek Orthodox priest to heads of national religious organizations to academic theologians. They were eager to join our discussion of the increasing intersection between biomedical research and religion.

We have even people of faith ready to support us, at least to some extent, and discuss their differences with us.

As a group, we pursued questions that touch on the fundamentals of the human scientific endeavor: Are science and scientific applications inherently flawed processes because the human beings behind this work are flawed? How much can humans ever know and understand? Are humans morally equipped to handle the great power conferred by technology and, specifically, biotechnology?

One participant said, "Christianity sees human beings as morally imperfect. We are corrupt and continuously corruptible." Thus, just as the scientific method embraces skepticism about the superficial appearances of nature, so does religion about the superficial appearances of human nature.

One theologian was particularly struck by the revelation in February that the human genome has only about 30,000 genes, a number that seems insufficient to account for the complexity of a human being. "A theological approach says that God has created an incredible ecology even at the level of the genome," he said. "Everything relates to everything. A lot of our environmental and agricultural models haven't fully appreciated that."

The group also shared passionate economic and social concerns about biotechnology. They wanted to know who benefits from our work and how we can manage the industry to ensure its advantages do not accrue just to the wealthiest nations or individuals.

As we wrapped up the meeting, the pastors and the academics were bubbling with ideas, many of them grass-roots-level proposals—writing Sunday school curricula on bioethics, educating seminarians, getting seminarians and clergy into our labs to get a more tangible understanding for these matters.

Medical biotech is hardly the only area where we can develop productive discussions with religious leaders and their followers. Consider the biotech solutions on the market and in the works for industrial pollution and waste; we would be fools not to explore the common cause we have with those who devote themselves to the biblical injunction to be good stewards of the earth. With agricultural biotech, we can safely intensify the production of crops for food, fibers, fuel and building materials. Doesn't the Bible tell us to feed the hungry, clothe the naked and shelter the dispossessed?

Our goals are simply to alleviate suffering: to treat and cure Alzheimer's, Parkinson's, breast and cervical cancers, and allow

---

Just as religious leaders recognize their responsibility to learn about biotechnology, we have a responsibility to work with them, to educate them and to learn from them.

---

many nations represented here to provide more than the barest levels of nutrition to their populations. Florence Wambugu of Kenya says, so simply and eloquently, "Those who protest biotechnology do so with a full belly."

Ninety-five percent of Americans surveyed in a Gallup poll this spring said they believe in God, 68 percent reported membership in a church, and 65 percent said religion answers problems. U.S. policymakers cannot ignore two-thirds of the public. Neither can our industry.

When Congress considers sweeping bills to ban human cloning, we need to reach people of faith and discuss the distinction between its reproductive and therapeutic applications—and the ethical objections they and we have. When the president withholds money for stem cell research that carries such great promise in treating Parkinson's, Alzheimer's, spinal cord damage, and other grave health problems, we need to discuss the competing moral issues as broadly as possible.

We will never overcome all objections and satisfy every concern. Fear of the unknown is powerful and persistent, and so we hear protests over biotech foods long after they are proved safe. We can't simply dismiss people's misgivings: There's something primal in people's relationship with their food, their bodies, and we should be thoughtful in responding to that.

Then there stands a principle: A devout Buddhist who would not countenance the killing of animals—even vermin—would find animal testing and the harvesting of animal organs reprehensible. As I said earlier, there is a fundamental difference between faith and science, and good science cannot follow all religious dictates.

I also know—from years of experience—that a lot of people in this industry and in this room enjoy a good argument, a good controversy. We succeed in part because we embrace mavericks, because we are mavericks. The prospect of consultation and consensus building on ethical and public policy questions isn't all that exciting. Yet it must be done. Just as religious leaders recognize their responsibility to learn about biotechnology, we have a responsibility to work with them, to educate them and to learn from them.

The companies, universities, foundations, and governments that support us have given us the chance to do this amazing, exciting science, and get paid for it, with the understanding that we will use this gift responsibly. That means being responsible in choosing which research to pursue—and which to forgo. That means being responsible in the conduct of that research, and then in the marketing and even more important, in the access to our technologies and products.

Our revolution is about more than science. Make no mistake, it touches the whole earth, potentially every individual, and we have to keep faith with global society. Only then will we be doing our jobs and delivering on the promise of our distinct revolution, which so far, we can all be very, very proud of.

At the very end of my meeting two weeks ago with the religious leaders and theologians, the former head of a prestigious seminary who is now leader of a national alliance of churches stated, "This has been a timely, significant meeting; I think we should look at it as the first second of a 24-hour discussion. We've got to lift this to scale." He said, "We don't want to go away today, on June 13, 2001, and then come back together in 2007 to have lunch together again. Yes, there are crazies on the right and left, and there are anarchists. But there is a core of thoughtful people who are religious, and we need to start a new wave of conversation. What you do is too important, too central to the human condition."

Ladies and gentlemen, let that conversation come up to scale right here, right now in San Diego, and let us continue forever to keep that faith.

Thank you.

Testimony at the Hearing on Stem Cell Research[2]

James R. Langevin

U.S. Congressman from Rhode Island (Democrat), 2000– ; born Providence, RI, April 22, 1964; bachelor's degree, Rhode Island College, 1990; master's in public adminstration, Kennedy School of Government, Harvard University, 1994; intern for Senator Claiborne Pell, Rhode Island State House; secretary, Rhode Island's Constitutional Convention, 1986; state representative, City of Warwick, RI, 1988–94; secretary of state, RI, 1995–2000; board of directors, Rhode Island American Red Cross, Tech Access, The Warwick Shelter, Rhode Island March of Dimes, and PARI Independent Living Center of Pawtucket, RI; member, Knights of Columbus, Lions Club, and Save the Bay.

Editors' introduction: On August 9, 2001, President George W. Bush approved federal funding for embryonic stem cell research that would be limited to existing stem cell lines. The ethical implications and medical benefits of studying embryonic stem cells were being increasingly debated throughout American society, with some, including Representative James Langevin of Rhode Island, arguing for more extensive research than the president proposed. Mr. Langevin, who had suffered a severe spinal chord injury when he was 16, was the first quadriplegic elected to the U.S. Congress. He therefore offered a unique perspective at a hearing on stem cell research before the U.S. Senate Committee on Health, Education, Labor, and Pensions. "Frustrated with the discovery of just how little room" President Bush's ruling "leaves for medical advancement," Mr. Langevin advocated "open[ing] the door to research on all excess embryonic stem cells derived from in vitro fertilization, and to do so with government oversight that ensures ethical research procedures."

James R. Langevin's speech: I would like to thank Chairman Kennedy, Senator Gregg, and the entire HELP committee for convening today's hearing on stem cell research. I am honored to join Senator Specter, Secretary Thompson, and these eminent cellular biologists in shedding light on the ramifications of President Bush's August 9 decision.

---

2. Delivered on September 5, 2001, at Washington, D.C.

The issue we face today is not whether to move forward with embryonic stem cell research, but how. How do we ensure that all unnecessary barriers to the research and development of lifesaving cures are removed, how do we establish parameters that provide ethical oversight of this most delicate issue, and how do we help as many people as possible as expediently as possible? Unfortunately, today these questions are being answered in the context of a policy that impedes the potential of this nation's leading scientists.

As many of you know, on November 7 last year, I became the first quadriplegic elected to Congress. While my physical condition does not define me, it does affect me on a daily basis, providing me with a unique perspective on stem cell research.

At the age of 16, I spent my summer vacation participating in the Warwick police cadet program. I had dreamed of being a police officer or an FBI agent my entire life. But on August 22, 1980, my dream was shattered. I stood in a locker room with a fellow cadet watching two members of the SWAT team examine a handgun. It accidentally discharged, launching a bullet that ricocheted off a metal locker and into my neck, severing my spinal cord and leaving me paralyzed for life—perhaps until now.

> *The issue we face today is not whether to move forward with embryonic stem cell research, but how.*

While embryonic stem cell research could give me the chance to walk again, please understand that I am here today not just for myself, but to alleviate the pain and suffering of millions of people whose lives could be saved, lengthened and dramatically improved by this research. Nearly half of all Americans could benefit from embryonic stem cell research, including 1 million children with juvenile diabetes, 8.2 million people with cancer, 60 million people struggling with heart disease, 4 million Alzheimer's sufferers, 10 million people fighting osteoporosis, 43 million arthritis sufferers, 230,000 people with spinal cord injury, and 30,000 Lou Gehrig's disease patients. Every family in America has been touched by these diseases and conditions, and now we have the opportunity to offer them real hope.

That is why I support using stem cells derived from excess frozen embryos that otherwise would be discarded to save, extend and improve lives. Every year hundreds of thousands of couples experience the joy of childbirth through in vitro fertilization, a process which necessarily creates more embryos than can be used. To relegate these potentially lifesaving cells to the trash heap after the arbitrary deadline of August 9 is simply wrong.

While I applaud the door President Bush opened with the new embryonic stem cell policy, I am frustrated with the discovery of just how little room it leaves for medical advancement. Despite NIH's recent disclosure of the 64 stem cell lines that existed before August 9, we are now learning that they are not all "robust" as once claimed, and some of these cells are still in development and cannot yet be classified as lines. Questions about the safety of using the cells in human trials are also surfacing because many researchers have mixed human cell lines with mouse cells, which poses the risk of infecting people with animal viruses. Finally, irrespective of the president's guidelines for the existing embryonic stem cell lines, the private sector in the United States, as well as the public and private sectors abroad, will continue to conduct research on stem cells that fall outside of the parameters established by the Bush administration.

What will we do when an embryonic stem cell derived from the in vitro fertilization process after August 9 leads to a cure for heart disease, the number one cause of death in this country? Will we deny 60 million Americans this life-saving cure? And worse, what if such a cure is found through the morally offensive procedure of creating embryos purely for harvesting stem cells? We must fund research on other cell lines besides the 64 cell lines identified by NIH, and we must provide strong oversight of this research to ensure that it is conducted by ethical means that do not force us to wrestle with similar moral quandaries in the future.

The administration's policy impedes unprecedented, life-saving research and raises critical ethical dilemmas that we must not ignore. Because embryonic stem cell research cannot deliver on its promise of therapeutic benefit for millions of people under this policy, I am compelled to oppose it. I understand the struggle to balance a prolife position with embryonic stem cell research. This was one of the most difficult decisions I've ever made. Having come so close to losing my own life, I am reminded every day of how precious a gift life is. And that is why I am prolife.

However, nothing is more life-affirming than using what otherwise would be disposed of to save, extend and improve countless lives. I urge my colleagues to open the door to research on all excess embryonic stem cells derived from in vitro fertilization, and to do so with government oversight that ensures ethical research procedures.

Thank you, Mr. Chairman.

Testimony at the Hearing on Human Cloning[3]

Stuart A. Newman

Professor of Cell Biology and Anatomy, New York Medical College, Valhalla, NY, 1979– ; born New York City, April 1945; A.B., Columbia University, 1965; Ph.D., chemical physics, University of Chicago, 1970; INSERM Fellow, Pasteur Institute, Paris, 1984; Fogarty Senior International Fellow, Monash University, Melbourne, Australia, 1989; visiting scientist, French Atomic Energy Center, Saclay, 1992, Indian Institute of Science, Bangalore, 1998, and University of Tokyo, 2001; consultant to the U.S. National Institutes of Health on both technical and societal issues; founding member, Council for Responsible Genetics, Cambridge, MA; has contributed to the fields of biophysical chemistry, developmental biology, and evolutionary theory; has also written on the social implications of biological research.

Editors' introduction: Stuart A. Newman testified at a hearing before the U.S. Senate Committee on Health, Education, Labor, and Pensions. The Senate committee's concerns were the dangers of cloning and the promise of regenerative medicine. The hearing was occasioned by the introduction of bills before the Senate and House of Representatives to enact bans on human cloning. Some 200 persons present at the hearing included senators and their staffs, journalists, scientists, public interest advocates, students, and representatives of the health care and biotechnology industries. The testimony was carried by C-SPAN. Professor Newman predicted that "cloning embryos for producing embryo stem cells will, by failing to deliver on its promises, inevitably lead to calls to extend the lifespan of clonal embryos so as to permit harvesting developmentally more advanced cells and tissues for research and potential therapies . . . up to and including full term clones from which to harvest organs."

Stuart A. Newman's testimony: My name is Stuart Newman. I have been a professor of cell biology and anatomy at New York Medical College since 1979, where I teach medical and graduate students and direct a laboratory in developmental biology. This is the scientific field that studies embryo development, cloning, regeneration, and stem cells. My work on the development of form and pat-

---

3. Delivered on March 5, 2002, at Washington, D.C., mid-afternoon in the Hart Senate Office Building. Reprinted with permission of Stuart A. Newman.

tern in animal embryos has been supported over the past 25 years by grants from the National Science Foundation and the National Institutes of Health. I am currently the recipient of two Federal grants.

Since my student days I have also been concerned with the uses to which scientific research is put. Having become convinced that scientists, who are beneficiaries of public resources, have a deep responsibility to anticipate what lies down the road in their own fields and to serve as a resource for the public on the complex issues around applications of scientific research, I joined with other scientists, social scientists, women's rights advocates, and environmentalists to found the Council for Responsible Genetics in the late 1970s. The Council is now the Nation's oldest organization scrutinizing and interpreting the new genetic technologies, and has worked to educate the public on the scientific and social hazards of proposals to introduce inheritable genetic modifications into humans, including the allied technology of human cloning. I have placed into the record several documents from the Council that relate to the issues at hand, including the Genetic Bill of Rights, which affirms, in part, that "All people have the right to have been conceived, gestated, and born without genetic manipulation."

I will state from the outset that I, and the Council for Responsible Genetics as an organization, unequivocally support a woman's right to make her own reproductive decisions. Therefore, while what I am here to tell you today calls into question technologies that manipulate, clone, and genetically alter human embryos, these views do not derive from any notion of the sanctity of the embryo, nor from attributing to it the status of a human being. Rather, our concerns derive from two distinct sources: (1) the irresponsible promotion of another scientifically questionable biotechnology, in conformity with what is now a recurrent pattern of playing to investors' hopes and patients' desperation; (2) the destructive social consequences of moving down the technological path that begins with embryo cloning.

Specifically, cloning embryos for producing embryo stem cells will, by failing to deliver on its promises, inevitably lead to calls to extend the lifespan of clonal embryos so as to permit harvesting developmentally more advanced cells and tissues for research and potential therapies. The same well-intentioned imperatives that make some of you unwilling to deny patients who hope for relief by means of embryo stem cells will make you, or your successors, susceptible to demands for increased access to improved products of this work, up to and including full term clones from which to harvest organs.

I will try to lay out how this will happen. Embryo stem cells are derived from embryos that are less than two weeks old—the now proverbial "clump of cells in the bottom of a Petri dish." If derived from a clonal embryo resulting from transfer into an egg of a patient's somatic cell nucleus, the stem cells will be a genetic match for the nuclear donor. Transplants derived from such stem cells will be compatible with the immune system of these patients. Please note, however, that this will be of little advantage to patients with type 1 diabetes, whose condition causes them to immunologically reject their own insulin-producing cells.

While such genetically matched cells may be tolerated by patients with other conditions, there are still likely problems. Two decades of research on embryo stem cells in genetically compatible mice has yielded a handful of studies with modest therapeutic results—in all cases less than what has been achieved with grafts of nonembryonic cells. Despite great efforts, embryo stem cells never become just one cell type or coherent tissue, but differentiate into disorganized mixtures of cell types. Most importantly, they are genetically unstable. If placed in adult mice they cause tumors. There is every reason to believe that human embryo stem cells, including those from cloned embryos, would cause cancer in human patients.

To overcome this, if it is indeed possible, will take years of research. Some say it's worth a try, and scientists and companies with patents on this technology are willing to make the attempt. However, science and medicine always gravitate toward better technologies. In fact, Dr. John Gearhart of Johns Hopkins University has isolated a different kind of human stem cell. These are derived from the developing gonads of 8–9-week human embryos, and could be obtained after elective abortion. Like the embryo stem cells, these so-called embryo germ cells can differentiate into all cell types. Most importantly, when transplanted into experimental animals they do not cause cancer.

On purely scientific grounds, embryo germ cells show greater promise than embryo stem cells. Now, if they were derived from clonal embryos they would be nearly perfect, again in a purely scientific sense. But interestingly, none of the advocates of permitting embryo cloning has raised the specter of growing clonal embryos for 8 to 9 weeks so that genetically matched embryo germ cells could be harvested. These embryos would, of course, no longer be clumps of cells in a Petri dish, and some supporters of embryo cloning here might object. Right now it would be a hot potato, but once we have clonal embryos for a while and have gotten used to the idea, who would turn a deaf ear to calls by patients and their loved ones for these superior therapeutics?

And once stem cell harvesting from two-month clonal embryos was in place, who could resist the pleas to extend the time-frame so that liver and bone marrow could be obtained from six-month clonal fetuses to cure sufferers of life-threatening blood disorders such as beta-thalassemia, or so that brain lining cells could be harvested from near-term fetuses to treat Parkinson's sufferers?

I emphasize that all of this makes perfectly good scientific and medical sense. The only thing that stands in the way is a sense of propriety concerning the uses to which developing human embryos and fetuses may be put. Some of you may draw the line at the tiny clump of cells; others at the two-month embryo; still others somewhat short of full-term. Wherever each of you decides to leave this particular train, there will be others who will assert their right to take it to the next station. After Dolly the sheep was cloned, a British scientist suggested, tongue-in-cheek, that inactivation of brain-inducing genes could be used to produce headless full-term human clones for organ harvesting. To his surprise, Britain's most prominent embryologist publicly replied, "Why not?" Short of saying no to embryo cloning, any line that you draw will be a moving boundary. Few in this room would go along with the more extreme possibilities, but what about future generations growing up in a world in which producing clonal embryos for spare parts is medicine as usual?

Not only this, but the scientific publications that will ensue if embryo cloning proceeds will enable those reckless individuals who have announced their intention to make full-term clones, and then genetically-"improved" clones, to do so. Those who think that han-

---

What about future generations growing up in a world in which producing clonal embryos for spare parts is medicine as usual?

---

dling clonal embryos as controlled substances in regulated laboratories will stop the transfer of the technology do not understand how science works.

This is my prediction: if embryo cloning is permitted, within a few years frustration over lack of progress in producing safe and effective therapeutics from embryo stem cells will lead to calls to permit harvesting of embryo germ cells from 2–3-month clonal embryos, and we may all find ourselves here again. The rest will be just a matter of time. But there are other possibilities. Stem cells derived from adult tissues and umbilical cord blood have already proved to be effective therapeutics in animal models and in clinical trials. There is less commercial interest around them since it is difficult to obtain patents on a patient's own cells. Correspondingly, however, these cells are immunologically compatible with the patient from whom they are derived. It will take much additional work to make this technology practical, but scientifically, and societally, I am convinced that this is the way to go.

Biotechnology and the Struggle for Human Dignity

Whatever Happened to the Human Race?[4]

Nigel M. de S. Cameron

Director, Council for Biotechnology Policy, and Dean, of Charles W. Colson's Wilberforce Forum; a naturalized citizen, born in the United Kingdom, living in Deerfield, IL; founder of the prolife journal Ethics & Medicine: An International Journal of Bioethics, *1983, and the Center for Bioethics and Human Dignity, Bannockburn, IL, 1994; helped found Americans to Ban Cloning, 2001; former provost and distinguished professor, Trinity International University, Deerfield, IL; consultant in ethics and public policy issues in the United States and United Kingdom; bioethics advisor on the U.S. delegation to the United Nations meeting on human cloning, 2002; has debated cloning on ABC's* Nightline *and testified before Congressional and Senate committees; authored* Abortion: The Crisis in Morals and Medicine *(1986) and* The New Medicine: Life and Death After Hippocrates *(1992); edited* Is Life Really Sacred? *and* Death Without Dignity.

Editors' introduction: Nigel Cameron, a widely acknowledged spokesman for the Judeo-Christian tradition in medicine and bioethics, addressed some 600 delegates during the opening general session of the 30th annual National Right to Life Committee Convention. Attending were grassroots volunteers and local, state, and national leaders of the right-to-life movement. Dr. Cameron has worked with political progressives, including prochoice and environmental leaders, in building a consensus against cloning and what they maintain are other biotech assaults on human dignity. In his speech, Dr. Cameron cautioned, "We now have power not simply to kill or to prevent procreation or to decide which man and which woman should join together . . . . We are now taking to ourselves powers that were designed to give us full design capacity over our own nature." The response to Dr. Cameron's speech was reported to have been excellent and served as a motivational springboard to the three-day-long convention.

Nigel M. de S. Cameron's speech:

---

4. Delivered on June 27, 2002, at Pittsburg, PA, in a hotel ballroom at 10:00 A.M. Reprinted with permission of Nigel M. de S. Cameron.

The Dolly Agenda

Dolly the sheep—the most famous sheep in the history of the world, the sheep who made all the newsmagazines—was born just a few miles from my former home in Edinburgh, a great Scottish contribution to the problems facing humankind. With the announcement back in February of 1997, five years ago, that a mammal had been cloned, we learned that a second front had been opened in the struggle—the worldwide struggle—for human dignity. Of course, as soon as the announcement had been made that a sheep had been cloned, nobody went on ABC *Nightline* to say, "Is it a good thing to clone *sheep*?"

We have long recognized that, in technology after technology, the firebreak between animals and humans is narrow. It may take a generation for it to be jumped, as happened with artificial insemination developing into in vitro. It may take much less.

Euthanasia, of course, is a classic example of standard fare in veterinary medicine now being applied to humans. And so as soon as Dolly the sheep was cloned, the question was, "Is this a good thing for *us*?"—because at the end of the day, if you can do it in an animal, you can do it to us. And if you have done it in an animal, there will be someone, somewhere who wants to do it to us.

In technology after technology, the firebreak between animals and humans is narrow.

As we look back over the precursor technology—the technologies that paved the way for this technology and these debates: artificial insemination, in vitro, that whole complex of questions, paving the way for this "new and improved" method of making human beings—(we remember) those old methods involved using human gametes, mimicking the natural processes. Here we have a whole new way to make a mammal in which asexual reproduction, reproduction without sex—copy shop reproduction—can be applied to one of our species. The significance of that announcement made five years ago, as we look back on it—as perhaps a hundred years we look back on it—will be seen as momentous, because with that announcement of what these scientists had done at this little place in Scotland at a little research institute that nobody had every heard of, an announcement that nobody was expecting, the second front was opened in the war on human dignity. And its implications have hardly begun to unfold.

Who would have guessed that less than 30 years after *Roe* let loose the dogs of war on our unborn, this new marriage of bioscience and the hubris—the overweening self-confidence—of human beings in their delight in manipulating their own nature—that these purveyors of a new view of human dignity would be setting the agenda and be drawing all of us into enormously complex, and hugely fateful, questions for the future of the human race itself?

Peter Singer Clears the Ground

Two weeks ago I was in Oakland, California, having a debate with the bioethicist Peter Singer. Peter Singer is a most engaging man, one of the most pleasant people you could meet. He's a vegetarian; he follows his principles; he gives away a lot of his money. And when you go into the room with him, a cold shiver goes down your spine. You and I have been saying all of our lives as we get into these debates,—"If you do this to the unborn baby, you will do it to the born baby." There really are discontinuities, but they are small when you compare them with the continuity. All that stuff we go around saying, he says, "You know, you're right!"

In front of 600 people, with demonstrators outside trying to stop people getting in, handicapped people, animal rights people—it was quite an occasion—he actually said, "If you can kill the handicapped child before it's born, then why don't give the parents a year to decide whether they want to have their handicapped child live, after it's born? It makes sense to me."

One of the prolife feminists in the audience—it was a very mixed audience—came up to one of my friends later in the evening and said, "You know, I think he has convinced me I can't support abortion." So Singer is a very unusual propagandist for the prolife cause!

He follows the argument to its logical conclusion, because, Peter Singer says, there is nothing special about being human. He clears the ground. The only thing that is special is what you can do: reason, consciousness, communication. And he says chimpanzees have a lot of this stuff and newborn babies don't.

We were asked in this debate by the moderator Michael Krasny, who is a radio personality in the Bay area, what it was we agreed on. I turned to Peter and said, "The one thing we agree on is that almost everybody in these bioethics discussions stands somewhere between where I am standing and where you are standing, and we both agree they are all inconsistent, and they are all wrong."

And I said, "I know that much controversy attended your coming to Princeton a number of years ago. I have to tell you, and as a utilitarian you will appreciate this, that I think there is great utility in having you involved in this debate because you put into words what the people who stand between me and you try to cover up."

I know there was all that protest about his coming to Princeton—and, from one point of view, it is appalling that our major universities will give a platform to someone whose ideas are so subversive to our vision of human dignity. On the other hand, Peter Singer clarifies the issues.

I was on a Christian radio program with him some years ago. He said he'd never before been on a Christian radio program so he was somewhat out of his depth. And the presenter began by saying, "Dr. Cameron, we've had you on before. You tell us what to think, about all of these things. You tell us what you think about Dr. Singer's latest book," And I said, "I don't want to say very much today. I want you to listen to him, because if I told you what he thought, you wouldn't believe me."

Now, you see, Peter Singer is, in a sense, wrapping up the logic of the old debate about what it means to be human and whether we may take innocent human life. And he is saying what we have been saying all along. Either one accepts the indivisibility of human dignity: Everyone who is member of our species—however tiny, however damaged—must be treated as one who is a member of the human species. He accepts the logic of our position, and he says, "That is not the case because *being human doesn't matter*. It's what you can do which matters; it's how *mature* you are that matters; it's whether you are in a position to *reason*."

The New Debate: Bioethics II

On the ground of that old debate, nesting in that old debate, we have a whole new debate. And as I try to clarify these things for myself, and when I teach and when I write, I come up with my own new terminology—hardly rocket science, but I have called these debates Bioethics I and Bioethics II. It certainly enables me to summarize what I am saying.

Bioethics I is the old debate—if you like, the Singer debate, the debate about whether being human matters. It is the debate about whether we take innocent human life, the abortion debate, the euthanasia debate, and all sorts of connections.

Bioethics II is not about whether we may take innocent human life. It is about whether we may make human life; whether we may manipulate human life; whether we may use human life for our ends; whether we may have command and control mechanism to determine human life.

Now, how you weigh Bioethics I and Bioethics II against each other, I do not know. I was on James Dobson's radio program last summer. We did, I think, two shows on these questions as the stem cell debate and the cloning debate were really coming on the political horizon. And I said this, and I was interested because I tend to press my point, I tend to overstate, sometimes to offend the people who agree with me by the way in which I press the position. In fact, Dr. Dobson asked me to repeat my position two or three times to get it just right to go on air, and I said, "We are moving from killing human beings who were made in God's image to making human beings in our own image, and it is by no means clear which of these is the greater crime." If you put yourself in God's position, and you look down on those who commit the old high crime of Cain and Abel—the crime of taking innocent human life—and on those who commit the new crimes of human hubris and bioscience—the crimes, if you like, of the Tower of Babel—I think there is no better image of the biotechnology industry than the building of that great tower to reach up to heaven and the power it will bring.

I think we see two sets of crimes against God and man. And we need to realize it is by no means clear that to take human life is worse to God than to make it. To seize hold of the Creator's role and determine for yourself what life shall be like is something we have hardly begun to consider.

> *It is by no means clear that to take human life is worse to God than to make it.*

And so in our civilization with its changing assumptions, its shifting loyalties, its ever moving worldview that threatens to go into moral free fall, we find the scientist and the venture capitalist coming together in a whole new project that will give us powers to do evil, as well as powers to do good—which we have never had before and which most of us had never before thought we could have. And so we come to terms with the implications of the birth of a sheep that will define a culture.

It was said that the one thing the Nazis lacked in their eugenic program was the science to give them the manipulative powers to do what they wished to do and create human nature according to their plan. And of course, as you look back into the old eugenics movement, both the Nazi variety and the very "civilized" variety in the United States and the UK, where the whole thing had been intellectually based, there wasn't an awful lot they could do.

It was an amazing folk movement here in the United States. They would have fairs at county fair grounds, eugenic fairs where blue-eyed blondes would be given prizes. You could praise the people who were fit, and you could say bad things about those who were not. You could sterilize. So you could prevent people from reproducing what was regarded as "defective" human stock. But you had to wait generations for all this to work. And so when the Nazis got their blue-eyed, blonde-haired guys to father children by women who fit the Aryan model, this was a long-term project.

What we have now in the new development of cloning, and the new technologies that will follow cloning, is a higher power, in a dimension than we can scarcely begin to grasp, to achieve the eugenic agenda. We now have power not simply to kill or to prevent procreation or to decide which man and which woman should join together, which were the only powers available before. We are now taking to ourselves powers that were designed to give us full design capacity over our own nature. That is at the heart of the new Bioethics II. That is the significance of the announcement about Dolly the sheep, and that is our agenda as those who fight for the dignity of human life in this next generation.

Let me open this out. There are three distinct phases in what has begun to take place, three different stages which, of course, all overlap with Bioethics I—Peter Singer questions with the issue of whether we take human life—that issue doesn't go away, as well we know. But added to it we have this new layer of conversation. And the cloning issue has by fate, or in the providence of God, given us the overlay of these two questions. It's the bridge issue, the watershed between the old bioethics issue agenda and the new. And that is why it has such remarkable importance to us, drawing us into the education in the new questions, which alone will enable us to understand the most radical threat to human nature that the world has ever known.

These three phases are in Bioethics II, in this second front opened in the war on human dignity. The first is a simple principle of manufacture, and that is what cloning is. Cloning is turning procreation into manufacture: the making of human beings.

Now we know that there are two dimensions to the cloning discussion. First there is the production of embryonic human beings to be used for laboratory vivisection, for experimentation or so-called therapy. And that is the motive of those who are pressing, and pressing, and pressing either to be allowed to do this on the grand scale or, at least, to prevent any legislative action which would stop them. But we have these two thrusts: the desire to produce embryos on an industrial scale for experimentation and a covert desire, a largely hidden desire, specifically for the purpose of live-birth cloned babies. Secondly, at the moment, everybody is saying there is not one vote on Capitol Hill in favor of producing live-born cloned babies. And that may be true—at the moment.

In the last year I have engage in a series of debates with another engaging ethicist, Gregory Pence. If you want to read a pro-cloning book by someone who is unashamed in his commitment to cloning babies, read Greg Pence's book *Who's Aftaid of Cloning*? Clono-phobia, I suppose, is the concept here. We're all clono-phobics in this room.

We've done this debate on college campuses. We've done seven or eight in the last couple of years. And Greg Pence just says, "What's wrong with this? It's a reproductive rights issue. Let people make their choices." And I say, "What about the clone? Who asked the baby? Every child has a right not to be born a clone." He says, "What about the parents?" And I say, "What about the baby?"

It is said there are no votes in favor of so-called "reproductive cloning." It's a misnomer, of course. All cloning is reproductive. But in favor of live-born baby cloning, it is very interesting to see what is going on behind the scenes; because, for example, the congressional testimony of the American Society for Reproductive Medicine, which is the trade organization of the scientists, has been very plain. It is not, in principle, opposed to cloning human babies. It is opposed to it at this time because of the dangers to the woman and also to the child who might be born because the science has so many problems facing it. It takes no position on whether the birth of clonal babies is good or bad. And these are the guys in the trade.

It doesn't take a lot to gain some historical perspective on the way things change over time. Those of us who are always accused of slippery slope arguments now find it rather easy to look back just a few years and say, "Well, don't you think we've been sliding?"

Charles Krauthammer, the columnist, is quadriplegic. He is Jewish, a physician, a very interesting man. He has taken a view in favor of experimenting on embryo stem cells, but a vigorous view opposing using cloning to create those embryos. He makes a powerful argument against cloning. Last summer everyone on Capitol Hill was saying, "We want stem cells, but we do not want clonal stem cells." That was the push. Even leading prochoice Democrats were saying, "We do not want to use cloning to produce stem cells." Now, of course, things have changed. And so Krauthammer's comment was, "This isn't a slippery slope. It's downhill skiing."

We have to gain some perspective. The *Washington Post* back in the mid-'90s editorialized that to create human embryos for experimentation, as opposed to using so-called "spare embryos," would be unconscionable.

As goes the cloning debate, . . . so we may expect will go all the other issues on the biotechnology agenda.

You gain a sense of how rapidly things change. We aren't saying that in a generation's time you never know what might happen. We are saying that in five years' time, or three years' time, or one year's time, how fast things go. And not least among the awful effects of September 11 was the postponement of Senate action on cloning from last fall, when it was expected and when we were in an immensely stronger position than we are now on that question. To catch up—Senator Sam Brownback's (R-KS) attempt to ban all human cloning has run into very serious problems. And it is not at all clear when we will be able have a vote on his initiative, or even on a modified form of it in a moratorium on all cloning, in the course of this Congress.

It is no surprise that the biotechnology industry has taken the view, which is my view, that this is a watershed question, because as goes the cloning debate, as goes the cloning question, so we may expect will go all the other issues on the biotechnology agenda.

We are aware that vast amounts of money have been flowing into advertising and lobbying. And major contributions to the Republican Party come from the biotechnology industry, as they seek to create a favorable environment for their agenda.

We are moving rapidly from a context in which the people who are doing the science earned $80,000-a-year teaching at state universities, to a context in which they own gene patents and sit on boards of potentially enormously wealthy companies. They are the people now sitting on the scientific panels and weighing research proposals and testifying on behalf of the scientific community. These enormous changes are little understood in public. And, of course, the media has quite depressingly sought to work immensely hard to bias almost every report coming out of this debate.

But to stand back again and look at the cloning question, the watershed issues, the opening of the second front in the battle for human life: Cloning is not the end; cloning is just the beginning. Dr. Antinori in Italy has been reported as saying he has five clonal pregnancies; almost certainly his showmanship is at stake here. I think it is hard to believe that he has mastered the science, which is eluding these major companies here in the States who can't make it work for human beings yet. But at some point we will hear of the birth of clonal babies, and we will first experience what it is to have members of the human species—they are the same as we are—who are also manufactures. They are commodities who are also people. The only parallel we have in our thinking—and this boggles our minds—takes us back beyond the Thirteenth Amendment into the experience we have of chattel slavery, when we had human beings who were also commodities. And as these technologies take off, and the commodification of human life focuses as the central question again, and again, the haunting of chattel slavery and Dred Scott will not go away.

Three Phases in the Remaking of Human Nature

I said there were three phases in this second front which has been opened in Bioethics II. The first is cloning, the basic manufacture of human beings. You have to have the one you want to manufacture; you've got to pick the one you want to copy, whether you are picking your favorite uncle or aunt, or whether you are picking some celebrity whose DNA you will be able to buy over the Internet in the way you can now get hold of eggs and sperm over the Net from highachievers and, ultimately, celebrities.

I was hearing the other day that there are now campuses in California, where in the student employment office, selling your eggs is listed as a way of funding your education. This has now become routine within our culture.

But to get a clone you have to have one you want to clone, and if the thing works, all you will get is a copy. That gives you great opportunity and, of course, radically demeans the one you have cloned, whatever your motives may be.

But the second phase lies beyond cloning. The second phase after *manufacture* is *design*. When the results of the human genome project finally begin to show their capacity for commercial applications, we shall be set for what is most simply described as inheritable genetic changes: ways in which you can make changes in every succeeding generation; ways in which you can change the nature of a child; ways in which you can begin to redesign what it means to be one of us.

I was at a conference last September, in fact in Boston, with a title "Beyond Cloning," organized by some progressive bioethics people who are by no means our friends on the abortion agenda, but who don't like cloning either. And the professor who began the conference said, "Well, what if you want to have a blue baby? Or what if you want to have a baby with wings? These are ridiculous examples, but they are the point." And his view was, the technology will be there, and how can we say it's wrong? It's a matter of time and money and marketing.

And you may know that so-called germline or inheritable genetic changes are different: This isn't using genetics to fix you up. This isn't the sort of micromedicine which will, little by little, become possible to cure your diseases genetically in a way that just deals with you. These are changes that will be inherited. Many of those who think most about those things know there is no line you can draw between inherited disease and fundamental human traits—what about shortness, increasingly seen in the disease category? It's all a matter of fashion, a matter of shape. Somebody once said that if we'd had inheritable genetic modification in Rubens's day, we would all be very large.

> *The principle will be whether or not we let loose these technologies to change human nature so you can have babies by design.*

Fashions change, but the principle will be whether or not we let loose these technologies to change human nature so you can have babies by design. If you've seen the movie *Gattaca*, you will have seen a remarkable vision of a society in which a combination of eugenic-based genetic discrimination in society, and design mechanisms not far beyond our present scientific knowledge, condition a culture. There is no better argument than watching the story.

So the second phase is that of design: being able to change and to shape. Yet this will not come to us in a package. We won't suddenly be told, "Right now you can design your babies. Do you want to do this or do you not want to do this?" This will be the moral vision of the West, once again, being cooked like a lobster; little, incremental changes. Pay $1,000, and get your baby an extra few points on the SAT. Or be sure that he or she will be within a narrow range of height; perhaps predispose your child not to have certain tendencies to overweight—subtle things, little appealing things. That is how these things will be marketed, one by one. The principle is that we will begin to be able to design human nature for ourselves.

Thirdly, going beyond that, we have something which presently seems to us so far outside our imagination as to be beyond thought. Yet there are those out there who are now thinking hard about how the blending of man and machine, the development of machines with humanlike characteristics, will blur the distinction between human life and the life of things. Some of you will have seen one of the most amazing stories in recent days of the use of nanotechnology implants in the brains of rats, so that rats can be used to go into burning houses with little TV monitors on their heads. You can control a rat with an implant in the rat's brain—marriage of the mechanical and the organic. Again the movies say it all. In Spielberg's *A.I.*, which I thought a poor movie with great effects, one of its themes was the blending of what in the movie are called "mecha" and "orga," the mechanical beings and the organic beings. This again will begin in small ways with salami-slicing, lobster-cooking opportunities for us to enhance what we can do and to determine what our children shall do and who they shall be.

We go from cloning, basic manufacture copying, to design so that our manufacturing of human nature can be according to our choosing. And that is the context in which two terms have been coined that probably you haven't heard. One is "post-humanism": the post-human future, getting beyond being human. The other is "trans-humanism": transcending our human nature. That is what some of the brightest minds in our culture are now thinking about, affecting us not just biologically, through changes in our genetics, but mechanically through the developments of artificial intelligence, cybernetics, the marriage of human and computer—which some people believe lies not too far ahead. Other people believe it will never be possible. But highly intelligent people are being paid a lot of money to work on the technology and the ideas.

So it seems to me this is a three-fold, three-phase challenge: cloning, basic copy; germline genetic intervention, so you can determine the nature, the genetic structure of human beings; and then finally blending of man and machine in small ways and big. These are the challenges. And I suggest to you that cloning is the watershed issue.

It's an international issue. Reference is made to the United Nations' discussion of a treaty on cloning. Interestingly, in almost every other major country in the world this debate is going our way. I am embarrassed to say that the United Kingdom, my former home, is a pariah state in its determination to use technologies unethically for economic benefit. But major countries around the world, liberal and conservative, are coming together and saying, "On this issue, we will stand in line. And we will say, 'No.'"

The European Convention on Biomedicine and Human Rights— the European bioethics treaty that many European countries have signed—bans the use of genetics to change human nature, germline interventions.

In the international context, cloning is the watershed issue. And I would suggest to you that as we move from Cain and Abel to the Tower of Babel, as we move from killing human beings to making human beings, we face the greatest moral challenge, perhaps not simply of our generation, but of any generation.

And it will fall to us, my friends. It will fall to us, under God. It will fall to us to seek to thwart, to constrain, and to deny absolutely the claim of those in the biotech industry and their political friends to have uncontrollable development of these technologies, because we believe man's greatest achievement is to be free, to be under God the creature he/she was made to be in the image of God. And if we go down that path, grasp the irony here—the greatest achievement of humankind, the taking to ourselves of powers not just over nature around us but over our own nature—the greatest achievement of humankind will have been to turn our own kind into our own commodity.

And thus in this marriage, if you like, of hubris, of Faust, this overweening confidence in self and desire to do what we choose to do, and Frankenstein the man-made man, the monster—the flowering of human nature will find itself in nothing other than the building of a new Tower of Babel, that finally will destroy this human nature that we seek to advance.

The second front opened five years ago with the announcement of the cloning of Dolly the sheep. We must work, and we must pray to ensure that here also we stand for human dignity. And we must ensure that every generation to come has the freedom of our human nature, God-given, and yet the preservation of which is now in the balance.

Thank you very much.

Cumulative Speaker Index: 2000–2002

A cumulative speaker index to the volumes of *Representative American Speeches* for the years 1937–1938 through 1959–1960 appears in the 1959–1960 volume; for the years 1960–1961 through 1969–1970, see the 1969–1970 volume; for the years 1970–1971 through 1979–1980, see the 1979–1980 volume; for the years 1980–1981 through 1989–1990, see the 1989–1990 volume; and for the years 1990–1991 through 1999–2000, see the 1999–2000 volume.

Abrams, Janet, and Laurie Girand, 2001–2002, pp135–138, S.T.O.P.'s Position on FDA's Efforts Toward BSE to Date

Ashcroft, John, 2001–2002, pp99–102, Remarks on the National Security Entry-Exit Registration System

Bailey, Antoinette M., 2000–2001, pp113–138, Thoughts on Building a House for Diversity

Buchanan, Patrick J., 2000–2001, pp139–145, To Reunite a Nation

Bush, George W., 2001–2002, pp11–18, Address to a Joint Session of Congress and the American People

Bush, Laura Welch, 2001–2002, pp26–27, Taliban Oppression of Women and Children

Cameron, Nigel M. de S., 2001–2002, pp178–188, Biotechnology and the Struggle for Human Dignity: Whatever Happened to the Human Race?

Chao, Elaine L., 2001–2002, pp105–109, State of the Workforce

Chavez-Thompson, Linda, 2001–2002, pp86–89, Immigration Reform

Cheney, Richard (Dick), 2000–2001, pp176–181, Remarks at the Annual Meeting of the Associated Press

Conko, Gregory, 2001–2002, pp139–148, Behind the Headlines: What Laymen Should Know About Everyday Issues in Science and Health

Daschle, Thomas, 2001–2002, pp110–122, America's Economy: Rising to Our New Challenges

Dingell, John D., 2001–2002, pp149–154, Food Safety and Bioterrorism Legislation

Donohue, Mary O., 2001–2002, pp50–56, Maria College Commencement

Donovan, John B., 2000–2001, pp105–109, Bringing Hope to Youth: Religious Education for Public School Students

Fanton, Jonathan F., 2001–2002, pp28–32, Chicago Council on Foreign Relations

Feldbaum, Carl B., 2001–2002, pp163–170, Keeping the Faith

Gephardt, Richard A., 2000–2001, pp90–97, Educating America: A National Challenge for the 21st Century

Ginsburg, Ruth Bader, 2000–2001, pp3–20, Remarks on Judicial Independence: The Situation of the U.S. Federal Judiciary

Girand, Laurie, and Janet Abrams, 2001–2002, pp135–138, S.T.O.P.'s Position on FDA's Efforts Toward BSE to Date

Giuliani, Rudolph W., 2001–2002, pp19–25, United Nations General Assembly Special Session on Terrorism

Guengerich, Galen J., 2001–2002, pp6–10, The Shaking of the Foundations

Harshbarger, Scott, 2000–2001, pp58–67, Regarding Election Reform

Henderson, Wade, 2001–2002, pp97–98, Statement at SEIU Immigration Press Conference

Hogan, Kathleen B., 2000–2001, pp161–165, Remarks at the Fifth Annual Green Power Marketing Conference

Jefferson-Jenkins, Carolyn, 2000–2001, pp49–57, Making Democracy Work

Jones, Julia Hughes, 2000–2001, pp43–48, Vote Theft 2000: Selecting Our Leaders Fairly and Honestly

Kabbani, Shaykh Muhammad Hisham, 2001–2002, pp33–40, Muslims Within the Democratic Framework

Kohn, Alfie, 2000–2001, pp110–116, Standardized Testing and Its Victims

Krikorian, Mark, 2001–2002, pp90–96, Immigration and Civil Rights in the Wake of September 11

Langevin, James, 2001–2002, pp171–173, Testimony at the Hearing on Stem Cell Research

Lee, Bill Lann, 2000–2001, pp33–40, Remarks to the National Consortium of Task Forces and Commissions on Racial and Ethnic Bias in the Courts

Lebow, Steven J., 2000–2001, pp151–158, There Are Giants in Our Midst

Loria, Christopher J. "Gus," 2001–2002, pp43–49, In Defense of Liberty

McCain, John, 2000–2001, pp68–73, Opening Statement on Campaign Finance Reform

McConnell, Mitch, 2000–2001, pp74–76, Proposing an Amendment to the Constitution of the United States

McGee, Liam E., 2000–2001, pp79–89, Education is Everybody's Business

Merrifield, Jeffrey S., 2000–2001, pp182–194, A Vision of Tomorrow, a Plan for Today

Moyer, Thomas J., 2000–2001, pp27–32, Cleveland City Club

Mullarkey, Mary J., 2000–2001, pp21–26, The Recent Presidential Election: The Residual Effects on the Courts

Murano, Elsa, 2001–2002, pp155–160, Taking Food Safety to the Next Level

Murkowski, Frank H., 2000–2001, pp170–175, A National Energy Crisis Is upon Us

Newman, Stuart A., 2002–2002, pp174–177, Testimony at the Hearing on Human Cloning

Pataki, George E., 2001–2002, pp3–5, Joint Session of the New York State Legislature

Pitt, Harvey L., 2001–2002, pp123–127, Remarks Before the Economic Club of New York

Powell, Colin L., 2001–2002, pp59–65, Acceptance of the 14th Annual Philadelphia Liberty Medal

Reed, Lawrence W., 2000–2001, pp117–129, A New Direction for Education Reform

Richardson, Bill, 2000–2001, pp166–169, Remarks on California's Electricity Event

Rumsfeld, Donald H., 2001–2002, pp68–70, Arlington National Cemetery Funeral Service for the Unidentified Victims of the Attack on the Pentagon

Sacconaghi, Michele Cavataio, 2000–2001, pp98–104, The Future Is Now: Education in the Internet Age

Schweiker, Mark S., 2001–2002, pp66–67, Flight 93: Our Heroes, Our Family

Stein, Dan, 2001–2002, pp73–85, U.S. Asylum Policy: Reforms Needed in Current System

Sweeney, John J., 2001–2002, pp128–132, Remarks on the Wall Street Rally

Yasin, Zayed Muhammed, 2001–2002, pp57–58, Of Faith and Citizenship: My American Jihad

Yates, Albert C., 2000–2001, pp146–150, Diversity: A Spirit of Community

Index

Abraham, Spencer, 96
Abrams, Janet, 135–138
Afghanistan, 13, 26–27, 29, 37
AFL-CIO, 87–89, 128, 131
agriculture and genetic engineering, 147
aid. *See* funding
airplanes
    passenger heroism, 7, 11, 47, 66–67
    safety measures, 17
al Qaeda, 13, 31, 117
American jihad, 57–58
American Muslims, 14, 24, 33–34, 38–39, 57–58
American Society for Reproductive Medicine, 183
Ames, Bruce, 144
animal testing, 142, 170
Annan, Kofi, 60, 61
Arctic National Wildlife (ANWR), 47
Arias, Oscar, 63
Ashcroft, John, 99–102
Asylum Corps, 77
asylum policy
    Cubans, status of, 84
    eligibility, 81–82, 83
    excessive claims, 76, 78–80, 81, 82
    immediate application requirement, 78
    loopholes in, 76–80
    quota increases, 80–81, 83
    reform proposals, 75–76, 82–84
    See also immigration

Barber, Benjamin, 7
Battle of Iwo Jima, 44–46, 48
Beamer, Todd, 11
Ben & Jerry's, 143, 144
bin Laden, Osama, 8, 13
bioethics
    blending of man and machine, 186–187
    clonal human births, 183, 185

    genetic manipulation, 175, 181–182, 185–186, 188
    God-like power from cloning, 164, 182
    manufacture of embryos, 173, 176–177, 183, 184, 185
    timing of embryo cell harvesting, 175–177
    use of "spare" embryos, 172, 176
biotechnology industry, 165–166, 168–170, 184
Biotechnology Industry Organization (BIO), 163
bioterrorism, 150–154, 159
border security. *See* security measures
bovine spongiform encephalopathy (BSE), 135–138
Brotherhood of Carpenters and Joiners, 105, 106
Brownback, Sam, 184
Buddhism, 170
budget deficit projections, 114
Burnett, Thomas, 7
Bush, George W., 11–18, 47, 64
Bush, Laura Welch, 26–27

Cameron, Nigel, 178–188
Canada, 117, 152
cancer, 143–144, 176
Cardozo, Benjamin, 56
Carson, Rachel, 143
Center for Immigration Studies, 90
Center for National Policy (CNP), 110, 111
CFA (Consumer Federation of America), 149
Chamberlain, Neville, 24
Chao, Elaine L., 105–109
character education, 51–55
Chavez-Thompson, Linda, 86–89
Chicago Council on Foreign Relations, 28
children
    character education, 51–55

crimes committed by, 53
support for September 11 survivors, 3
Taliban-inflicted suffering, 26–27
See also schools
China, 80
chlorine, 146
Christian fundamentalism, 166–167
Churchill, Winston, 67
civil liberties groups, 31, 32
civil rights, 87–89, 91–94, 97–98
cloning
as pivotal discovery, 179, 182–183,
185, 187–188
"Dolly" (sheep), 179, 182, 188
ethical issues. *See* bioethics
reproductive, 165–166, 169, 183, 185
therapeutic, 165–166, 169, 172
CNP (Center for National Policy), 110,
111
Colombia, 77
community service, 55, 64–65
Competitive Enterprise Institute, 139
Conko, Gregory, 139–148
Consumer Federation of America (CFA),
149
corporate fraud response
AFL-CIO lawsuit, 131
funding, 125
information disclosure, 125, 126, 127
political accountability, 132
reform proposals, 126–127, 130–132
SEC investigations, 124
Council for Excellence in Government,
105, 106
Council for Responsible Genetics, 175
Council on Foreign Relations, 32
Creutzfeld Jakob disease, 136
crime in U.S. society, 53, 55–56
Cuba, 84

Darwin, Charles, 166–167
Daschle, Thomas, 110–122
Declaration of Independence, 61–62, 63,
65
defense spending, 12, 114, 122
democracy
citizenship and, 21, 54–55, 62–63
in Afghanistan, 27, 37
Islam and, 34–39
political change and, 30

terrorists' views of, 14
See also Declaration of Independence;
human rights
Democratic Party economic plan, 115–122
Department of Justice (DOJ), 154
Department of Labor (DOL), 106, 107,
109
deportation policies, 78, 92, 93–94
Dingell, John D., 149–154
dioxins, 143–144
disease and cloning, 166, 169, 172
Dobson, James, 181
DOJ (Department of Justice), 154
DOL (Department of Labor), 106, 107,
109
"Dolly" (sheep), 179, 182, 188
Donohue, Mary O., 50–56

E. coli, 135, 136, 157
Ebbers, Bernie, 129
economic growth
Democrat stimulus plan, 115–121
energy industry and, 48, 120–121
fiscal discipline and, 112, 118
interest rates and, 118
September 11 effects on, 114
tax cut effects, 113–114, 116, 119
education. *See* schools
Egypt, 13, 30
Einstein, Albert, 165
embryonic cloning. *See* cloning
energy
oil exploration, 47
reliance on foreign oil, 30, 47, 121
U.S. economy and, 48, 120–121
Enron, 129
Entry-Exit Registration System, 99–102
Environmental Protection Agency (EPA),
144
epidemiology, 141–142, 159
ethical issues in biotechnology. *See* bioethics
ethnic profiling, 91
eugenics, 165, 182, 186
European immigration policies, 101
evolution and religion, 166–167

Falwell, Jerry, 8
Fanton, Jonathan F., 28–32
farming and genetic engineering, 147
Federation for American Immigration

Reform (FAIR), 73–76, 80, 83–84
Feldbaum, Carl B., 163–170
Flight 93, 47, 66–67
Food and Drug Administration (FDA)
    bioterrorism legislation and, 150–
        151, 153–154
    food safety practices, current, 136–
        137, 151–152
    pharmaceutical review process, 145
    recommendations to, 137–138, 152–
        154
    USDA assistance to, 158
food safety
    bioterrorism and, 150–154, 159
    FDA current practices and, 136–138,
        151–152
    funding for, 153, 156
    genetic engineering and, 146–148
    mad cow disease and, 135–138
    recommendations for, 137–138, 152–
        154
    security measures, 151–154, 158, 159
    USDA initiatives, 156–160
France, 101
fraud, corporate. *See* corporate fraud
    response
Freedom Corps, 64, 65
freedom. *See* democracy
fundamentalism
    Christian, 166–167
    Islamic, 8, 13, 14, 34
funding
    corporate fraud response, 125
    defense spending, 12, 114, 122
    for food safety, 153, 156
    for security measures, 118, 122, 153
    for stem cell research, 171–173
    for terrorist organizations, 38–39
    for victims of September 11 attacks, 3,
        16, 64, 122
    humanitarian aid, 13
    political, from biotechnology industry,
        184

Galileo, 167–168
Gearhart, John, 176
Genetic Bill of Rights, 175
genetic engineering, 146–148, 165

genetic manipulation in cloning, 175,
    181–182, 185–186, 188
Girand, Laurie, 135–138
Giuliani, Rudolph W., 19–25
Glick, Jeremy, 7
Global Crossing, 129
globalization and labor force, 120
Greenspan, Alan, 106, 111, 115
Guengerich, Galen J., 6–10

Hadith, 36
Hamas, 117
Havel, Vaclev, 63
Henderson, Wade, 97–98
heroism
    daily acts of courage, 56
    in Battle of Iwo Jima, 44–46, 48
    in September 11 attacks, 3–5, 7, 11,
        20, 47, 54, 63–64, 66–67
History of the Islamic Schools of Thought
    (Zahra), 35
Holocaust, 8
    See also Nazim
Homeland Security Office (U.S.), 15
    See also security measures
Howard, George, 18
human rights
    as birthright from God, 61–62, 63
    civil rights, 87–89, 91–94, 97–98
    oppression
        in the Middle East, 13, 26–27, 30
        in Uzbekistan, 30–31
        of women, 13, 26–27
    terrorism and, 20, 21, 28–31, 64
Human Rights Watch, 29, 30, 32

Ignatieff, Michael, 29
immigration
    influx size, 84, 95
    policy
        asylum. *See* asylum policy
        civil rights and, 87–89, 91–94,
            97–98
        deportation, 78, 92, 93–94
        in Europe, 101
        post-September 11 changes, 91–
            93, 97–98, 99–102
        union movement and, 87–89
    welcoming climate vs. level of, 84, 94–
        96
    See also security measures

Immigration and Naturalization Service
(INS), 80
culture of approval, 82
I-9 enforcement system, 89
overwhelmed by backlog, 76
imported food safety. *See* food safety
interest rates and economy, 118
International Religious Freedom Act, 31
Islam, traditional, 14, 27, 34–39
Islamic extremism, 8, 13, 14, 34
Islamic Jihad (Egypt), 13
Islamic Movement of Uzbekistan (IMU),
13, 31
Islamic organizations, 38–39
See also specific organizations
Iwo Jima Battle, 44–46, 48

Jefferson, Thomas, 60, 61, 62
jihad, 13, 57–58
Jihad vs. McWorld (Barber), 7
jobs. *See* labor force
Jordan, Barbara, 78, 90

Kabbani, Muhammad Hisham, 33–39
Karimov, Islam, 31, 32
Karzai, Hamid, 37
Kerik, Bernard, 20
Kim, Dae Jung, 63
Koran, 36, 38, 58
Krauthammer, Charles, 184
Krikorian, Mark, 90–96

labor force
globalization effects, 120
immigration worker rights, 87–89
projected shrinkage, 107–108
skills training importance, 107, 119
unemployment rates, 107
Langevin, James R., 171–173
Lay, Ken, 129
Lazarus, Emma, 9
Leadership Conference on Civil Rights
(LCCR), 97
Learned Hand, 54
liberty. *See* democracy
libertyunites.org, 16
Lincoln, Abraham, 63
Loria, Christopher "Gus", 43–49

MacArthur Foundation, 29
mad cow disease, 135–138

Mahmoud, Abdul Halim, 36
Mandela, Nelson, 61, 63
Maria College of New York, 50, 55, 56
Max, D. T., 11
Maximum Tolerable Dose methodology,
142–143
McGuire, Peter J., 105
meat safety. *See* food safety
media sensationalism, 139–140
medical research. *See* research
Meissner, Doris, 77
Mexico, 152
Middle East and human rights, 13, 26–
27, 30
military spending, 12, 114, 122
moral relativism, 19, 23
Moynihan, Patrick, 55
Mt. Suribachi, 44, 45
Muhammad, founder of Islam, 34, 35, 36
Murano, Elsa, 155
Muslim people. *See* American Muslims;
Islam, traditional; Islamic extremism

National Crime Information Center
(NCIC), 102
Nazism, 8, 24, 182
Newman, Stuart A., 174–177
9/11. *See* September 11 attacks

Office of Homeland Security (U.S.), 15
See also security measures
oil, reliance on foreign, 30, 47, 121
organic food, 144

Panetta, Leon, 111
Paracelsus, Philippus Aureolus, 143
Pataki, George E., 3–5, 54, 55
Pence, Gregory, 183
Pennsylvania crash site, 47, 66–67
See also September 11 attacks
Pentagon attack, 68–70
See also September 11 attacks
Peru, 146
pesticides, 143–144, 145, 147
Philadelphia Liberty Medal, 59, 60, 63
Pitt, Harvey L., 123–127
plants and pesticides, 143–144, 147
policy
asylum. *See* asylum policy
changes after September 11, 23, 91–
93, 97–98, 99–102
immigration. *See* immigration, policy

research influence on, 145–147, 158
Powell, Colin L., 59–65
Precautionary Principle, 146
profiling, ethnic/religious, 91
public service, 55, 64–65

Qaeda, al, 13, 31, 117
Qur'an, 36, 38, 58

racial profiling, 91
Reeves, Richard, 7
reform proposals
    asylum policy, 75–76, 82–84
    corporate fraud, 126–127, 130–132
    food safety, 137–138, 152–154
religion
    diversity with faiths, 34
    faith and citizenship as complementary, 57–58
    faith and tragedy, 8, 16
    freedom watch list, 31
    Gallup poll on beliefs, 169
    science compatibility with, 164–170
    virtues as framework, 51–52
    See also Buddhism; fundamentalism;
        Islam, traditional
religious profiling, 91
research
    context in, 141, 142–143
    influence on policy, 145–147, 158
    media sensationalism and, 139–140
    product safety implications, 140–141,
        145–147
    R&D support, 119–120
    stem cell, 171–173, 176–177
    validity evaluation, 141–142
retirement security, 108, 121, 128–129,
    131
    See also Social Security
Ridge, Tom, 15, 118
Roosevelt, Theodore, 47, 50–53
Rosenthal, Joe, 45
Roth, Kenneth, 29
Rubin, Bob, 111, 115
Rumsfeld, Donald H., 68–70
Russia, 117

Safe Tables Our Priority (STOP), 135–
    138

safety measures
    airplanes, 17
    food safety. See food safety
    in the workplace, 108–109
    research findings and, 140–141, 145–
        147
    See also security measures
Salmonella, 136, 156, 157
Saudi Arabia, 30
schools
    character education in, 55
    college vs. high school outcomes, 107
    evolutionary biology instruction, 166–
        167
    violence in, 53, 55
Schreir, Harold, 45
Schweiker, Mark, 66–67
science
    government vs. corporate payroll,
        184–185
    public responsibility, 175
    religion compatibility with, 164–170
    technology transfer dangers, 177, 179
scientific research. See research
Scopes, John, 167
Scotland, 179
Securities and Exchange Commission
    (SEC)
    about, 123
    financial statement requirements,
        125
    reform proposals, 126–127
    WorldCom investigations, 124
security measures
    air safety, 17
    Entry-Exit Registration System, 99–
        102
    exit controls, 102
    fingerprinting, 92, 101
    for food safety, 151–154, 158, 159
    funding for, 118, 122, 153
    immigrant tracking, 93, 101
September 11 attacks
    casualities, 20, 70
    civilian responses, 3–5, 7, 11, 20, 47,
        54, 63–64, 66–67
    economic effects, 114
    emergency spending following, 122

international support, 12, 16, 21
multinational victims of, 12
national unity affected by, 5, 8–10, 12, 20, 25, 47
Pennsylvania crash site, 47, 66–67
Pentagon, 68–70
policy changes following, 23, 91–93, 97–98, 99–102
security response. *See* security measures
war against terrorism following, 14–16, 122
"seven virtues", 51–52, 55
Silent Spring (Carson), 143
Singer, Peter, 180–181
skills training for jobs, 107, 119
Social Security, 108, 109, 121–122
  See also retirement security
Statue of Liberty, 9
Stein, Dan, 73–85
Steinbrenner, Mo, 111
stem cell research, 171–173, 176–177
  See also cloning
stock market, 124, 126, 127, 129
STOP (Safe Tables Our Priority), 135–138
Summers, Larry, 111
Suribachi, Mt., 44, 45
Sweeney, John J., 128–132

Taliban, 13–14, 26–27
Task Force on School Violence, 55
tax cut effects on economy, 113–114, 116, 119
terrorism
  bioterrorism, 150–154, 159
  democracy and, 14
  economic/political pressure against, 13–14, 32
  financial support for, 23, 38–39
  human rights and, 20, 21, 28–31, 64
  international networks, 13
  security response. *See* security measures
  U.S. war against, 14–16, 122
  See also September 11 attacks; *specific groups*
Thun, Michael, 142
Tillich, Paul, 7, 8
trade

global, effect on jobs, 120
  with repressive regimes, 30, 32
transmissible spongiform encephalopathy (TSE), 135–138
Turkmenistan, 31

unemployment rates, 107, 115
union movement and immigration, 87–89
United Flight 93, 47, 66–67
United Kingdom, 136–137, 187
United Nations, 20, 22–23, 187
United States
  citizenship significance, 21, 57–58, 60, 62–63
  crime in, 53, 55–56
  economic/political pressure on terrorism, 13–14, 32
  Islam, sentiments on, 14, 24
  Muslim society in, 14, 24, 33–34, 38–39, 57–58
  national unity and September 11 attacks, 5, 8–10, 12, 20, 25, 47
  oil, reliance on foreign, 30, 47, 121
  trade with repressive regimes, 30, 32
  war against terrorism, 14–16, 122
United States Department of Agriculture (USDA), 156–160
Uzbekistan, 13, 30–31, 32, 118

violence, 30, 53, 55–56
  See also terrorism
Von Essen, Tom, 20

Walesa, Lech, 60, 61
Wambugu, Florence, 169
war against terrorism, 14–16, 122
Who's Afraid of Cloning? (Pence), 183
Wilhelm, John, 86, 87
Winnick, Gary, 129
women
  asylum policy and, 81, 82
  oppression in Middle East, 13, 26–27, 30
workplace safety, 108–109
World Trade Center attacks. *See* September 11 attacks
World Trade Center Memorial Scholarship, 3
World Trade Center Relief Fund, 3
World War II, 7, 44–46

World War III, 7
WorldCom, 124, 129, 131

Xenotransplantation, 165

Yasin, Zayed Muhammed, 57–58

Zahra, Abu, 35